ROCK

AN ILLUSTRATED HISTORY

ROCK

AN ILLUSTRATED HISTORY

STEPHEN BARNARD

SCHIRMER BOOKS

To Eril, with love and affection

Author's acknowledgements

I was lucky to have been born with rock'n'roll – in the same week in 1954, I now realise, that Bill Haley entered the US chart with 'Rock Around the Clock' and Elvis made his first-ever commercial recording in 'That's All Right, Mama'. This book is the end product, therefore, of over thirty years of growing up with pop music, and my thanks go first and foremost to my parents, who fuelled my first interest in popular music and always encouraged me to write, and to my brother John, who influenced my tastes to a far greater extent than he has probably ever realised. Sincere thanks are also due to the editorial staff of *Let it Rock* and *Cream* magazines – and especially Charlie Gillett – who gave me space to write about many of my past and then-current favourites in print for the first time during the pre-punk Seventies; and to the adult education department of London's City University, who allowed me to give classes on what must have seemed an eccentric subject for academic study – pop history – and thereby research and explore many of the themes developed in these pages. Finally, I must thank Lorrie Mack, my editor, for her perceptive reading of the text and her valuable comments on it, and Eril, my wife, for her support, understanding and tolerance of innumerable late nights during the writing of this book.

Stephen Barnard
London N13
June, 1986

First published in Great Britain 1986
by Orbis Book Publishing Corporation Limited
a BPCC plc company, Greater London House,
Hampstead Road, London NW1.

Schirmer Books
A Division of Macmillan, Inc.
866 Third Avenue, New York, N.Y. 10022

Cataloging in Publication Data
available from the Library of Congress
Printed in Italy

printing number
1 2 3 4 5 6 7 8 9 10

ISBN 0-02-870251-4

Printed in Italy

Photographs were supplied by Cyrus Andrews, Apple/EMI, Associated Press, Graham Barker, Barnaby's Picture Library, BBC, John Beecher, Peter Benjaminson, Arthur Berlowitz, Blues Unlimited, Rob Burt Collection, Capitol Records, CBS, Colour Library International, Country Music Foundation, Crackerjack Photography, Andre Csillag, Culver Pictures, Ralph Denyer, Adrian Devoy, Henry Diltz, EMI Records, Erica Echenberg, Flair Photography, Flashbacks, David Gahr, Chris Gardener, Charlie Gillett, Mick Gold, Ronald Grant, Gijsbert Hanekroot, Phil Hardy, Martin Hawkins, Island Records, Jazz Music Books, Peter Kanze Collection, Kindlight Ltd, Kobal Collection, G. Lautrey, J. P. Leloir, London Features International, Janet Macoska, Melody Maker, Memphis Press-Scimitar, Bill Millar, David Morosoli, Motown Records, Michael Ochs, Peter Newark, Old Time Music, Steve Petryszyn, The Photo Source, Pictorial Press, John Pidgeon, John Platt, Barry Plummer, Polydor, Popperfoto, Press Association, N. Ralph, Rare Pics, RCA, RCA/VICTOR, David Redfern, Rex Features, Steve Richards, Christian Rose, Tom Sheehan, Shooting Star, Steven Shore, D.J. Smith, Smudger, Star File, Syndication International, Thames Television, Times/Picayune, John Topham Picture Library, U.P.I., Paul Vernon, Virgin Records, WEA Records, Alfred Wertheimer, ZEFA.

Contents

INTRODUCTION

The story of rock is much more than
just that of a particular musical style.
It is a story that parallels and reflects
the growing confidence, maturity and
economic independence of the post-
war young generation — its changing
aspirations, its unquenchable thirst for
novelty and fashion, and its rising
political consciousness. It is a story
of exploration and enterprise, of
innovation and imitation, on the part
of musicians, songwriters, producers
and promotion men alike — the story
of how the music industries on both
sides of the Atlantic came to terms
with the demands of a new audience
through the relentless exploitation of
new sounds and new recording
technology. In thirty years, rock has
grown from a minority music —
lambasted for its anarchic spirit
and abused for its roots in the
unsophisticated ethnic styles of blues
and country — into perhaps the most
vital form of modern popular culture.
The following pages relate, through
the key events in rock history and the
careers of rock's main protagonists,
how this extraordinary evolution
came about.

CHAPTER 1

ROCK 'N' ROLL IS HERE TO STAY
The roots of rock

A revolutionary synthesis of black R & B and white country formed the rallying cry of Fifties youth

Opposite page: the young Elvis on stage, working the magic that made him king of rock 'n' roll

Right: Glenn Ford gets to grips with juvenile delinquency in the form of Sidney Poitier – a still from the film The Blackboard Jungle, *released during 1955. In featuring Bill Haley's 'Rock Around the Clock' over the credits, the film forged a link in the public mind between rock 'n' roll music and teenage criminality*

In the beginning, there was rock'n'roll – an unashamedly primitive musical style that gave voice to the frustrations, fantasies and obsessions of teenagers the world over. From the early Fifties onwards, rock'n'roll provided unmistakable proof of the younger generation's new-found commercial clout, while the sexuality of its rhythms and the rebellious edge of its lyrics challenged adult society's standards of propriety and order. No matter that its musical roots were almost as old as America itself, rock'n'roll had youth appeal because it promised not only change, but a liberation from an age of restricted pleasures and controlled emotions.

Looking back on the Fifties in her 1973 book *Trips*, Ellen Sander wrote: 'We got a long hard look at how it was out there, competitiveness motivating a dreary lifestyle, money being an end not a means, nations hustling ultimate doom – and it stunk. Everything else that was happening was beyond us, forced upon us by circumstances beyond our control. But our music was ours'. To millions like her, rock'n'roll was a music of both revolt and escape, a celebration of ephemeral excitement, sexual hedonism and individual gratification. Its promotion of the 'eternal now' of sensuous, self-absorbed fun rejected all that Calvinist America stood for – the work ethic, financial prudence, stability, romantic love, and – if you accepted and lived by these values – the promise of rewards in later life.

Those who dismissed rock'n'roll at the time as a harmless novelty missed its significance by miles: the expansion of its popularity was inseparably linked to the growth of teenage culture. The very word 'teenager' was a Fifties concoction that gained currency as the American media became increasingly youth-obsessed. Much newspaper space was devoted to the alarming rise in juvenile crime, books on adolescent psychology flooded the stores, and Hollywood produced a glut of films that seemed to depict the very condition of youth as a social evil. The teenage 'problem', some said, was actually a consequence of America's post-war affluence: because of widespread prosperity and almost full employment, teenagers now had more disposable income than ever before, but nothing identifiably 'young' to spend it on. They had to find their own kind of excitement and create their own sense of style, the models for which they found in

THE ROOTS OF ROCK

Above: both Marlon Brando and James Dean (inset) personified, in their various film roles, the adolescent alienation that fuelled the emergence of rock 'n' roll in the Fifties

the sleazy glamour of rock'n'roll and the very films that Hollywood pretended were shocking exposés of widespread juvenile delinquency.

The film industry at least acknowledged the existence of teenagers as a separate consumer market – something American television, with its family orientation and dependence on big-money sponsors, failed to do for years. Well before rock'n'roll hit the headlines, American youth saw in certain Hollywood films – or more particularly, their stars – a real source of identification. In *The Wild One* (1953), Marlon Brando played the leader of a motorcycle gang intent on terrorising an archetypal American small town; in *Rebel Without a Cause* (1955), James Dean took the role of a brooding, unreachable outsider who rejects parental authority. The latter production's title became instant media shorthand for mid-Fifties youth, while

Dean's violent death before the end of 1955 sealed the film's very powerful symbolic significance.

It was another film, *The Blackboard Jungle*, that brought rock'n'roll national exposure overnight and established a clear link in the public mind between the music and delinquency. Released in 1955, it featured good guy teacher Glenn Ford battling for the respect of would-be hoodlums in a Bronx high school – while, over the opening credits, Bill Haley and the Comets could be heard performing the first great rock'n'roll anthem, 'Rock Around the Clock'. The track had been issued a year earlier and had sold moderately; now, on the back of the film, it reached Number 1 in the American chart and single-handedly launched an anti-rock, anti-teen bandwagon upon which politicians, newspaper columnists, churchmen and parent-teacher associations were only too quick to jump.

THE ROAD FROM RHYTHM AND BLUES

Below: Louis Jordan, R&B star of the Forties, whose racy brand of 'jumpin' jive' was a particular influence on Bill Haley's sound. Jordan's producer, Milt Gabler, supervised many of Haley's early rock'n'roll recordings

Quite apart from rock'n'roll's supposed links with juvenile problems, adult America just could not relate to the hell-for-leather raucousness of its sound. While rock bore superficial similarity to the big-band 'jumpin' jive' of Louis Jordan and the cowboy-hat country-boogie of Tennessee Ernie Ford, both highly popular in the Forties, it drew most of its energy from sources outside the musical mainstream – notably the black blues and white country music traditions associated particularly with the American South. Lacking sophistication and subtlety, such idioms were alien to cultured American ears – on top of which they stirred up all manner of deep-rooted political, social and racial prejudices stretching back to Civil War days.

Such was the structure of the American record market that only rarely did discs made specifically for the black or country markets actually reach the national chart: limited-scale distribution by the record labels involved and the strict music policies of radio stations meant they received virtually no exposure. The story of rock'n'roll is in part that of how these ethnically divisive market structures were undermined – a process that began as early as 1949, when teenagers started to turn away from the stodgy fare of America's middle-of-the-road radio networks and tune in to the black stations based in the big urban centres. There they heard an undiluted diet of raunchy, electrifying rhythm and blues, most of it locally recorded and presented with outrageous pizazz by extravagantly verbose black disc jockeys. Soon, white kids were seen going in to the black ghettoes to buy the discs they had heard, a trend that prompted some of the more aware presenters at white radio stations to question their own music choices.

One of these was Alan Freed, who presented classical and light music programmes on station WJW in Cleveland, Ohio. In June 1951, he persuaded the management to give him a nightly rhythm and blues (R&B) show aimed specifically at white teenagers and titled 'Moondog's Rock'n'Roll Party'. The term 'rock'n'roll' was an invention of record store owner Leo Mintz, inspired by a sexual metaphor frequently heard in blues lyrics: he suggested that Freed avoid using the words 'rhythm and blues'

Below: Alan Freed, the first disc jockey to acknowledge and successfully exploit the new teenage taste for black music. Besides championing rock 'n' roll on his radio programmes, he staged the earliest multi-artist rock shows and played himself in a string of late Fifties rock films

because of the racial stigma attached to them. The show was a breakthrough, attracting high ratings within weeks and also setting a new style in presentation, for white radio at least. Borrowing freely from the black jocks' example, Freed would introduce each record in a hoarse jive patter and thump his fist on a telephone book in time with the beat. Every show was a performance, an event in itself, and in time other presenters on other stations adopted the same lively approach.

Promotion and payola

Freed recognised that R&B appealed most to teenagers because it was a deliciously abandoned form of dance music,

and as such a world apart from the formula-ridden records of singers like Eddie Fisher, Guy Mitchell and Patti Page that so dominated the national chart. Capitalising on his understanding of the emerging market, he became the first true rock'n'roll entrepreneur and even attempted to copyright the term at one point. In March 1952, he staged the first of many major rock concerts, the Moondog Coronation Ball: a racially mixed crowd of 25,000 showed up and broke down the doors to hear black stars like the Moonglows and the Dominoes. Dark threats of criminal charges followed, purportedly as a result of this violence, though clearly the authorities' main concern was that Freed had breached the

unwritten segregation laws at Cleveland entertainment venues. By 1954, he was promoting rock'n'roll on a national scale for the first time, via the syndication of his show by New York station WINS; he continued skirmishing with the establishment and building his empire, investing freely in artists and labels, using his show to launch them and accepting co-credits for songs – like Chuck Berry's smash hit 'Maybelline' – that he played no part in writing.

His legacy to rock'n'roll was crucial. He helped change the face, or rather the sound, of American radio, by influencing stations everywhere to adopt a teen-based rock music format, and he elevated the disc jockey to an all-powerful position as arbiter of taste, to be courted, cossetted and often kept financially secure by the record companies – especially those small, independent R&B labels who now found a totally new market open to them. National acceptance of rock'n'roll depended, finally, on radio exposure of these labels' products; 'payola', or payment for airplay, was often their only means of securing plays in the face of the superior marketing techniques of their big New York-based rivals – some of whom took to releasing whiter-than-white 'cover' versions of R&B songs which, because of better distribution, could outsell the originals.

The size, style and musical outlook of these independents (or 'indies', as they were called) varied enormously. Some were opportunists cashing in on a particular trend, while others specialised in local or regional R&B sounds – black vocal groups with gospel leanings, blues shouters, the jump blues stars of New Orleans – with a long tradition and proven appeal to black listeners. Among the most significant for rock'n'roll were King in Cincinnati, Specialty and Imperial in Los Angeles (though many of the releases of both these labels were actually

recorded in New Orleans), Atlantic in New York and Chess in Chicago – all of whom were quick to appreciate that R&B could be successfully adapted and subtly transformed with the tastes of young white listeners in mind. It could, in short, be made even more marketable.

The Domino effect

This appreciation marked a turning point in the development of rock'n'roll as a distinctive style. It could be clearly seen in the recordings of Imperial's Fats Domino, who started the Fifties as a leading R&B hitmaker and a fine exponent of the piano-based jump blues, which as a classic New Orleans style had antecedents in Dixieland jazz, Creole blues and

Below: the genial giant of New Orleans rock 'n' roll, Fats Domino, who adapted better than most black stars to the demands of the expanding white teen market

boogie-woogie. The chief characteristics of these early, local hits were Fats' mumbled, distant, vocal delivery, a pounding piano and top-heavy percussion – 'The Fat Man' (1950), a million seller in the R & B market, was typical. As his discs began selling nationally, starting with 'Ain't That a Shame' in 1955, a clear commercial formula emerged: his lazy, lugubrious and faintly melancholy vocal came much more to the fore, while the rolling saxophone riffs arranged by Domino's studio partner Dave Bartholomew gave the tracks they worked on an irresistible good-time quality.

Domino's transition from R & B hero to rock'n'roll star was achieved almost effortlessly, setting a pattern that other New Orleans acts – Little Richard, Lloyd Price, Smiley Lewis, Clarence 'Frogman' Henry – all attempted to follow. All made use of the talents of the city's famed sessionmen and the facilities of Cosimo Matassa's celebrated J & M studio, a Mecca for R & B musicians and producers since its opening in 1945. Domino, however, remained in a class of his own for years. His rock career appeared to be

Top left: New Orleans producer Cosimo Matassa, whose J&M Studio was responsible for dozens of national and regional hits for such artists as Fats Domino, Lloyd Price and Little Richard

Above: some of Matassa's sessioneers, who formed one of the most notable house bands of the Fifties, pose for the camera

Left: Pat Boone, a clean-living white crooner who found unlikely fame as a rock 'n' roll star with cover versions of R&B hits by New Orleans-based performers

threatened, initially, by the massive promotion given to ballad singer Pat Boone's rather embarrassed covers of his songs, but the efforts of disc jockeys like Alan Freed – who refused to play what he called 'watered-down steals from the new Bing Crosby' – ensured that the Domino originals returned huge sales. An obvious point in his favour was that he was, in certain respects, a highly traditional artist: he did not embody the explicit sexuality that was normally associated with R & B and was presumed to offend white sensibilities, and his tubby form and avuncular personality guaranteed him appearances on national television denied to other, more handsome and sexually charismatic black performers like Clyde McPhatter.

The lesson was that black sounds had to be rendered acceptable to make a really sustained impact on mainstream

Below: Little Richard, whose extravagant theatricality and ecstatic, lascivious singing represented rock 'n' roll at its wildest and most comic

American music – and that inevitably favoured those artists who were amenable to change, who had the vision to appreciate what white audiences wanted, and who conformed to certain pre-conceptions of what a black entertainer should be. The wild success of Little Richard – loud, brash and madly theatrical, with songs like 'Tutti Frutti' and 'Ready Teddy' that were totally devoid of any meaning – might seem to contradict this rule, yet his very outrageousness neutralised any threat he posed. To many, he was a frenzied caricature of an R&B singer, too ridiculous to be dangerous. He was an important rock'n'roll stylist and certainly the music's first great showman, but it is for the comedy of his stage act rather than the quality of his hot-gospel delivery that he is now best remembered.

Street corner serenades

In its earliest form, rock'n'roll was synonymous with R&B, but it also encompassed elements of black gospel music – most notably in the 'doo-wop' singing style of black vocal groups who sprang up by the thousand in the Fifties. With its gospel base, doo-wop lacked the raunch or drive of secular R&B, but the sweetness of its harmonies and the devotional nature of its songs made it far more accessible to white audiences. Many of the groups quite literally came together on the street corners of black neighbourhoods, trading harmonies in the manner of the Ink Spots and the Mills Brothers: both were key influences and career models, their phenomenal following among whites in the Forties having brought them the kind of all-American success denied to blacks in most other avenues of life.

The term 'doo-wop' was a phonetic interpretation of one of the many vocal phrases with which a group would back its lead singer, and part of its popularity

with young blacks could be put down to the fact that it needed no instrumental accompaniment and therefore no financial outlay. The voices were everything and the churches – traditionally at the heart of black communities in America – provided the perfect training grounds. The Ravens and the Orioles were among the first to find major success at the start of the Fifties, their records being the first discs that white radio stations reached for when confronted by teenage demand for black music. Part of the policy behind encouraging doo-wop as opposed to hard R&B was diversionary, and its popularity even inspired a string of rather insipid imitation records by white high-school kids. 'White doo-wop', however, was a fleeting craze.

Doo-wop's place in the rock'n'roll story has always been slightly anomalous, its sentimentality and emphasis on the ballad form seeming to contradict the

Above: the legendary Ink Spots, easily the most popular and influential black vocal group of the century, pictured in a radio studio during 1940. Their success in a white record market gave encouragement to scores of younger street-corner quartets and quintets

energy and aggression of R&B-influenced rock. Yet its influence was felt in the long term: groups like those signed to Detroit's Motown label, who began in classic doo-wop fashion, would later forge a link between gospel, R&B and pop elements and in so doing lay the foundations for both Sixties soul music and the music of the Beatles. In the Fifties, doo-wop simply represented the acceptable face of black music – a point admirably illustrated by the presence of the Platters, who made their name with classy, supper-club interpretations of old-time ballads like 'My Prayer', in the first rock'n'roll exploitation movie, *Rock Around the Clock*.

Above left: the Ravens, the most likely pretenders to the Ink Spots' crown during the late Forties and early Fifties. Despite considerable success, they were eclipsed by the brilliantly professional and astutely managed Platters (left), who found a new home for the doo-wop sound in the sophisticated setting of America's supper clubs and cabaret centres

17

record companies and artist management alike. Ownership at all levels of the music business, including that of several influential R&B-based independents, was concentrated in white hands. Yet there was a creative as well as economic aspect to white interest in R&B that became most evident in country music circles, especially among young white musicians who had grown up near black communities and knew its qualities at first-hand. Blending black rhythms with the melody of country, they brought a new dimension to rock'n'roll and secured its future as a commercial force.

At first sight, white involvement in black music in the early Fifties verged on appropriation: not only did the interest of white listeners inspire the modification of black sounds, but white demands also coloured the treatment of the music and its makers by media,

Like R&B, country was a community

music with its own values, heroes and institutions, including radio stations and record labels dedicated to pleasing a low-income audience generally neglected by the national media. Essentially it was the music of the poor white Southerner, and so traditionally of only marginal importance to the record industry, although commercial expansion of the field did begin in earnest after World War Two. Several of the major labels established offices and studios in Nashville, initially to record country's top radio performers for Southern consumption, while the city's biggest music publisher Acuff-Rose signed a lucrative deal to supply Columbia Records with a steady flow of suitable songs for their massively successful roster of artists. Masterminded by Mitch Miller, Columbia's formidable artists and repertoire manager (also known for his *Sing Along with Mitch* albums), the deal ensured that America would steadily become used to hearing country music in a pallid and much sentimentalised form.

Public awareness of country – then often derisorily labelled 'hillbilly' – music was therefore greater than that of R&B, but many of its most popular figures like Roy Acuff, Ernest Tubb and Hank Williams remained largely unknown outside the South. Nor was there much appreciation nationally of the distinctions between country styles, from the western swing of Bob Wills – who mixed traditional fiddle and steel guitar accompaniment with jazz instrumentation – through the bluegrass music of Bill Monroe to the guitar-based honky tonk sound of the Texan drinking dens. It was out of these three styles, all dance musics of different regional appeal, that something called country-boogie emerged – a style that incorporated elements of black boogie-woogie music and boasted some fabulous guitarists in the Delmore Brothers, Merle Travis and Jack Guthrie.

Haley moves in

Country-boogie was the field into which Bill Haley moved around 1950, after some years of making a living as leader of a minor-league hillbilly band. Particularly influenced by black bluesman Joe Turner, Haley broke new ground by grafting country arrangements on to songs that had already sold well in the R&B market. In time, he dropped the fiddle and steel guitar from his line-up altogether in favour of saxophone and electric guitar; in live performance, too, his band simulated some of the exuberance of black contemporaries like the Louis Jordan band, completing a potent mix

Below: Bill Haley, the man whose success opened the flood-gates to rock 'n' roll. He was originally the leader of a hillbilly band whose approach owed much to the 'western swing' styling of Forties favourites Bob Wills and his Texas Playboys (opposite page)

that transferred well to record. His was one of several jobbing bands on the northern country and western circuit to take the same course, but he had the astuteness to smarten the band's image – their name was changed from the home-spun Saddlemen to the flashier Comets, and they took to wearing a stage uniform of tartan jackets and bow ties – and deliberately gear his repertoire towards the younger of his dance-hall clientele.

In going this far, Haley left country music far behind, but tracks like 'Shake, Rattle and Roll' (a Joe Turner R&B hit expunged of all its sexual references in Haley's version) and the monumental 'Rock Around the Clock' stood out as the first commercial syntheses of R&B and country. It was a contrived marriage of styles, much of the credit for which should go to Haley's manager Dave Miller and his producer Milt Gabler, who had produced many of Louis Jordan's hits in the Forties and deliberately sought to re-create the free-rolling drive of those recordings. His aim was to create a sound that was perfect for the dance-hall environment, but just as important to the success of 'Rock Around the Clock' and other Haley hits was something intangible – the way they captured a certain emerging spirit, an impatience with the world. The lyrics, too, with their smattering of R&B-derived jive talk – 'See You Later, Alligator' was a classic example – and constant references to the dance floor, marked the songs as identifiably and immovably teenage in appeal. Although he was no musical innovator, Haley's sound had the right ingredients and paved the way for other, more subtle versions of the R&B-country blend.

The Sun sound

Haley's involvement in country had always been peripheral; his territory was not the cities and towns of the South but the northern conurbations, home of exiled Southerners whose perception of country was nostalgic and romanticised. In musical terms therefore, Haley's influence on the country scene was only fleeting. Much more significant in broad terms were the commercial and creative strides being made, quite independently of anything Haley was doing, by white

Right: the stage gymnastics of the Haley band at its peak – new and exciting at the time, if somewhat comic in retrospect. Haley's career as a top-line artist was brief, his status as 'king of rock 'n' roll' quickly threatened by the emergence of Elvis Presley (pictured with Haley, below). They appeared on the same bill in Cleveland in 1955, the year before Presley's national breakthrough

producers, musicians and singers on the fringes of the country music industry. Memphis, Tennessee, one of the most cosmopolitan cities in America and a major recording centre for both blues and hillbilly musicians since the Twenties, was the focal point for much of this activity. It was there, in 1950, that a white radio engineer named Sam Phillips established the Sun recording studio, his initial aim being to record tracks by Tennessee bluesmen for leasing to blues labels in Chicago – home of many Southern-born blacks since the migrations of the Thirties and Forties – and elsewhere.

The Sun record label developed naturally out of the studio's success, and Phillips kept to a similar policy of recording only blues because that was where his own passion lay. He nevertheless appreciated the growth of teenage interest in black styles: among Sun's first local commercial successes were novelty blues numbers by black disc jockey Rufus Thomas and the four-man Prisonaires, a black vocal group from the state penitentiary. With hits and publicity came

aspiring hit-makers – including a young truck driver, Elvis Presley, who won himself an audition after using Sun's private recording service to cut a birthday disc for his mother. On the face of it, Presley was of no use to Sun – not only was he white, but his hero was Dean Martin and his singing style apparently suited to country or gospel. Sessions with Sun's resident musicians, bassist Bill Black and guitarist Scotty Moore, confirmed this until, during a break from recording, all three began to relax by playing some straight blues. The sound was a revelation: at his most relaxed, even abandoned, with the grittiest blues numbers, Presley sang with an authenticity that was almost chilling.

A white boy singing the blues – a perfect musical match, added to which Elvis had, despite or perhaps because of his shyness, a kind of detached sexual charisma. 'That's All Right, Mama', an Arthur Crudup blues number recorded during that first session, was released back to back with a bluegrass number, Bill Monroe's 'Blue Moon of Kentucky':

Above: the famous Sun label, bearing the title of one of its most historic releases

Below left: Sun boss Sam Phillips cuts a disc, watched by Elvis and session men Bill Black and Scotty Moore

Below: Sam shows Elvis a guitar chord

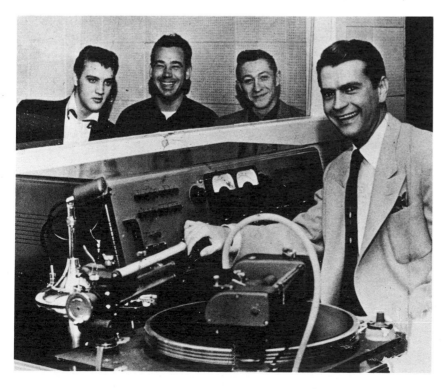

Presley handled both with a confidence that suggested exposure to blues *and* genuine down-home country from an early age. The record sold well locally and Elvis went on the road as 'the Hillbilly Cat' – an uneasy billing that illustrated the difficulty both show promoters and radio stations had in categorising him. Even Phillips himself was unsure of precisely how to market him – taken together, Presley's first Sun recordings showed a very eclectic singing talent at work. Only after Bill Haley's 1955 breakthrough did it occur to anybody, least of all Elvis himself, to call what he was creating rock'n'roll.

Elvis goes national

Between 1954 and 1956, Elvis' fame grew steadily in the South, although his appearance on the country music world's Number 1 radio show, the Grand Ole Opry, was not a success. Despite his command of the country idiom, he was too much of an individualist to comply with the demands of hillbilly tradition; as one contemporary described his performing style, 'He was a sight to see, let alone hear. No cowboy rig like the others, but rainbow-dazzle sports clothes, a

satin stripe down the trousers, drape jacket with collar up, longish hair in a duck tail. A very dangerous Dapper Dan, very common'. Scotty Moore managed him for a while, then Nashville-based Bob Neal, until a one-time fairground barker and arch-hustler named 'Colonel' Tom Parker recognised his potential beyond the confines of establishment country. Parker, for all his sharp dealing and devotion to the show business ethic, was at least attuned to the mood of the times: he saw in Elvis an explosive mix of danger and deference that, whatever

Above, above left: young, lean and unquestionably charismatic – Elvis Presley pictured in 1955, on the verge of countrywide fame

specific musical bag he fell into, cried out for a national platform.

In a relatively short time, Elvis grew too big for Sun. His records were beginning to break nationally, but there was no way that Sam Phillips – with his limited facilities and lack of organised distribution in the northern states – could cope with the increasing demand. So in 1956, under pressure from Parker, Sun effectively sold Presley to the highest bidder – the major RCA Victor. Phillips received $35,000, a sum that gave his label a sound financial base for the future. The move was another key turning point for rock, not only because it was the means that brought the unquestioned king of rock'n'roll before an international public, but because it signalled the first recognition by America's record industry that rock'n'roll was indeed here to stay. After that unprecedented (and, for the time, astonishingly expensive) deal, rock'n'roll

entered the big-money league, no longer the product of a handful of uppitty independents but the property of record companies who realised that fighting against the teenage tide was to risk their positions in the market place. Inevitably, however, the very accommodation of rock'n'roll into the mainstream would alter both its content and its character.

Left: the cover of Elvis Presley's first album for RCA, released in 1956

Below: Presley with Colonel Tom Parker, who took him from Sun to RCA and turned the Elvis phenomenon into a multi-million dollar industry

ROCKABILLY AND BEYOND

The bosses at RCA took their investment in Elvis Presley very seriously indeed. Under artists and repertoire boss Steve Sholes they had already made big inroads into the country music field, and it was with leading Nashville producer and guitar virtuoso Chet Atkins that Presley was placed. The brief, however, was very specific – to re-create the atmosphere and vitality of those early Sun recordings. Hip, young rock'n'roll songwriters with a proven track record were brought in to provide material, notably Jerry Leiber and Mike Stoller, composers of hits for the Drifters and the Coasters. The very earnestness of the task led to a certain loss of spontaneity and air of contrivance on some tracks – that distinctive echo-chamber sound on the Sun recordings was a consequence of the recording environment, not a decorative gimmick – and there was no doubt that Presley's style was now more focused, more self-conscious, even verging on self-parody at times. But the dynamism and electricity of 'Heartbreak Hotel', his first RCA release, was undeniable; a little later, 'Don't Be Cruel' topped the American pop chart, the country chart *and* the R & B chart, a first-time feat that graphically demonstrated the nonsense inherent in dividing American music along racial lines. Elvis, it appeared, had united young people of different races and backgrounds behind one common musical banner.

His impact was enormous, on many different levels. As a performer, he had all the glamour and personality that Bill Haley had lacked: not only was he good-looking, he had style and a shy grace that belied the frenzy and sexual horseplay of his stage performances, which were apparently influenced by the black gospel preachers of his native Tupelo, Mississippi. His rags to riches story was a reflection of the American dream. He was a symbol of and for American youth, the

Left: Elvis could call on the songwriting expertise of a string of first-rate composers and lyricists; among them Mike Stoller (left) and Jerry Leiber (right). Their compositions for Presley included 'Hound Dog' and 'Jailhouse Rock'

country boy who made it to Hollywood, apparently without compromising – someone who had played the system and won. After Presley, every would-be rock performer would try to capture that blend of sly sexuality, self-deprecation and surly separateness that was his unique trademark.

On a musical level, Presley was the catalyst for the growth of rockabilly, loosely defined as the white Southerner's rock'n'roll – a style based upon the fusion of black influences with the more free-wheeling, good-time elements in country music. Rockabilly – literally, rock plus hillbilly – was the kid brother of country-boogie, its tone set by both Presley and those musicians who came to Memphis to record for Sun in the wake of his success. All shared Presley's background and his innate feel for blues and country. Carl Perkins, Sun's biggest name in the year or so following Presley's departure, was typical: 'The man who taught me guitar was an old coloured man. See, I was raised on a plantation in the flatlands of Lake County, Tennessee, and we were the only white people on it. For white music, I liked Bill Monroe's bluegrass

Above: Carl Perkins (at microphone), like many other graduates of the Sun school of rockabilly, recorded his own material almost exclusively

stuff; for coloured music, I liked John Lee Hooker, Muddy Waters, their electric stuff. Even then I liked to do Hooker songs Bill Monroe-style, blues with a country beat'.

The crown pretenders

Perkins was one of the great rockabilly guitarists but his reluctance to perform live, after a car crash on tour that killed his brother, cost him lasting commercial success. Nevertheless, his record 'Blue Suede Shoes' (1956) topped both the country and R&B charts (and reached Number 2 nationally), and was one of the first songs to tap the vein of unabashed narcissism at the heart of the teenage lifestyle. Capturing the same spirit but with even greater abandon was Jerry Lee Lewis, a Louisiana fireball who sold six million copies with 'A Whole Lotta Shakin' Goin' On', only his second Sun release. The Lewis style was Perkins-style rockabilly plus a pumping, impromptu piano and soaring, self-confident vocals. A wild man on stage, he was a sort of rock'n'roll Elmer Gantry, a hot gospeller whose intentions seemed decidedly satanic, and ultimately it was his abrasiveness and refusal to bow to convention – he was quietly dropped by Sun after the controversy concerning his marriage to a 13-year old cousin – that cost him the chance of assuming Elvis' rock'n'roll crown.

Sam Phillips' other signings included Charlie Rich, who had all Presley's feeling for blues and country but none of his ambition or drive; and Johnny Cash, who was never happy with Phillips' determination to restrict him to rockabilly when he preferred to record folk songs and religious material. Cash eventually departed to Columbia in another major deal, as Mitch Miller's sop to those in his company who wanted their own Elvis Presley. As it happened, Cash was allowed to develop as a country performer, while Miller continued to narrow his interpretation of rock so it encompassed only the time-honoured tradition of having top mainstream acts record either R&B or country songs. Guy Mitchell's 'Singing the Blues' (1956) was a classic example, a very clever copy of the Presley RCA sound, complete with vocal backing in the manner of the Jordanaires (virtually ever-present on Presley recordings after 'Don't Be Cruel') and an echo-laden production sound. The song itself had been a major hit in the country market for Marty Robbins, who Columbia also promoted as a surrogate rock'n'roll star a little later in the decade.

The search for a second Presley occupied the waking hours of record company chiefs – especially those of the majors – for the best part of two years, to little avail. While MGM eventually placed their faith in a Sun reject with the distinctly un-rock-like name of Conway Twitty, Capitol had short-term success with Gene Vincent, yet another young hillbilly performer to model his whole singing style on Elvis. The million-selling 'Be Bop a Lula' (1956) showed how well he had absorbed the lessons of his mentor's success: again, the production deliberately evoked the atmosphere and sound of 'Heartbreak Hotel', complete with flutter-echo and a mannered but engaging vocal hiccup. His fame was transient, since his career degenerated through heavy drinking and a series of management blunders, but he was no mere copyist. Never a glamour boy and, image-wise, a far cry from the certainties of the Elvis machine, he fared particularly well in Britain, where he gave working class youngsters – the Lennon, Townshend generation – something with which they could strongly identify.

Opposite page: Elvis grooming the famous slicked-back hair. Many Presley imitators attempted to ape his appearance as well as his music

Below: Gene Vincent and the Blue Caps pictured in The Girl Can't Help It, *a 1956 movie showcase for more than a dozen top rock 'n' roll acts*

It was debatable whether Gene Vincent or many other of the post-Presley discoveries could really be described as rockabilly singers. In the words of writer Martin Hawkins, rockabilly was 'hyperactive country-boogie with a strengthened rhythm, jumping guitar solos derived from R&B, and hot-potato-in-the-mouth vocals' – features more prevalent on the records of artists like Sonny Fisher, Mac Curtis and Charlie Feathers, hitmakers none of them, than on those of the more publicised Presley soundalikes. Rockabilly increasingly became a catch-all term applied to anything in the rock'n'roll vein sung or played by white artists. Inevitably, too, it was confused with a more poppified form of country music, exemplified by the smooth Nashville productions of the Everly Brothers, and the jaunty teenage lullabies of Ricky (later Rick) Nelson.

In the three years from 'Rock Around the Clock' (1955) to 'Dance to the Bop' (1958), Gene Vincent's last big American hit, rock'n'roll had changed – not so much in appeal, but in character and definition. There were already clear signs that the music was becoming softer and sweeter, and that its aggressive spirit was being tamed: the entry of a singularly compliant Elvis Presley into the US Army during 1958 was, in this sense, symbolic. Record industry exploitation of the young market was becoming much more sophisticated and intense, as new independent companies entered the fray and the teen music rosters of the majors began to expand. Perhaps the key change, however, was in the market itself – now more evenly split between the sexes, a little older, and with an insatiable appetite for music that, like the teen magazines springing up in the wake of Elvis, reflected teenage concerns more obsessively than ever.

HIGH SCHOOL USA
From rock into pop

When the made-to-order teenage pop song was born, young America temporarily left rock 'n' roll behind

Right: Chuck Berry, a witty and affectionate chronicler of teenage life in scores of classic, much-covered rock 'n' roll songs

Opposite page: Buddy Holly, rock music's first great singer/songwriter

In 1957, Chuck Berry scored his third *Billboard* chart hit with an uncompromising anti-school song, 'School Days', in which he depicted the classroom as a confining, regimented environment peopled by mean-looking teachers and bullying fellow pupils. His message, though, was an optimistic one: 'Hail hail rock'n'roll / Deliver me from the days of old', he sang, identifying the music as not only a source of release but as the very enemy of the kind of traditional values that education propagated.

Only two years later came an indicator of just how much had changed within rock. The Atlantic label released 28 different versions of Tommy 'Bubba' Facenda's 'High School USA', each of which mentioned the names of high schools in particular American cities. The record was symptomatic of much about the late Fifties rock business – its incessant digging for teenage themes, its passion for novelty, the razor-sharp marketing sense of many of its operators – but it was the content, the message, that was so different from Berry's hit. Offering a vision of a delinquent-free world in which inter-school chauvinism was defined as the key outlet for teenage energy, the record seemed a negation of everything that rock'n'roll had once stood for.

'High School USA' was a typical product of an industry arrogantly sure of its audience and back in control (after the upheavals caused by rock'n'roll) of its own direction. It was typical, too, of a general descent into trivia, an inevitable

result of the intense exploitation of the teen market that followed the initial rock boom. Record companies came to anticipate more sharply the changing tastes of young record buyers: as trends were assessed and the money-spinning gimmicks or effects of particular discs noted, so rock records became increasingly self-conscious, self-referring and stylised. Imitation became rife – and the process was accelerated as more labels emerged, attracted into the market by the prospect of a quick return on capital, and television began to play an active role in the star-making machine. And as power in the industry began to centre on a new type of professional – artists and repertoire heads on the look out for a new pretty face, song-writers adept at fashioning songs to match the image of a

Right: Neil Sedaka, writer and performer of a new kind of cute, cleverly-constructed teenage love song

Below: Chuck Berry's importance to the development of rock was crucial. When the first wave of city beat groups began forming in Britain during the early Sixties, all of them sought to emulate Berry's clanking, metallic guitar style and to perfect carbon-copy cover versions of his best rock'n'roll recordings

certain performer, producers with a faultless ear for a hit sound – so the haphazard, instinctive quality of classic rock'n'roll was lost.

Even the terminology gradually changed. With the appearance of string arrangements on teen records and the preponderance of ballads in the charts of 1958/59, 'rock'n'roll' was no longer appropriate to the kind of music being made. 'Pop' became the new catch-all term. There was a shift, too, in the nature of the pop song itself, as lyricists – taking their initial inspiration from the likes of Chuck Berry – became increasingly aware of the possibilities that the teen-age culture offered them. Conveniently ignoring the anti-establishment edge of Berry's work, they played up the para-phernalia of the teen scene instead of exploring its undercurrents – hence the innumerable songs about junior proms, pony-tails, drive-in movies, and even the teenage death wish, translated into awe-somely morbid songs like Mark Dinning's 'Teen Angel' (1960), where the heroine dies snatching the ring her boyfriend gave her from the path of a train. The language of the pop song changed, from the party-doll vocabulary of the rockabilly song to the quaint angels-and-devils metaphors of a writer like Neil Sedaka, holed up in a steamy New York office creating hit songs for a living.

Despite all this, however, it is possible to see the late Fifties and early Sixties as a period of retrenchment, when after the violent breakthrough of the mid-Fifties, the music eased itself into national ac-ceptance as the primary means of ex-pression for the young and settled into an unshakeable position. Certainly the deadening hand of big business pushed music into safe formulas, but the ground-work was being laid – by artists like Buddy Holly and the Everly Brothers, and numerous young musicians and singers – for future triumphs.

CHRONICLERS
OF THE TEEN SCENE

Perhaps the key feature of the whole late Fifties teen culture was its degree of self-awareness – its delight in its own passions and concerns, the insatiable appetite of teenagers for reading about themselves, watching themselves on television, comparing notes with each other on fashions and trends. The first songwriter to capitalise on this was Chuck Berry, who created a kind of mythology out of the minutiae of teenage life and became almost the poet laureate of rock'n'roll.

Berry emerged in the mid-Fifties out of Chicago R & B, the toughest of blues schools, with the endorsement of blues

legend Muddy Waters and a contract with Chess, the city's premier independent label. He always insisted that his conversion to rock'n'roll was motivated purely by economics – 'the dollar dictates what music is written' was one of his favourite and most characteristic sayings – but it inspired a body of songs that came the closest of any in the Fifties to

Below: Berry on stage during one of the package tours that helped to shape his career

31

Above: Muddy Waters (with guitar) at the Chess studios in Chicago

Above right: Chuck Berry, who owed his first recording break to Waters' patronage, on a UK tour in the mid-Sixties

capturing how it felt to be young, white and at odds with the adult world. That it took a black musician with an impeccable blues pedigree to achieve this, at a time when white musicians and singers were busy emulating black sounds, was one of rock's nicest ironies.

With a clear, precise voice that ensured every word of his songs could be heard – not a facet for which blues singers were renowned – and a guitar sound influenced as much by rockabilly as straight R & B, Berry's records had no trouble gaining airplay on white radio. Even as his first hit, 'Maybelline', reached Number 5 in the American chart during 1955, it was widely believed that he was a white artist. The crux of his appeal however, was his songs, which not only drew on specific white teenage concerns for their subject matter, but offered a wry, sympathetic commentary upon them. He wrote of the growing pains of adolescence in 'Almost Grown', the drudgery of the workplace in 'Too Much Monkey Business', the promise of sexual adventure that automobiles embodied in 'Maybelline' and 'No Particular Place to Go', and the comedy of a rock'n'-roll-crazed couple's teenage wedding in 'You Never Can Tell'. By identifying himself with such themes, he engaged the emotions of teenage listeners far more readily than any of his R & B-based black contemporaries.

Berry also celebrated in his songs the sheer energy and release inherent in rock'n'roll itself. 'Rock'n'Roll Music', 'Roll Over Beethoven' and 'Reelin' and Rockin'' were variations on the same message – rock transcends the mundaneness of the workaday world – while 'Johnny B. Goode' charted in epic fashion the rags-to-riches rise of a backwoods guitar star. At their best, his songs had a panoramic quality, rejoicing in Americana – 'Back in the U.S.A.', 'The Promised Land' – and glorying in its artefacts, from juke boxes to fast cars,

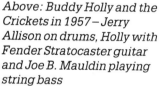

Above: Buddy Holly and the Crickets in 1957 – Jerry Allison on drums, Holly with Fender Stratocaster guitar and Joe B. Mauldin playing string bass

Above right: Holly in a 1958 publicity pose, sporting his famous horn-rimmed spectacles

Right: Holly and band in full song during a performance for the BBC in London

from autographed star pin-ups to the latest dance craze. The tone of such compositions was consistently comic and more than a touch journalistic: he wrote and sang with the detached, relaxed amusement of an open-minded outsider, standing slightly apart from his subjects and reporting what he saw.

Tex-Mex teendreams

Chuck Berry would remain a rock hero for years, thanks to the durability and continuing relevance of his magnificent repertoire, but his lyrics placed him as a commentator on the teenage scene, not a participant in it. Buddy Holly's perspective was different; as a young white boy from small town America – Lubbock, Texas – he could write from within the teen experience and personalise many of the themes that Berry touched upon. The result was rock'n'roll music of a different character – more down to earth, introspective, self-concerned and shot through with an unusual degree of emotional honesty. Always direct, even cynical, in their stance – 'That'll Be The

Day' (1958) was the ultimate lover's put-down – Holly's songs took the form of intimate dialogues between friends or lovers ('Well All Right', Listen to Me'), or nervous, soul-searching soliloquoys ('Everyday', 'Heartbeat'). His song constructions were simple, in part derivative of the country music he began his career performing, but he had a telling ear for the casual, everyday phrase and a refreshing ability to avoid the obvious rhyme or linguistic effect – except in his hit 'Peggy Sue', which was recorded as a self-mocking exercise in vocal technique.

Below: Norman Petty, under whose management Holly's career prospered

Bottom: joint honeymoon in Acapulco for Buddy Holly with Maria Elena and Crickets drummer Jerry Allison with Peggy Sue – who inspired one of Holly's biggest hits

Ordinariness was important to Holly. He fashioned lyrics with which the average kid on the street could identify, and he assiduously avoided promoting himself as a personality or a pin-up, to the extent of wearing his horn-rimmed glasses on stage. This somewhat cultivated lack of lustre extended to his recordings, both those he made as a solo artist (for Coral) and as a member of the Crickets (for Brunswick). Produced by Norman Petty, Holly's manager and sometime composing partner, at his studio in Clovis, New Mexico, they were as basic as the rockabilly fashion dictated, while featuring imaginative use of Tex-Mex rhythms and percussive effects – an ingenious hands-on-knees accompaniment on 'Everyday', for example. Only when Holly split with the Crickets and severed his connections with Petty in late 1958, did his music become soft-centred to the point of mawkishness; moving to New York, he spent the last months of his life writing and recording material in a much more mainstream vein, forsaking the rock'n'roll focus of his earlier work in favour of ornate orchestrations and clever but indulgent vocal overdubbing.

Holly's career was desperately short – he died in an air crash while on tour in February 1959 – but during that time he stood out as the undisputed leader of the second wave of rock performers, those following Presley and the other Sun pioneers but not necessarily sharing the same experience of, or interest in, black sounds. Holly took his cue from rock'n'roll itself, not its sources, and from the Tex-Mex music of the Mexican border country, which inspired the urgent, rhythmically insistent and flamenco-like guitar sound on 'Peggy Sue' and 'Not Fade Away'. Perhaps his greatest contribution to rock, though, was his pioneering of the beat group set-up: having first forged his style within the limitations of a guitar-drums duo (formed with Jerry Allison), he expanded upon the tight-

knit, self-contained base of that sound within the framework of the three- and later four-man Crickets. The Beatles, in particular, would owe much to him – their very name was Cricket-inspired.

Smalltown dreamers

Holly was only 22 when he died. Younger still and working in a similar rockabilly-influenced vein were Don and Phil Everly, two singing brothers from Brownie, Kentucky. They had a country music background of some distinction, having been stalwarts of local radio in their home state since their early teens, and they made their debut on the *Grand Ole Opry* just prior to their national breakthrough in 1957. They also had ideal backing for a duo straddling the country and rock camps: their business affairs were handled by Wesley Rose, head of the Acuff-Rose publishing house, which also provided them with an exclusive repertoire. Their recordings – although released through Cadence, a New York independent – were all produced in Nashville by Chet Atkins, late of Elvis Presley's RCA sessions and a man in the throes of revolutionising the country scene with a new recording format known as 'the Nashville Sound'. This format simply threw out the steel guitar and fiddle accompaniments that had been so much a part of country records for years and replaced them with piano, percussion and rhythm guitar backing; Everlys hits such as 'Bye Bye Love' were among the first to feature it.

The Everly Brothers could rock when required – their versions of Little Richard's 'Lucille' and Roy Orbison's 'Claudette' proved it – but their particular niche was a kind of countrified teen ballad, to which their young and sweetly controlled high-register harmonies were especially suited. Even in 1957, there were few publishers offering this kind of material – the best teenage songs were

Above: three favourite sons of smalltown America, pictured in conversation during 1958 – Buddy Holly (left), Phil and Don Everly

Left: Boudleaux and Felice Bryant, songwriters extraordinaire, holding success in their hands. Their songs for the Everly Brothers brilliantly encapsulated the aspirations and anxieties of white American teenagers during the mid to late Fifties

invariably those written by performers for their own use – but Acuff-Rose had a songwriting team in Felice and Boudleaux Bryant who applied themselves to the task with customary Nashville professionalism. 'Bye Bye Love', the cutely risqué 'Wake Up Little Susie', and the faintly masturbatory 'All I Have To Do Is Dream' were all their compositions, while even the hits that Don and Phil themselves composed – 'When Will I Be Loved' and 'So Sad' among them – had similar form and content.

The brothers found a formula very early in their rock career and stuck to it, though they often found interesting variations on

Above and right: Phil and Don Everly – twin guitars, shimmering vocal harmonies, good looks and oceans of brilliantine. Their public face hid animosity that culminated in an acrimonious break-up on stage during 1973. They reunited ten years later for a Royal Albert Hall concert

it with spirited revivals of old-time standards like 'Temptation' and 'Don't Blame Me', classic rock'n'roll songs like 'Be Bop a Lula', and classy, continental-style ballads like the impressive 'Let It Be Me'. Mostly their songs were exquisitely-crafted vignettes about problems in school, girlfriend troubles, traumas with parents – the concerns of small-town teenagers with reputations to keep and self-respect to nurture, yet nonetheless fascinated by the game of love. More than any other act of the period, they seemed the true voices of decent-minded, put-upon American youth. In time they, like Presley, made their big move to a major company – in their case, the new record division of Warner

Left: Chet Atkins (holding guitar) with two fellow architects of 'the Nashville sound', pianist Floyd Cramer and saxophonist Boots Randolph. Atkins lent his formidable production skills to hits by Elvis Presley, Jim Reeves, Don Gibson and the Everly Brothers (below) between 1956 and 1964, besides recording the occasional instrumental hit in his own right

Brothers, the giant Hollywood film and television corporation – but with it came no perceptible change in style or shift in popularity. Under no pressure to mature in the conventional career sense, they remained popular for as long as their formula remained acceptable. Only with the coming of the Beatles, whose harmonies bore a distinct Everly Brothers influence, did their long hit-making run begin to falter.

There was another quality to the Everlys' music that helped take the 'teenage sound' – as the industry was by now preferring to label rock – into a different league. Theirs was not a sound rooted in the dance floor or juke joint, but rather one meant for solitary listening. Everly records expressed more intimate moods and sentiments than those hitherto acknowledged by rock, and as such were heard best on bedside record players or dressing table radios. Like Buddy Holly, the Everly Brothers did much to broaden rock from a social to a personal, even domestic music, relevant to more than just the leisure activities of teenagers. That the record industry sought to exploit this new factor through the growing phenomenon of the teen idol was not their fault.

THE TEEN IDOL ERA

Record companies, and especially those in the independent sector, were quick to learn as the Fifties wore on. The mass burst of creative activity that was the rockabilly boom gradually gave way to a concern for formula and a new concentration on non-musical factors – the image and television presence of a singer, his appeal to the fast-growing female audience, his potential in films and in the wider world of showbusiness. Musically, the most important ingredient in this new commercial mix was repertoire in the style of the Everly Brothers and their contemporaries – songs that explored the ups and downs of teenage romance but in far less subtle fashion, provided by a production line of songsmiths whose chief talent was imitation.

The obession with image was another by-product of Elvis' huge success, and his career seemed to offer newer idols like Tab Hunter, Paul Anka and Frankie Avalon a clear model for progress. By 1958, the Presley rebel image had been undermined by increasingly stylised hits and his apparent penchant for ballads; he had entered the US Army in a flurry of patriotic publicity and his Hollywood films were not the smouldering, James Dean-inspired teen pleasers that many had expected. He was no longer primarily a rock'n'roll star: his success showed that it was equally important, for career durability, to master other musical styles and develop one's skill as an all-round entertainer.

Below: adoring female fans gather for an open-air performance by Paul Anka in 1958. Anka's rock 'n' roll roots were tenuous, but he crafted his songs – like the million-selling 'Diana' (1957) – to appeal to any teenager who had ever wept into his pillow over a love that never blossomed

His absence on Army service cleared the way for others to fight for centre-stage. Robbed of their prize asset for two years, the teen magazines looked around hungrily for other acts to promote and found a succession of new record labels – most based in the northern cities – willing and able to supply them. Television, too, played a crucial role in discovering new stars, beginning with Ricky Nelson, who found national fame after appearing in his parents' situation comedy show and recording a hit version of Fats Domino's 'I'm Walkin''. Soon after, he signed to Domino's Imperial label and was launched as a kind of junior Elvis, with amiable grin and gentle, country-flavoured teen songs to match. His rise was paralleled by that of Paul Anka, who also had television backing in the form of ABC Records, the record label subsidiary of ABC-TV. He was not so much a junior Elvis as a would-be Sinatra, complete with smart suit, big-band accompaniment and big-city management; making his chart debut with 'Diana' in 1957 and following that with a string of highly conventional self-composed ballads, he was identified with rock only because of his extreme youth and the teenage

orientation of his lyrics. Although influential in their use of cha-cha rhythms and pizzicato-like guitar sounds, his records bore hardly a trace of classic rock'n'roll.

Bopping on Bandstand

Singers in the Anka mould found an ideal platform in *American Bandstand*, a television show that had begun before the Presley era yet only really came into its own with the teen idol trend. Broadcast live every day from studios in Philadelphia, the show was pitched directly at America's high school audience and so gave advertisers a ready means of marketing all manner of teen-related goods. The format had stars dropping by to talk about themselves and mime to their latest record, while dancers recruited from the local high schools competed with one another to create new dance steps for the rest of America to imitate. Hosted by the super-smooth Dick Clark, who also selected the artists and records for exposure on the show, it promoted a sanitised version of rock by favouring balladeers over rock singers and reducing the music to the level of a harmless novelty. With his daily homilies about

Above: Annette Funicello and Frankie Avalon, co-stars of innumerable early Sixties 'beach party' movies, caught in a clinch. Like Ricky Nelson, Avalon progressed into film work once his days as a teen idol were numbered, but his lack of personal charisma and simple acting ability ensured his movie career was a short one

Above left: Ricky Nelson, one of the first teen idols to owe his success entirely to television. After a long run of pop hits, he tried his luck in films and then moved into the country music field, achieving critical acclaim but only limited commercial success. He died in a plane accident on the last day of 1985

Frankie Avalon, whose lack of voice and any kind of stage presence – so woefully apparent on 'De-De-Dinah', 'Venus' and 'Bobby Sox to Stockings' – failed to stop him enjoying a brief year of *Bandstand*-inspired fame. He and those who followed him – Fabian, Bobby Rydell, Freddy Cannon, Charlie Gracie – all had girl appeal in the Italian-American heart-throb tradition of Sinatra, Vic Damone and Philadelphia-born Al Martino, but their links with rock were tenuous. Most were performers to whom teen music was simply a means to an end, a pad from which to launch a career as a cabaret entertainer or film star. The worst of them were no more than puppets, told what to sing and how to sing it by worldly-wise managers who had more than a hint of sharp practice about them.

Bandstand attracted an audience of over 20 million at its peak and so demanded a fast turnover of acts. Across America, groups came together in schools or colleges, cut a record at a local studio, and dreamed of getting the *Bandstand* call. Some did: the late Fifties was a great era for one-off hits and novelty discs that contributed to fads of the show's own creation, while the passion for dance crazes brought momentary national exposure to a string of instrumental groups. What the programme

Above: Bobby Rydell, one of several young Italian-American singers to take the pop spotlight between 1959 and 1963. His career was boosted spectacularly by appearances on the American Bandstand *television show, whose host Dick Clark (top right) survived a major 1959 probe into his business affairs by a congressional committee investigating corruption in the music industry*

respecting one's betters and living a clean, wholesome life, Clark attempted to re-invent the teen culture, rendering the once-threatening onslaught of teendom safe by playing up its saccharinity.

Bandstand's impact on the music scene was major. The programme's Philadelphia base encouraged local entrepreneurs to start their own labels and scour the high schools for singers with the requisite youth and good looks. Chancellor, set up by Bob Marcucci and Peter De Angelis, was one such: their discovery was a tough street kid named

failed to show, however, was precisely how cut-throat the record business was becoming in the light of such intense promotion and recording activity – and political concern over this very question prompted a Congressional inquiry, completed in 1959, into the involvement of the media in the music industry.

The inquiry revealed what some had suspected all along – that bribery or 'payola' was rife throughout American radio, and that Dick Clark had misused his position as host of *Bandstand* to push records, songs and artists in which he or his companies had financial interests. Clark himself came off lightly – he divested himself of all outside interests and was able to carry on as the show's presenter – but others, particularly in radio, became casualties. Alan Freed, rock'n'-roll's first great proselytiser, was prosecuted and died just a few years later, penniless and out of work. The net effect was that radio stations tightened their playlists, disc jockeys were denied the automatic right to choose what they played, and regionally-produced discs were ignored in favour of dependable formula records by known artists.

Hearing or reading the evidence put forward during the inquiry – of how record companies regularly had disc jockeys on their payrolls as 'consultants'

in return for airplay, how advertising agencies and publishing firms were established as 'fronts' for clandestine financial deals, and how gifts of cars, clothing and sexual favours had become part of the music business lifestyle – it was almost possible to agree with Harriet Van Horne's assertion in the *New York Telegram and Sun* that 'the whole rock'n'roll craze was artificial and contrived. Contrived by corrupt men . . . systematically greasing the palms of greedy disc jockeys. Collusion and deception all the way down the line'. Coming on top of the death of Buddy Holly, the shaming of Jerry Lee Lewis, the arrest of Chuck Berry on a child abduction charge, and Elvis Presley's less than triumphant return to recording after his sojourn in the army, the sense of disillusion among those committed to rock as a music was palpable. Many teenagers, horrified both by the Philadelphia idols and the payola findings, deserted rock for the more dignified world of folk.

The payola inquiry did have a cleansing effect on the industry, although in chart terms it just meant that the chaotic kitsch of the *Bandstand* years was replaced by an overwhelming blandness. The programme's role as a star-maker became more and more peripheral, its only major contribution to early Sixties pop being a series of ephemeral dance crazes, among them the Chubby Checker-popularised Twist. Looking beyond Philadelphia, however, the spirit of rock'n'roll could be seen to resurface occasionally – notably in the work of Roy Orbison, Del Shannon, Bruce Channel and other singer-writers whose musical approach was generally not dictated by producers or managers. In New York and Detroit too, label owners, producers and artists were beginning to forge a happy compromise between the demands of the pop production line and individual innovation and expression.

Left: the shady dealings of pioneer rock 'n' roll disc jockey Alan Freed finally caught up with him at the close of the Fifties, when congressional investigations into 'payola' destroyed his career. He died, penniless, in 1965

SOUNDS FROM THE STREETS

The pop reputation of New York, like that of many other cities, was built on a white interpretation of the black R&B sound. This took two forms. First, there were those white singers and groups who copied the black vocal group sounds with increasing confidence as the Fifties went on – street corner outfits like Dion and the Belmonts and (a little later) the Four Seasons – kids mostly from the poorer Italian neighbourhoods, for whom vocalising was both sociable recreation and free self-expression. This strain of New York pop produced a crop of hits in the early to mid-Sixties. Secondly, there was the involvement of white producers and arrangers in the recording and career direction of black singers and groups, centred initially on the white-owned independent label, Atlantic.

Jerry Leiber and Mike Stoller, two white songwriters who had been providing material for black acts since the start of the Fifties, spearheaded this involvement by creating a string of comic masterpieces for the Coasters from 1957 onwards. They took almost total control of the recording process, writing the songs – funny if rather stereotyped representations of black street culture – and creating arrangments to match. Tracks like 'Yakety Yak' and 'Shoppin' For Clothes' were sometimes the product of as many as 60 takes and countless splices, though the resulting mix of call and response patterns, disbelieving bass voice and spluttering saxophone breaks always sounded spontaneous.

With the Drifters, a popular black act re-constituted by Atlantic in 1959 after various personnel upheavals, Leiber and Stoller developed this style of technical overlay to an even greater degree. Adding latin rhythms, string accompaniment and all manner of production effects, they wrote and produced the million-selling 'There Goes My Baby' (1959) – easily the most contrived mélange of sounds yet heard in rock, yet the most imaginative

Below: the Drifters, who were transformed by producers Leiber and Stoller from a superior but relatively obscure R&B outfit into makers of machine-tooled, precision-tuned vocal group hits for the white pop market

Below right: street corner serenaders Dion and the Belmonts, from the tough Italian quarter of New York, whose masterly command of the black vocal idiom brought them a string of early Sixties hits

use that had yet been made of the studio technology. Stylistically and technically, the disc – and subsequent Drifters releases like 'Dance With Me', 'This Magic Moment' and 'Save the Last Dance For Me' – set new standards. Particularly influential was their introduction of the *baion* rhythm into pop: this was a rhythm akin to the samba and bossa nova, with the accent placed on the offbeat, and virtually every producer and songwriter working in New York during the early Sixties incorporated it into his thinking.

New York production line

The success of the Drifters' records had immediate repercussions. It encouraged the quick growth of a service industry, as Leiber and Stoller turned more to other arrangers and songwriters to develop their ideas still further and keep up the flow of hits: Burt Bacharach and Hal David wrote and arranged a number of Drifters releases and met Dionne Warwick, later to give their extraordinarily complex compositions an international stage, during one such recording session. Phil Spector sat in on many sessions and effectively served a production

apprenticeship with Leiber and Stoller; and Gerry Goffin and Carole King, unquestionably the most recorded songwriting team of the early Sixties, wrote for

Above: Burt Bacharach with Dionne Warwick. Theirs was one of the most inventive and productive musical partnerships of the Sixties, as both applied lessons learned during their respective associations with Leiber and Stoller

Left: the team that cut some of the most ingenious R&B discs of the Fifties. Surrounding Leiber and Stoller at the piano are, from left, associates Lester Sill and Jerry Wexler, the four members of the Coasters, and Atlantic label boss Ahmet Ertegun

the Drifters and for other New York groups of similar ilk.

One such was an all-girl group, the Shirelles, who recorded for Luther Dixon's Scepter label and scored a huge pop hit towards the end of 1960 with Goffin and King's 'Will You Still Love Me Tomorrow'. A ballad written in the Drifters' style but more appropriate, because of the lyric's sentiments, to a female voice, its success sparked off a craze for girl group records that took a solid three years to dissipate. In that time, many new, small independent labels emerged in New York to cash in on the boom, providing a fertile training ground for such important arrangers and producers as Bert Berns, George 'Shadow' Morton, Steve Venet and Jeff Barry. The girl group fad proved a major factor, too, in the rise of Aldon Music, a publishing house based in the Brill Building on Broadway that specialised exclusively in teen-type material. The Aldon staff of songwriters were mostly teenagers themselves, high school kids from the middle-class Jewish suburbs. Contracted on a nine-to-five basis, their brief was to create songs to order, rather in the manner of the infamous 'song

factories' of pre-rock'n'roll Tin Pan Alley. Aldon could claim an impressive roster of talent – Neil Sedaka and Howie Greenfield, Barry Mann and Cynthia Weil, Jerry Keller, Goffin and King themselves – and such was the company's success rate that a subsidiary record label, Dimension, was set up with Carole King, the Cookies and Little Eva (formerly King's babysitter) as its principal acts.

The girl groups themselves were largely anonymous trios or quartets who were allowed little say in what or how they performed. Many were brought into the

Below: a 1962 press advertisement blazing the trail for two of Don Kirshner's most successful Dimension label releases, Carole King's 'It Might As Well Rain Until September' and Little Eva's 'The Locomotion'. Carole also co-wrote and co-produced, with husband Gerry Goffin (below right), the 1961 chart-topper 'Will You Love Me Tomorrow' for the Shirelles (right)

studios direct from schools or youth clubs, and were happy to be manipulated by some fast-talking producer if it meant earning good money touring on the strength of the resulting hit. The *sound* of these records was their most important feature: groups came and went by the hundred – the Chiffons, the Cascades, the Honeys, the Toys, the Angels, the Murmaids, Reperata and the Delrons and countless others – yet what lingered was not any sense of their personalities as singers, but the dazzling match of shrill, young female voices, black and white, to the elaborate aural designs of the men behind the recording consoles.

The Spector sound

The most influential manipulator of the girl group sound was Phil Spector, the Leiber and Stoller protégé who arrived in New York after spells in the Teddy Bears – whose 'To Know Him is To Love Him' was the archetypal high school hit of the *Bandstand* era – and with Phoenix-based producers Lester Sill and Lee Hazlewood, the men behind guitarist Duane Eddy's run of hits. Productions for Gene Pitney ('Every Breath I Take') and the Paris Sisters ('I Love How You Love Me') in 1961 indicated his potential, and later that year he joined Sill in forming the Philles label. Their first two hits – 'There's No Other (Like My Baby)' and 'Uptown' by the Crystals – were mundane by Spector's later standards but were each the product of endless remixing and overdubbing. Buying out Sill, he moved his base of operation to his native Los Angeles and began working exclusively in the Goldstar studio, where he found a handful of session men and arrangers – notably Jack Nitzsche – particularly amenable to his ideas. With the voices of the Crystals, the Ronettes, Darlene Love and Bob B. Soxx and the Blue Jeans as his raw material, he fashioned what became known as the Spector 'wall of sound' – a

dense, three-dimensional effect achieved by placing together layer upon layer of musical sound. 'Mine is a Wagnerian approach to rock'n'roll', he told the pop world, 'I'm writing little symphonies for the kids'.

Still drawing on songs by the Aldon circle of writers, he graduated from epic girl group hits like the Ronettes' 'Be My Baby' (1963) to productions featuring two top R&B acts, the Righteous Brothers and Ike and Tina Turner, whose success in the pop market had so far been minimal. Their maturity and command of the R&B idiom gave a new edge to Spector's style and their respective hits 'You've Lost That Lovin' Feeling' (1965) and

Above: Phil Spector, pictured at his opulent California home. Dubbed 'the first tycoon of teen' by journalist Tom Wolfe, Spector turned the production of three-minute pop records into a fine art during the early Sixties and did much to focus attention on the burgeoning west coast recording scene. After retiring over the US failure of Ike and Tina Turner's 'River Deep Mountain High' he returned to prominence in the Seventies with his work on the Beatles' Let it Be LP and releases by George Harrison and John Lennon

Above: Phil Spector (right) captured during a mid-Sixties recording session. His regular arranger Jack Nitzsche (left) was himself an important backroom figure in west coast pop, writing and producing hits for a succession of internationally popular artists

'River Deep, Mountain High' (1966) were both powerful, consummate musical statements – not only dazzlingly atmospheric and ingeniously designed recordings, but perfect examples of how the grit and soul of vocal R&B could be allied to pop values without suffering any consequent loss of passion.

Spector was a seminal figure in record production, but he also brought a new sharpness to pop marketing. When most labels were expanding their rosters and hiring staff to handle specialised tasks like publicity or talent-scouting, Spector took charge of every record at each stage of its production, from first take to final pressing. Rather than release a handful of singles at the same time, as many of his fellow independents did, he issued one a month to stop the sales of one harming another. Refusing to follow the common independent's practice of using a major label's pressing facilities, he handled all his own manufacturing and distribution and so saved on production costs. He was also one of the first pop producers to mix his productions specifically with airplay on transistor radios in mind – he

would turn up the treble to create a ring-ing sound that was certain to catch the ear of a casual listener.

Early Motown

Spector's development of the girl group and vocal R&B sounds was paralleled elsewhere, most influentially by Berry Gordy Jr's Detroit-based Motown cor-poration. Gordy began his career writing and producing one-off hits for local acts and leasing them to established labels. In 1960, he set up his own Motown and Tamla labels and soon after secured his first million sellers in the Miracles' 'Shop Around' and the Marvelettes' 'Please Mr Postman'. In 1962, these and numerous other local labels were absorbed into the one umbrella corporation, instantly giving Gordy access to such outstanding vocal talent as Junior Walker, Jimmy and David Ruffin, the Temptations and the Spinners. With his music publishing sub-sidiary, Jobete, he quickly made the corporation self-sufficient in material and encouraged talents like Smokey Robinson of the Miracles, Lamont Dozier and Eddie and Brian Holland to write for and pro-duce other Motown acts. With his opera-tion geared wholeheartedly to the white pop market, he quickly established Motown as not only the most profitable independent label in America but also the first black-owned business organisa-tion of any kind to make a major impact on the nation's industry.

Motown *was* a production line, but it allowed individual talent to flourish. Motown releases also had a clear identity that distinguished them from the

The faces of early Motown. Above: the Marvelettes presided over by the sleek, ever-smiling Gladys Horton (top)

Top left: Motown founder and controlling force, former Ford assembly-line worker Berry Gordy Jr

Left: Smokey Robinson (at left) during a record session

Motown struck gold when the Supremes (right) were teamed with writer-producers Lamont Dozier and Brian and Eddie Holland (bottom right). Other Motown acts used the team's material with regularity, including Martha and the Vandellas (below)

sometimes bland concoctions of the New York labels, namely their strong gospel feel. Detroit had long been a recording centre for church choirs and groups, and Gordy drew on this tradition by copying the accompaniments used in church singing and the call-and-response vocal patterns heard on gospel records: the Supremes' 'Baby Love' and Martha and the Vandellas' 'Dancing in the Street' (both 1964) were key examples, each featuring an entreating lead singer and an answering chorus singing above a solid R&B beat. In contriving to marry R&B and gospel, Gordy created not only great dance music but an early strain of what soon came to be labelled 'soul' music – the growth of which is described in Chapter 7.

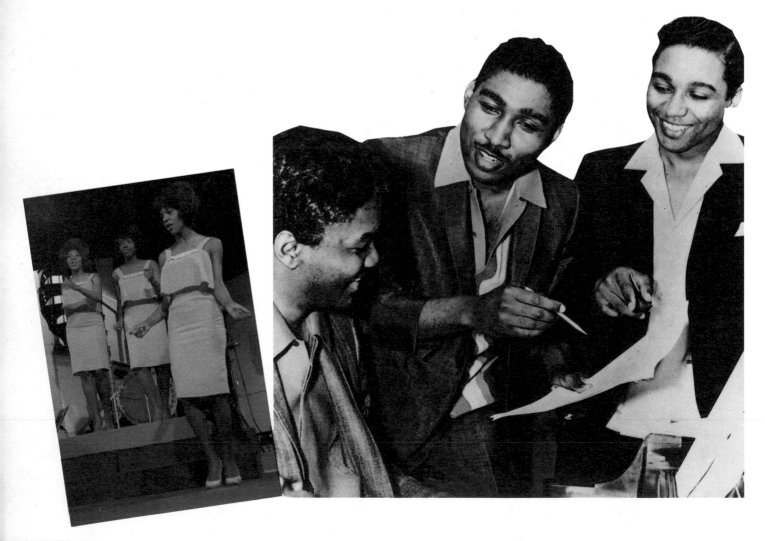

Below: Hitsville USA, the original studios of Berry Gordy Jr's Motown Corporation in downtown Detroit, Michigan, and the home of countless worldwide hits until Gordy moved his base of operations to Los Angeles in the early Seventies

Gordy and Spector were part of a new American breed – independently-minded pop entrepreneurs whose creations rose above the commonplace because of their own marketing guile, visionary flair and almost manic obsession with musical detail. They had counterparts in other areas, yet American pop as a whole had the air of a slumbering giant in the early Sixties, dominated not by individual singers or groups with strong musical personalities but by fragmented 'sounds' and crazes and finely-hewn, all-purpose teenage love songs in the Aldon style.

No-one, least of all those involved in the record industry itself, expected matters to change. The search for a second Elvis had long since been given up; rock'n'roll was already a source of nostalgia on radio – 'oldies but goodies' were a key part of early sixties programming – and many of the companies who had made a killing in rock were returning to strengthening their middle-of-the-road rosters and cultivating, once again, the adult market. The impetus for change in American pop could not come from within but from outside – and it was a group of British musicians who provided that boost, by creating something new, vital and ultimately world-shaking out of all the diverse ingredients of ten years of rock. Through the Beatles, America was put back in touch with its rock heritage.

CHAPTER 3

ENGLAND SWINGS
The rise of British beat

British youth's love affair with all things American sowed the seeds of a pop revolution the world over

Opposite page: the Dave Clark Five were among the most successful of the astonishing number of British beat groups to emerge in the Beatles' wake. Their so-called 'Tottenham Sound' briefly challenged Merseybeat towards the end of 1963

Below: Bill Haley (centre) received an ecstatic reception from the British fans on his arrival for a UK tour in 1957. This picture was taken aboard the train specially hired by the Daily Mirror for the occasion, which brought Haley and his entourage from Southampton to Waterloo station in London

No-one could have predicted during the Fifties that British-made pop music would one day rule the world. Compared to America, Britain was strictly second division – a pop backwater lacking the special cultural conditions that spawned rock'n'roll across the Atlantic, with neither America's racial mix nor its regional diversity, and with no equivalents to those independent record labels and local radio stations that helped make the United States such a cauldron of pop activity. On top of this, there was a basic lack of belief within the home record industry – born of years of experience – that Britain could ever better the brash American product that so dominated the charts and enlivened the BBC airwaves. In a culture still recovering from the effects of World War Two, and used to playing second fiddle to the Americans in everything from Olympic sport to world politics, it was to America that the populace inevitably turned in search of glamour, entertainment and simple relief from all the drabness.

America was regarded with a mixture of resentment and awe, especially by teenagers. Growing up in an atmosphere of recession, rationing, belt-tightening and prolonged nostalgia for the values of the war years, young people of all classes saw in America a beguiling vision of how life should really be lived. Hollywood played a vital role in this: the people in its films looked tanned and wealthy, the girls were sexier, teenagers in particular seemed able to get everything they wanted – they even drove *cars*. Films provided models of behaviour and of dress: Teddy Boys, working class youths who were fond of starting fights at dance halls and roaming the streets in packs, took their uniform of greased-back hair, sideburns, bootlace tie and natty frock coat from the bad guy characters of Hollywood westerns. And it was at the cinema during 1956 that British teenagers first saw their rock'n'roll heroes in action, when the Bill Haley film *Rock Around the Clock* attracted what the newspapers called 'undesirable elements' and inspired the hitherto unheard of phenomenon of jiving in the aisles.

The infatuation with all things American ran deep. Rock'n'roll seemed at first just another manifestation of it, like the craze for traditional or 'trad' jazz that had preoccupied students and middle-class teenagers with college ambitions since early in the decade, but it had a broader

significance. Trad had youth appeal but, as part of a movement dedicated to the reverential re-creation of old American jazz forms, it hardly ranked as the dynamic young sound of the Fifties; by contrast, rock, as we have seen, was the first music with specific teen appeal, and this struck deep at the leisure industry's long-held perception of the British record-buying, radio-listening, cinema-going audience as one amorphous whole. Just as it did in America, rock held out the possibility that teenagers could actually become a commercial force – and it had the advantage of bringing in its wake a ready-made, fully-formed version of a youth culture that British teenagers were keen to adopt and emulate.

Above: New York teenagers queue for a rock 'n' roll concert in 1957. Affluent, devil-may-care, super-cool and cocky, American adolescents were regarded by their British counterparts with awe and envy

ROCK, SKIFFLE AND THE COPYCAT PRINCIPLE

Although Bill Haley's 'Shake, Rattle and Roll' had reached the British chart two years earlier, 1956 was the year in which rock'n'roll took off in Britain on a grand scale. In bewilderingly quick succession came the premiere of *Rock Around the Clock*, the sudden emergence of Elvis Presley – with 'Heartbreak Hotel' and 'Blue Suede Shoes', both Top Ten hits during June – and the launch of Britain's very first home-grown rock star in Bermondsey-born Tommy Steele. The music's impact seemed total: by the end of the year, even favourite crooner Frankie Vaughan was high in the chart with a cover of 'Green Door', a rock'n'roll hit in America for Jim Lowe.

Of these events, the arrival of Tommy Steele received the most positive attention. He was bravely spoken of as Britain's answer to Elvis, but he had no real rock credentials beyond a confident handling of country and western material – he had toured USAF camps in Britain as a member of a country band – and some familiarity with American guitar styles. His rise was closely plotted by his managers John Kennedy and Larry Parnes, whose publicity stressed Steele's working class background while playing up his supposed popularity among high society debs. Such approval seemed important in the class-conscious Fifties and certainly won him some inches in the country's gossip columns, but within a year he was already talking of leaving rock behind for a career in musical comedy and summer season.

Steele's example prompted others to

try the rock'n'roll route to stardom and had the side-effect of turning the 2 Is coffee house in Soho, where he was reportedly discovered, into holy ground for all aspiring rock performers. It was there, according to popular myth, that the country's top agents and record company chiefs lurked, constantly on the look out for the best new imitators of

Above: Wally Whyton and the Vipers in action at Soho's 2 Is coffee bar. The Vipers were one of the few skiffle groups to achieve chart success

Above right: Marty Wilde, a protégé of promoter Larry Parnes, whose status as natural heir to Tommy Steele's rock 'n' roll crown was quickly challenged by both Cliff Richard and Adam Faith (right). Wilde, Richard and Faith all began their careers in Vipers-style skiffle outfits

Presley; the subsequent success of Cliff Richard, Adam Faith, Terry Dene and Marty Wilde, all 2 Is regulars at some point, made the prospect all the more believable as the Fifties went on. If its attractions were exaggerated, it was nonetheless true that any newcomer could at the very least share the camaraderie of a young community of musicians for nothing more than the cost of a cup of espresso. More importantly, the fame of the 2 Is influenced coffee houses all over the country to introduce music, so giving local performers priceless opportunities to develop their talents.

Washboards and folk songs

There was a certain irony in the depiction of the 2 Is as the cradle of the British rock scene, as the cafe had begun life as a jazz venue and had been, for much of 1956, the home of that year's other major teenage fad – skiffle. Jazz buffs tended to look on skiffle, an offshoot of the trad scene, with patronising protectiveness; rock, to their ears, was a counterfeit form of American music, unworthy of the kind of intellectual consideration that skiffle could claim and fit only for morons like Teddy Boys. Rock fans retorted by calling skiffle wet and weedy, and the widely reported mutual antipathy between Tommy Steele, lone voice of British rock, and Lonnie Donegan, founder and propagator of the skiffle boom, added further spark to the argument.

Skiffle had other supporters, too, in teachers and clergymen who saw the do-it-yourself music-making that Donegan encouraged as a healthy alternative to rock'n'roll, a means of diverting teenagers away from the spurious pleasures of the dance hall and the juke box. And skiffle was easy to play: a form of American jug-band music first introduced by Donegan in his days with the Ken Colyer and Chris Barber jazz bands, the only instrumentation it required was a guitar plus whatever came to hand – washboards, tea chests and broom handles with strings attached were generally favoured. Its repertoire of old American folk songs was easily learned, and there were briefly thousands of skiffle groups up and down the country, based in schools, churches and youth clubs, who all sang poignantly of life on the road and the hardships of the chain gang. The inspiration came mostly from Donegan himself, whose record sales in Britain during 1956 and 1957 matched those of Elvis Presley, but a key event in the spread of skiffle was BBC-TV's decision to launch *6.5 Special* as their Saturday night youth programme. Not only did the show feature many skiffle acts, its sponsorship of skiffle contests did more than anything to encourage the formation of new groups.

For all the approving attention it received, skiffle made only a minor impression on the charts: Donegan apart, only the Vipers, Nancy Whiskey and expatriate American bluegrass guitarist Johnny Duncan achieved big sellers. Skiffle was something to play rather than buy, and its importance lay in planting the idea of playing an instrument – and consequently of making one's own music – in millions of young minds. Its reign was brief, but it was skiffle's very success in achieving its aims that hastened its decline: those teenagers who had mastered the guitar chords found the standard skiffle line-up limiting and its repertoire inappropriate to their own lives or feelings. For such newly-skilled musicians, it was the American rock'n'roll acts who offered the way ahead, with their electric guitars, super-slick musicianship and teen culture songs.

The American way

This drift to rock'n'roll on a participatory level had two effects. In the short term, some of the ex-skifflers made an instant

bid for fame and found it: their understanding of, and affection for, rock'n'roll generally gave their records a more credible quality than those of Tommy Steele and his immediate contemporaries. Over a longer period, the ex-skifflers in areas outside London began developing their skills locally, with like-minded musicians, in a live dance hall or club environment. All continued to take their inspiration from America and its seemingly limitless supply of new rock'n'roll acts. Gene Vincent, Buddy Holly and Eddie Cochran were particular influences, for their voice, songs and guitar playing respectively; all toured Britain during the late Fifties or early Sixties and made a direct and lasting impact on young people.

Above: the Lonnie Donegan Skiffle Group, with its leader pictured second from right. When the skiffle era began to fade, Donegan switched uneasily to comedy material – 'Does Your Chewing Gum Lose Its Flavour', 'My Old Man's a Dustman' – before beginning a second career in cabaret

Left: British rock 'n' roll stars unashamedly based their performing styles on those of their American counterparts. Gene Vincent (extreme left) and Eddie Cochran (extreme right) were favourite models of would-be rockers Joe Brown (second left) and Billy Fury (second right), both of whom were signed to Larry Parnes' management stable

The instinctive approach of both British record companies and British artists, in the face of such relentless and high-quality American competition, was to imitate as closely as possible. The time-honoured practice of covering American material was therefore continued: Decca's discovery Terry Dene recorded Marty Robbins' 'A White Sports Coat' and Sal Mineo's 'Start Movin''; Marty Wilde at Philips covered two Jimmie Rodgers hits, 'Honeycomb' and 'Oh Oh I'm Falling in Love Again'; and Columbia's great hope, Cliff Richard, cut a version of Bobby Helms' 'Schoolboy Crush', only to see a disc jockey on Radio Luxembourg promote its flipside, 'Move It', and turn that into a very creditably placed debut hit. Almost alone among Britain's Presley followers, Cliff was allowed to develop his career without further recourse to American covers, but he quickly achieved a very special position within the British pop hierarchy and in time left rock'n'roll behind for sedate ballads and jaunty high-school pop in the American vein.

Cliff was one of many British rock'n'-rollers to come under the influence of television producer Jack Good, who originated *6.5 Special* before moving to ITV in 1958 to create a teen music show much more in line with his conception of rock'n'roll as a theatrical spectacle. The result was *Oh Boy!*, a fast-paced, humorous, all-music show presented before a live and frequently noisy audience – and one that gave a kind of corporate identity to the British rock scene, by joyfully making a virtue out of its very fake-Americanism. His treatment of Cliff was typical: to give him a distinct American look, yet not one that was too obviously a Presley copy, Good ordered him to shave off his Elvis-like sideburns, take on a new wardrobe of pink jacket and matching tie, black shirt, grey suede shoes and luminous socks, and rehearse a new set

Opposite page, top: Jack Good, producer of 'Oh Boy!', whips his audience into a frenzy during a recording of the show. Good gave television time to a long line of young British rock 'n' roll hopefuls, among them Adam Faith (né Terry Nelhams, far left), Vince Eager and Billy Fury (left)

Opposite page, bottom: Cliff Richard, a regular British hit-maker of over 25 years standing, brings his famous pink Oh Boy! jacket out of retirement for a Fifties-style TV show in 1981

of pained-looking on-stage movements down to the last flickering of an eyelid.

Oh Boy! became a natural showcase for those acts signed to Larry Parnes' management company, all of whom had stage names evocative of wild, untamed youth – Marty Wilde, Dickie Pride, Vince Eager, Duffy Power – while others like guitarist Joe Brown and small-voiced singer Terry Nelhams (renamed Adam Faith) won their first exposure on *Oh Boy!* offshoots like *Boy Meets Girl* and *Drumbeat*. Collectively, the British rockers and heart-throbs represented a modest but encouraging flowering of talent: the problem with most of them was not only their deference to American styles but also the attitude of their record companies and producers, many of whom were veterans of the dance band years who had no feeling for rock. Even the more sympathetic producers and arrangers who came into the industry during the late Fifties – men like Johnny Worth and John Barry, who wrote and produced Adam Faith's hits – were most interested in creating a clinical, measured formula based on re-interpretations of American sounds. In Faith's case, the pizzicato strings and hiccupping vocal effects of Buddy Holly's 'It Doesn't Matter Anymore' were aped endlessly; Helen Shapiro's discs, produced by Norrie Paramor at Columbia, bore an unmistakable Brenda Lee stamp; Anthony Newley sounded on disc like a pastiche of Paul Anka, Bobby Rydell and innumerable other American idols.

More wayward talents did occasionally produce outstanding examples of grit and invention, like Johnny Kidd and the Pirates with 'Shakin' All Over' and independent producer Joe Meek with his dazzling studio creations for the Tornados, but the overall mood within the British record industry at the turn of the Sixties was one of complacent self-sufficiency. American supremacy in pop continued to be taken for granted, and Cliff Richard's failure to dent the US consciousness during a much-publicised visit there in 1960 simply confirmed what everyone knew already – that Britain's music scene was too parochial, its products too closely based on American models, to ever take on much of an international dimension. All that however, was soon to change.

Below: Duffy Power, one of the lesser lights of Larry Parnes' celebrated management stable

BEATLEMANIA BECKONS

Below: the Shadows. Their line-up changed on several occasions during the Sixties, but Hank Marvin (centre) and Bruce Welch (right) were ever-presents. Both hailed from the north-east of England but found work after moving south and playing at the 2 Is club

Two British acts of the early Sixties did hint, in widely differing ways, at the revolution to come. The Shadows, Cliff Richard's backing group, began recording in their own right in 1960 and immediately set a fashion for instrumental groups: theirs was an accomplished, clinically-executed sound built around Hank Marvin's serene lead guitar work and Jet Harris' booming bass lines, which fulfilled the demand for American-style instrumental virtuosity yet represented a peculiarly British triumph in creative, independently-minded pop thinking. Marvin was a particular influence on every home-based guitarist who followed – he was the first in Britain to play a Stratocaster, the make of guitar favoured by Buddy Holly – while on a wider level the Shadows were the first British group to promote the idea that a group could be an expressive unit in itself, rather than just a collection of

faceless musicians who were quite literally in the shadow of a dominant and charismatic lead singer.

Billy Fury, too, though seemingly just a rather superior product of the Larry Parnes stable, had a fiercely individual streak, and he was virtually the only northern voice in a scene inhabited by home counties faces. This fact, plus his passion for classic American rockabilly and his ability to write his own material, made him a local hero to the beat groups of his native Liverpool. His success between 1959 and 1963 – when he was second in popularity only to Cliff Richard – showed what a local name could achieve on a national scale, and gave an early sign of the very special potential within that most cosmopolitan, energetic and music-mad of cities.

And Liverpool *was* a case apart, a law unto itself in a pop music sense. For a start, it had stronger American connections than any other British city, which meant local tastes developed in a peculiar way: seamen in the Merchant Navy, which accounted for much of the city's work-force, continually returned from New York, New Orleans and other American ports with records unheard by the rest of Britain. These included rock-'n'roll and R&B discs both classic and obscure, among them many that were not even widely-known in America, and they formed the basic repertoire of the city's emerging rock groups. Such groups were mainly one-time skiffle outfits who, as amateurs or semi-professionals, were able to play a set local network of youth clubs, jazz and blues cellars, dance halls and pubs. Few entertained ideas about making the big time, since to gain access to record companies or promoters required throwing in their jobs and moving to London, where there was no guarantee of success.

The combination of unique exposure to a wide range of musical influences,

and enforced isolation from the musical mainstream of London meant that Liverpool in the Fifties became an extraordinary melting pot of musical sounds, all synthesised in a live context by young musicians in front of equally young audiences whose only demand was good, solid dance music. With its strong R&B base, what the Liverpool groups played came closer to the spirit of early American rock'n'roll than anything that the London-based record labels could offer. Equally important to the success of the Liverpool scene was the encouragement given by a handful of local jazz club owners who switched to beat music,

Below: Billy Fury, Liverpool's first major pop force. His career under Larry Parnes' management began with an audition in Marty Wilde's dressing room during the interval of a Merseyside one-nighter

Right: the Beatles captured at the Top Ten Club, Hamburg, during 1962

Below right: Manfred Weissleder, owner of the Star Club, the first in Hamburg to be opened specifically for rock 'n' roll enthusiasts

thus echoing the transformation of the 2 Is in London; particularly popular was Ray McFall's Cavern Club in Mathew Street, which ran lunchtime sessions and – being unlicensed – had no age restriction to enforce. There was even a local paper devoted to the beat scene, *Mersey Beat*, which was run on a shoestring by local lad Bill Harry, and carried chatty features and local gig information.

Beatle beginnings

During 1961, *Mersey Beat* estimated that Liverpool had 350 beat groups and printed the results of a poll showing the Beatles to be the most popular of them all. Their local rise followed a familiar pattern: guitarists George Harrison and John Lennon, drummer Pete Best and bassist Paul McCartney all had lower middle class upbringings and experience in various skiffle and beat groups since leaving school. Together they served a memorable apprenticeship – like several other Merseyside bands before them – at a club in Hamburg's notorious Reeperbahn district, where they perfected their crowd-pleasing skills before an older, more disorderly and demanding audience than they had previously been used to. Reportedly unreliable and undisciplined, they were dropped by manager Alan Williams but found a replacement in the unlikely figure of Brian Epstein, head of the record department in his family's Liverpool store, who had no previous experience of artist management and seemed altogether too prim and too cultured for such a role.

Nevertheless, he learned quickly. He engineered a modest but effective publicity campaign, trailing the Beatles' second trip to Hamburg as a 'European tour', and arranged dates for them beyond Liverpool. With an eventual recording contract in mind, he persuaded them to exchange their leather outfits for smart lounge suits and to tone down their

language during gigs. On his insistence, they stopped clowning around on stage and began singing straight to the microphone. Actually persuading a record label to take an interest in them proved more difficult, because of the record industry's anti-provincial bias. Decca pondered for a while but chose instead to sign Dagenham's Brian Poole and the Tremeloes, who auditioned the same day. The only company to offer a deal was Parlophone, a subsidiary of EMI best known for its novelty releases, whose chief, George Martin, had long been on the look-out for a group to emulate the

success of Cliff and the Shadows at Columbia. He initially saw their future in precisely those terms – to the point of seriously considering giving either McCartney or Lennon the role of a Cliff-type front man – but they greeted the idea with scorn and insisted on following their own judgement from the start. They rejected Martin's choice, 'How Do You Do It' by professional songsmith Mitch Murray as their first single, and put their faith in their own 'Love Me Do'. With Ringo Starr replacing the sacked Pete Best on drums, and more than a little help from Brian Epstein, who bought up

10,000 copies to ensure it a chart placing, the record scraped into the Top 20 during December 1962. Just two months later, the exuberant follow-up 'Please Please Me' reached Number 2 and ushered in what can only be described as a new musical era.

Club sounds, northern songs

From then on, the Beatles' rise was relentless: 1963 brought three Number Ones and ended with a Royal Variety Show appearance and the country in the thrall of what the *Daily Mirror* called 'Beatlemania' – an all-consuming public

Above: the Grosse Freiheit, Hamburg, by night. The Beatles and numerous other Merseybeat bands played the clubs of this notorious district between 1961 and 1963 – the Star Club's sign is just visible under the neon TABU

fascination with every aspect of their being, fuelled by newspapers fighting an intense circulation war. Their impact was bewildering, but it had much to do with the sheer freshness and vitality of the music itself and the lack of any obvious roots in then-current chart styles. Their music *sounded* different: unlike much chart pop of the early Sixties, theirs was not the clinical, pre-planned product of a management team but very much self-styled and self-determined. Their early music was a response to the club and dance hall environment they knew so well, a form of dance music fashioned out of the rock and R & B repertoire that every Merseyside group plundered and that was best experienced live. This beat club ambience pervaded their first album, *Please Please Me*, most obviously in their versions of songs that had always been Cavern favourites – the Isley Brothers' 'Twist and Shout', the Cookies' 'Chains', the Shirelles' 'Baby It's You'.

Of most significance was the way Lennon and McCartney put the lessons of those original R & B releases into practice when writing their own material, and this was the quality that instantly set them apart from nearly all their Liverpool rivals. Not only did they base their harmony sound on that of black girl groups like the Shirelles, they modelled their earliest songwriting efforts on the work of Gerry Goffin and Carole King, master suppliers of girl group material. Their lyrics followed the conversational mode used so ably by Goffin in such songs as 'Don't Say Nothing Bad About My Baby' and 'It Might As Well Rain Until September': early Beatle songs were almost conversations in themselves, addressed to some anonymous third person rather than a partner – 'I Saw Her Standing There', 'She Loves You', 'And I Love Her', '(I'm in love with her and) I Feel Fine'. And as the emphasis in the Beatles' career changed from live to recording work, so they used

Right: the first UK album, Please Please Me, *released in January 1963 took the lads to the brink of international stardom in 1964 (below)*

Under the guidance of Brian Epstein (opposite, top), the Beatles threw off the wildcat image of their Hamburg days (below, inset) and refined their stage act – to the point of wearing suits (below) and bowing in unison (opposite, below)

what they had learned to develop a distinctive – and instantly recognisable – commercial style. 'Please Please Me' established something like a formula, 'From Me To You' copied it almost exactly and took the form of that classic hit-maker's ploy, a message to the fans, while 'She Loves You' (released in August 1963) showed to what extent their sound had crystallised in a few short months. The 'yeah, yeah, yeah' phrase, first used by the Beatles (as by the girl groups) for decorative effect, here became the song's pivotal feature – its hook. Even more cunning was the way the McCartney-Harrison falsetto was strategically placed at the end of the *third* verse rather than the first, to build up anticipation. The record bordered on self-imitation yet contrived, successfully, to sound irresistibly fresh; it was quintessential early-period Beatles – joyous, knowing and totally assured.

BEAT ACROSS BRITAIN

As musicians and songwriters, the Beatles clearly belonged to a new breed of pop artist: one of the effects of their fame was that singers in the Cliff Richard vein looked and sounded instantly dated. But they had an impact that extended far beyond the music world, to the point of becoming symbols of national optimism. There was a real sense during the Beatlemania autumn of 1963 that the Beatles were offering something fresh and new to Britain in the aftermath of the Profumo scandal, which had opened the

establishment to shame and ridicule and all but brought the Conservative Government – in power since 1952 – to its knees. As personalities, the Beatles seemed to embody a rejection of the old order in morals and politics, and their northern wit and intelligence formed an antidote to the dullness, restrictiveness and hypocrisy that had prevailed in British society since the Fifties.

The timing of their arrival was perfect. As part of what Derek Jewell (in a 1963 *Sunday Times* article) called 'that questing, confident, cool, sharp and unshockable stream which has come out of the grammar schools in the last decade', the Beatles both reflected and inspired among the nation's young a new mood that had its roots in that age group's growing economic independence. Their rise coincided, too, with a new burst of creativity in other areas of the popular

Below: the Merseybeats at the Cavern Club, Liverpool, in April 1963, when A&R men were just becoming aware of the depth of Liverpool talent

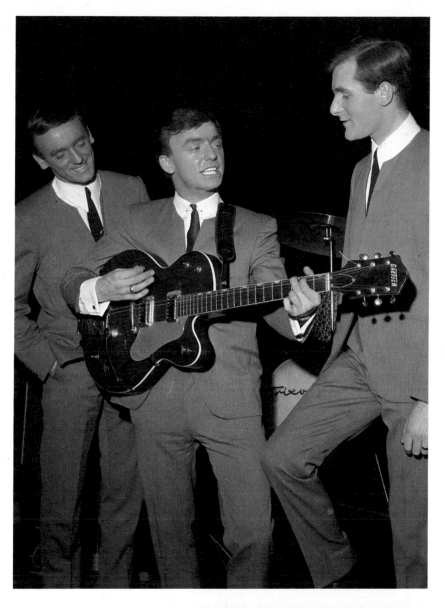

arts – notably in television, where glossy US imports now had to compete for ratings with down-to-earth proletarian dramas like *Z Cars* and *Coronation Street*, many of which depicted the working-class north as the spiritual heartland of Sixties England. Satirical programmes like *That Was the Week That Was* and magazines such as *Private Eye* legitimised the lampooning of public figures including even the untouchable Royal Family, while the anti-establishment tide threatened to culminate in the election of the Labour party – whose leader, Harold Wilson, represented a Liverpool constituency. The message was one of change – and the ultimate importance of the Beatles was that they altered Britain's downbeat image of itself.

The music spreads

In the short term, though, the effects of the Beatles' sudden and unpredicted success were most keenly felt within the record industry. The immediate thoughts of recording executives inevitably turned to finding their own Beatle lookalikes: reports of A&R men and agents piling off trains at Liverpool's Lime Street Station and asking directions to the Cavern became legend, and within weeks of 'Please Please Me' virtually all of the city's top beat acts had been signed. Some fared well – the Searchers at Pye, the Merseybeats at Fontana, and those Liverpool acts like Gerry and the Pacemakers that Brian Epstein contracted to his growing management stable – but the majority seemed unable to reproduce the exuberance of their live performances in a studio context and were dropped very quickly. Meanwhile, the effect on the Liverpool scene itself was catastrophic: suddenly barren of their beat talent, the clubs closed, and many of the key background figures in the local scene moved down to London to take up positions within the Epstein organisation.

Above: the Beatles' most serious rivals, Gerry and the Pacemakers, whose first three single releases made UK chart history by reaching Number 1

Right: the Searchers, like Gerry and the Pacemakers, enjoyed huge success in Britain and the US, but neither outlived the Merseybeat boom as chart acts

For a while, the Merseybeat sound figured prominently in the chart: Gerry and the Pacemakers, the Searchers, Billy J. Kramer and the Dakotas and Cilla Black all had Number Ones, the latter two with Lennon and McCartney songs. With the market's passion for groups showing no sign of abating, the record companies next focused their attention on Manchester, for no reason other than its proximity to Liverpool, and Freddie and the Dreamers, the Hollies and Herman's Hermits were all brought to London in quick succession. Although the Manchester scene did not have quite the cohesion or communal identity of Merseybeat, it did boast groups with an easy professionalism and an amenability – not always matched by the Liverpool outfits – to the suggestions of their respective recording managers. For this reason, they tended to enjoy more lasting chart success than their Liverpool counterparts, who were perhaps too much in the shadow of the Beatles to develop as musical personalities.

In time, the craze for beat groups took on the look of a social phenomenon, and there were indeed acts springing up in towns all over Britain as part of what seemed a kind of mass musical democratisation. Many won recording contracts, and every provincial town seemed to enjoy its brief moment of glory between 1963 and 1966, as local boys made good – the Troggs from Andover, the Barron Knights from Dunstable, the Nashville Teens from Weybridge, the Poets and Lulu and the Luvvers from Glasgow, the Zombies from St Albans, Unit Four Plus Two from Hertford, the Paramounts from Southend, and many more. Only a few became anything more than one-hit wonders, and most played a traditional mixture of rock'n'roll standards, current chart hits and possibly, if they were brave, a few of their own compositions. There was occasional talk

of a locally unique 'sound' in the Merseybeat mode, but these tended to exist only in the imaginations of record company publicists. The Dave Clark Five, for instance, were applauded as creators of a so-called Tottenham sound when 'Glad All Over' reached Number One late in 1963, though the only particularly distinctive feature of their records was their use of heavy, almost military drum rhythms.

British beat was a static form that allowed its musicians very little room to progress: as dance music, it put a premium on competence rather than

Is there life after Liverpool? A&R managers found the answer in the Manchester beat scene, from which they plucked the likes of arch-professionals the Hollies (top) and comedy group Freddie and the Dreamers (above)

More stars of the beat boom:
Herman's Hermits (far left), a
Mickie Most discovery; Billy
J. Kramer (left), a Brian
Epstein protégé; and Cilla
Black (below), another
Epstein star to enjoy the
capable musical direction of
Parlophone boss George
Martin (pictured with her)

dazzling instrumental or vocal virtuosity, and it provided no real outlet for personal musical expression. In the end, it became almost as restricting as skiffle had been in the Fifties; for some of its more imaginative musicians, far more interesting paths were being laid elsewhere – particularly in the London-based R&B movement, where young instrumentalists and singers were digging right back into the origins of rock'n'roll and developing their technique and improvisational skills. The Beatles, too, the original instigators and popularisers of the whole British beat movement, were already moving into new musical waters by the end of 1964 and challenging others to follow them.

America falls

The beat boom was just one aspect of the manner in which the Beatles revitalised the British pop scene during and after 1963. Record sales soared and the market expanded, encouraging record companies to invest still further in new talent. Beatle songs were much covered and copied, and the Beatles began a trend towards self-sufficiency – in career direction as well as choice of material – that became the norm as the decade went on. Their enthusiastic endorsement of initially obscure American sounds, notably Tamla Motown releases and the productions of Phil Spector, played a large part in the growing UK popularity of

R&B, of Motown itself and of the new soul music. And their records, increasingly drawing on sounds that were outside the realms of standard beat music – feedback at the beginning of 'I Feel Fine', a Rickenbacker guitar on 'A Hard Day's Night' – did much to broaden the perceptions of musicians, fans and industry figures alike as to what pop could be.

But the Beatles' greatest achievement, and the one from which the whole of the British entertainment world benefited,

was to take America by storm. Hitting the US charts early in 1964 with 'I Want To Hold Your Hand' and following it up with a staggeringly successful string of television appearances, the Beatles overturned years of American ignorance of British pop and led the way for what was described as a 'British invasion' of the US airwaves. There were rumours that the Beatles' breakthrough in America was engineered by radio stations in New York and that Epstein had plotted each step with meticulous detail, but there was no doubting the instant impact that they made. Quite apart from the astonishing presence of six Beatle records in the American Top Ten during the same week (in March 1964), American department stores were soon chock-a-block with Beatle toys, clothes, notebooks, pens, furniture, ornaments and musical instruments to which Epstein's American merchandisers put Lennon and company's names. Analysing the Beatle obsession became a popular American hobby, the common view being that they were a new kind of star – not the glamorous and deferential star of American convention, but ordinary boys who didn't give press conferences to a prepared script, who thumbed their noses at pretension and refused to be impressed by the more gaudy aspects of stardom. Looking deeper, others suggested a correlation between the assassination of President John F. Kennedy, the numbing aftermath and the growth of American-style Beatlemania just weeks later. At one of the lowest points in the nation's history, were Americans looking abroad for something new, youthful, positive, to take their minds off the tragedy? Brian Epstein thought so. 'They have this extraordinary ability to satisfy a certain hunger in the country', he told a US journalist. 'We are the antidote, the medicine man, dispensing the balm for a very sick society.'

Whatever the reason for this sudden responsiveness to British music – a form of music that was, paradoxically, an Anglicised hybrid of a variety of mainly black American styles – its effect on the home music industry was major. Whereas British artists had once confined their ambitions to topping the bill at the Royal Variety Show or achieving a gold disc, they now found their money-earning potential immeasurably increased. The United States, after all, meant not ballrooms and clubs but Carnegie Hall, Las Vegas, baseball stadiums, coast-to-coast TV and airplay on 6,000 different radio stations. On a broader level, the ensuing involvement of British record companies in the American market turned British pop into a multi-million dollar business – and it was ostensibly for their contributions to the export trade that the Beatles were awarded their MBEs during 1965.

The Beatles' success – and that of acts like Gerry and the Pacemakers, Peter and Gordon, the Animals, Manfred Mann, Freddie and the Dreamers, Herman's Hermits, the Rolling Stones and others who followed them to the top of the American chart – was a culture shock for Americans who had long prided themselves on their mastery of the entertainment world. Some American groups now attempted to look and sound English to win recording contracts, while even the likes of Frank Sinatra and Ella Fitzgerald felt obliged to record Lennon and McCartney songs. Others, meanwhile, heard and admired what the Beatles were doing and began creating music with a distinct Anglo-American edge. The Beatles had ended America's supremacy in pop music, but for some the most creative period in the music's short history was only just beginning.

Opposite page: a relaxed rehearsal for Britain's greatest musical exports during a US tour – far from the screaming hysteria that greeted their live performances on the same trip (inset)

Below: the line-up of the world's greatest group: George Harrison on lead guitar; John Lennon on rhythm guitar; Ringo Starr on drums and Paul McCartney on bass

TALKING 'BOUT MY GENERATION
From British blues to raga rock

Out of the clubs of swinging London sprang new sounds, new fashions and new attitudes that changed the face of popular culture

Opposite page: Eric Burdon of the Animals, one of several UK groups to take R&B into the transatlantic pop charts of 1964-67

Below: Britain led the world in fashion during the mid-Sixties; in that time, London's Carnaby Street was transformed from a quiet thoroughfare into the home of all things trendy

By mid-1964, Britain's propensity for producing new, exciting, internationally marketable pop groups seemed limitless – and the release of the Beatles' brilliantly inventive first feature film, *A Hard Day's Night*, and the growth of London's Carnaby Street as a world fashion centre enhanced the UK's reputation as home of a sharp, self-assured and super-confident youth culture.

American teenagers in particular seemed as besotted with the attractions of 'swinging England' as British kids had been with all things American just a few years earlier, and the profusion of new US groups with mop-top haircuts, fake-Scouse accents and imitation Beatle tunes was just one indication of the extent of English influence. In the US, such was the demand for British pop product over the home-made variety that the very profitability of the record industry was threatened, with record labels spending most of their time, money and energy not in encouraging native talent, but in securing licensing deals for the release of UK-originated material.

But British pop itself was already beginning to change, in character and content. Not only was the basic beat sound undergoing progressive embellishment at the hands of the Beatles and producer George Martin, record companies were starting to raid London's well-established but hitherto ignored jazz and blues clubs for young R&B groups to promote as quasi-beat acts. Decca, desperately anxious to live down the stigma of having rejected the Beatles, set the pattern by hurriedly signing top club act the Rolling Stones, but none of the record labels involved had much appreciation of the distinct differences between the Stones' brand of R&B and the more dance-based sounds of the provincial beat groups. Although the Stones were initially launched in Beatle-style suits and scored their first major hit with a Lennon and McCartney song, 'I Wanna Be Your Man', it very quickly became clear that they were a new kind of group – one less interested in playing R & B-inflected dance music than in using the R & B mode to make what amounted to an anti-establishment statement. Entering the mainstream pop world in a harmless beat guise, the Stones and their successors proceeded to subvert pop conventions in an alarming and potentially revolutionary fashion. The consequences for pop on both sides of the Atlantic were to be enormous.

Groups like the Rolling Stones differed from their beat contemporaries in musical approach, appeal and – most important of all – their attitude to the entertainment world in which they were required to work. Musically, while the

provincial groups drew on particular aspects of R & B – mainly the black vocal group sound, laced with mid-Fifties rock'n'roll – to create crowd-pleasing music perfect for dance halls, their London counterparts were dedicated to re-creating the supposedly more 'authentic', commercially 'untainted' styles of blues masters like Muddy Waters, Little Walter and Jimmy Reed. While beat musicians and fans hailed from mostly working class backgrounds and saw their music as no more than entertainment, the London R & B groups consisted mainly of art school students from the middle-class suburbs, who shared with their largely college-based following an intellectual interest in the

Below: an early line-up of the Rolling Stones. Ian Stewart (second from left) was replaced by Bill Wyman but became the group's trusted road manager. All the Stones were R&B fanatics, with Mick Jagger (below right) a particular devotee of the great Muddy Waters (bottom)

sources of their music and in American black culture generally. They took their music *seriously*: a beat group could move from dance hall dates to pantomimes and seaside shows, but for R & B bands this represented the worst kind of selling out, the ultimate compromise with the tacky world of show business. The very look of the respective groups spoke volumes: while the Hollies could wreath themselves in smiles and suits in their quest for acceptance, the Stones deliberately cultivated an anti-social image with their sneers, scruffy clothes and long, unkempt hair.

THE RISE OF LONDON R & B

during the late Fifties by bringing over Muddy Waters and other blues greats to appear with his band. Their use of amplified as opposed to acoustic accompaniment was a revelation to many, including Britain's premier blues buffs, Alexis Korner and Cyril Davies, who had founded London's Blues and Barrelhouse Club. With Korner on guitar and Davies on harmonica, they joined Barber for half-hour R & B sessions during his residency at the Marquee club, and the response was so positive that they were encouraged to form their own permanent R & B group. Already deeply disillusioned with the reactionary nature of the trad jazz scene – to which Barber, for all his sense of musical adventure, remained

Below: Blues Incorporated in 1962 – from left, Alexis Korner, Jack Bruce and Cyril Davies – with Mick Jagger (vocals) sitting in. Also included in this line-up was Dick Heckstall-Smith on the saxophone

Such non-conformist attitudes were fully in keeping with the general anti-establishment line that jazz musicians had always maintained, and it was as a factional offshoot of London's jazz scene that the R & B movement began. The godfather of this movement was the trombonist Chris Barber, who challenged the conservatism of trad jazz followers

Above: Georgie Fame with his Blue Flames, who made their reputation at the celebrated Flamingo Club (above right) in London's Wardour Street

committed – Korner and Davies effectively cut themselves off from the jazz mainstream by concentrating solely on R & B repertoire. Barred from most of London's established jazz venues because of their wholehearted use of amplification, they set up their own R & B club in a basement near Ealing Broadway tube station on the western outskirts of London, and installed their new combination – called Blues Incorporated – as its house band.

Opened in 1961, the Ealing Blues Club soon attracted a large, young, musically aware coterie of followers, and its success persuaded the owners of those venues that had previously resisted R & B to revise their policies. With the increased popularity of the club came problems, culminating in a split between Korner and Davies over the former's increasingly relaxed, catholic interpretation of what exactly constituted R & B: while Korner favoured the use of brass sections and did not object to fledgling R & B groups performing Chuck Berry or

Bo Diddley numbers, Davies was most interested in reproducing the gritty simplicity of Muddy Waters' Chicago recordings of the Fifties, and formed the R & B All Stars to do just that.

At the same time, a third 'school' of London R & B emerged, centred on the Flamingo All-Nighter Club in Wardour Street, Soho. There, former rock'n'roller and Larry Parnes protégé Georgie Fame was pioneering a sound that drew heavily on the jazz styling of Mose Allison and the gospel-tinged style of contemporary American soul artists. Performing regularly to an audience of predominantly black American servicemen on weekend passes from out-of-town USAF bases, Fame and his band the Blue Flames – formerly Billy Fury's backing band – in turn influenced other acts with a similarly sophisticated, good-time approach to R & B. These included Chris Farlowe and the Thunderbirds, Zoot Money's Big Roll Band and Tony Knight's Chessmen, all of whom enjoyed successful stints at the Flamingo after Fame gave up his residency there.

The Stones begin to roll

The London R & B scene flourished while trad jazz, which had become heavily commercialised at the start of the Sixties with the chart success of Kenny Ball and Acker Bilk, declined in appeal. Alexis

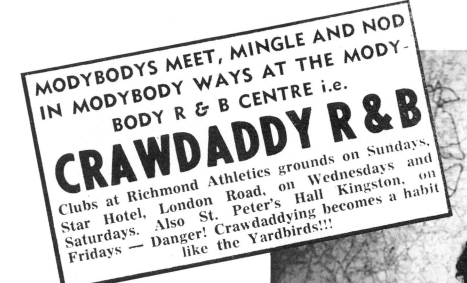

MODYBODYS MEET, MINGLE AND NOD IN MODYBODY WAYS AT THE MODY-BODY R & B CENTRE i.e. **CRAWDADDY R & B** Clubs at Richmond Athletics grounds on Sundays, Star Hotel, London Road, on Wednesdays and Saturdays. Also St. Peter's Hall Kingston, on Fridays — Danger! Crawdaddying becomes a habit like the Yardbirds!!!

Korner was a key figure in giving active encouragement to young R & B outfits, of whom Little Boy Blue and the Blue Boys from the Dartford-Sidcup area were just one. Bassist Dick Taylor formed the group in 1962 with fellow blues fanatics Mick Jagger and Keith Richards (who dropped the final 's' at his manager's request, then re-instated it during the 1970s). They were soon joined by Cheltenham Art College student Brian Jones, who was inspired to move to London after meeting Korner at a college gig. Various personnel changes later, with Jagger having already made a name for himself as an occasional vocalist with Blues Incorporated, the group developed as a true working unit and adopted the name 'Rolling Stones' after a Muddy Waters song. They made their performing debut at the Marquee in July 1962, and directly after that secured their reputation as the best young band on the R & B circuit with a residency at Giorgio Gomelsky's Crawdaddy Club in Richmond. In time, too, they were attracting not just the expected student clientele, but snazzily-dressed 'mods' from the council estates, who applauded the Berry and Diddley numbers as vociferously as the more purist blues fans in the audience booed them.

Although the Stones began as imitators, dipping freely into the repertoire

Top: a small ad for the Crawdaddy, one of London's foremost R&B venues during the middle years of the Sixties. The club was run by Giorgio Gomelsky (above) a jazz journalist and R&B impresario, who booked the Rolling Stones (left) in their early days and later went on to manage the Yardbirds

Right: Rolling Stones sharp-shooting manager Andrew Loog Oldham with the late Brian Jones

Below right: Keith Richards celebrates deification with his legendary companion – a glass of whiskey

of 19-year-old freelance publicist Andrew Loog Oldham, who had worked for Brian Epstein's NEMS organisation and fancied his chances of marketing a band as the antithesis of everything the ceaselessly cheerful and good-humoured Beatles represented. In Oldham, the Stones found a kindred spirit, a razor-sharp young hustler who proved his management worth by not only turning their disdain for authority into a selling ploy, but negotiating a recording deal with Decca that gave the band a degree of musical autonomy unprecedented in British pop. Acting on the advice of his mentor Phil Spector, Oldham insisted on recording the Stones independently, in studios of his or their choice, and then leasing the tracks to Decca for a fixed period; everything other than pressing and distribution – from choice of material through to publicity and promotion – remained the sole responsibility of Oldham and his group.

Rock heroes, public enemies

The Stones' recording career began uncertainly, with Oldham's inept production work betraying both his lack of previous studio experience and his fixation with apeing the Spector 'Wall of Sound', but their first American visit in

of Willie Dixon, Jimmy Reed, Berry and others, their relative lack of deference towards their blues sources and their refusal to stand in the shadow of their idols set them apart from their fellow R&B bands from the start. While other groups accentuated the musical qualities of R&B, earning respectful silences whenever the lead guitarist re-created a Muddy Waters guitar break, the Stones played on the music's innate sexuality and gave it contemporary relevance. It was this quality that fuelled the interest

the summer of 1964 set the tone for their best and most characteristic studio work. Booking into the legendary Chess studios in Chicago, they cut a handful of tracks with the same back-room boys – including ace engineer Ron Malo – who had worked with their great blues heroes. Their completely new arrangement of 'It's All Over Now', a minor American R & B hit for vocal group the Valentinos, emerged from these sessions and became the group's first British Number One just a few weeks later. Sounding relaxed, cocksure and totally at home in this most hallowed of blues environments, they quickly moved on from cleverly re-interpreting R & B material to creating their own. Taking their inspiration from blues lyrics, which by tradition were heavy with sexual imagery and sung almost exclusively by males, Jagger and Richard struck a pointedly anti-romantic pose in their compositions and frequently portrayed women in a submissive role. 'Under My Thumb', 'The Last Time', 'Yesterday's Papers' and 'Stupid Girl' positively gloried in male supremacy, while even mellower songs like 'Lady Jane' and 'Ruby Tuesday' revealed a contemptuous indifference to female emotions. At the time, with public attention focused on the newly-available contraceptive pill and the sexual licence it appeared to grant young people, such songs were widely interpreted simply as celebrations of sexual freedom, and their sexist implications went unchallenged.

The Jagger-Richard team proved at their best when railing against more general and less personal targets, as in the brilliantly conceived '(I Can't Get No) Satisfaction', which topped both UK and US charts during the steamy late summer of 1965. This was a savage indictment of materialism and the advertising world in particular, which sounded sensationally subversive when heard on American Top 40 radio, played between precisely the

kind of detergent and cigarette commercials that the lyric harangued. Featuring an introduction and fuzz-tone guitar riff inspired by the first few bars of Martha and the Vandellas' Motown classic, 'Dancing in the Street', the record was protest rock in the genuine sense – insolent and angry rather than self-pitying and anguished. It was also the perfect musical encapsulation of the

Mick Jagger blows up a storm on an early edition of Ready Steady Go! *(left) and sits out a rehearsal at the Decca recording studios during 1964 (below)*

Stones' now notorious public image, which stories of concert riots, fist fights, sexual misbehaviour and drug abuse had helped cement. Representing the eccentric, threatening extreme of swinging, liberated, promiscuous mid-Sixties London life, their notoriety gave them a credibility among rock fans that the Beatles, increasingly discontented projectors of a safe and universally acceptable image, tended to lack.

Nevertheless, there was a sense in which the Stones' very truculence obscured the quality of their musicianship – especially that of Brian Jones, the most obsessively anarchic and wilfully obnoxious Stone of all, whose musical ideas and instrumental eclecticism were never quite allowed full rein on the group's albums. His command of dulcimer, marimba and Indian sitar on *Aftermath* (1966) gave that album an almost ethereal aura that suggested the group were moving well beyond the R&B style. That promise dwindled, however, with the dilettantish splurge of *Their Satanic Majesties Request* (1967), which found the Stones for once trying to beat the Beatles at their own self-consciously experimental vein. As their extra-

musical exploits sparked off what seemed like an orchestrated campaign of victimisation by the authorities, climaxing in the conviction and brief imprisonment of Jagger and Richard for drug offences, so too did all the mayhem distract attention from what was unquestionably their greatest achievement – that of putting undiluted, uncompromising R&B, more 'black' in character and more rebellious and incendiary than rock'n'roll itself had ever been, into the best sellers lists. Of all the white groups in the history of rock to emulate the black sound, the Rolling Stones came closest to capturing the guts and grime of real down-home rhythm and blues. More than this, they made it relevant to the young, white, suburban middle classes.

The Stones in mystical pose, at the time of the release of Their Satanic Majesties Request . . . *(above left), and feigning decadence during their* Beggar's Banquet *period (above)*

CLUB SCENES, CAPITAL SOUNDS

The impact of the Stones could be measured as early as the winter of 1964, by the number of lookalike groups emerging in the R&B clubs, all of them sporting ever-lengthening hair and pouting, guitar-less lead singers in the Jagger mould. Their most obvious imitators were the Pretty Things, founded at Sidcup Art College by one-time Stone Dick Taylor, who signed to Fontana in May 1964 and had a string of minor hits. If the Stones sent army majors rushing for their pens to write letters of protest, the Pretty Things had them reaching for their bazookas, but their heavily ironic name and sub-moronic behaviour seemed covers for a basic lack of musical imagination. Certainly no-one, least of all those who frequented the R&B clubs,

Below: The Kinks, from Muswell Hill in North London, graduated from a caveman-like R&B sound to songs of social satire. They are pictured here during a British television show in 1964

took them very seriously and – despite later producing some interesting experimental albums, notably *S.F. Sorrow* in 1968 – they never lived down the tag of poor man's Stones.

Muswell Hill R&B boys the Kinks seemed destined for a similar fate in 1964, when the Stones-like 'You Really Got Me', complete with clanking, over-the-top guitars and a shrieking vocal climax, brought them a Number One and labelled them as purveyors of a primitive heavy metal sound. Tales of wrecked hotel rooms and on-stage fisticuffs between the group's two most volatile members, brothers Ray and Dave Davies, reinforced the caveman impression, but their allegiance to R&B was never that great and from 1965 onwards their releases indicated a complete change of musical direction. Settling into a lazy, even soporific good-time style that echoed the best of the mid-Sixties American jug bands, the Kinks became the vehicle for the idiosyncratic vision of lead singer and resident songwriter Ray. Painting melancholy little word pictures of London life in 'Dead End Street', 'Well Respected Man' and the elegaic 'Waterloo Sunset', he was one of the first mid-Sixties songwriters to blend rock with satirical social comment. His songs were mostly superb comic summations of the Carnaby Street/swinging London era: 'Dedicated Follower of Fashion' poked fun at the clothes freaks who lived to be seen in the Sunday colour supplements, while 'Sunny Afternoon' – with its bored millionaire's narrative and languid references to country houses, tax problems and runaway girlfriends – could have been about Mick Jagger himself.

Mann-made hits, Animal tracks

The Kinks enjoyed considerable chart success without ever achieving the mass adulation and cultural credibility of the

Stones. In the immediate aftermath of the Stones' success, only two groups from London's R&B circles seemed to have the right blend of musicianship and commercial appeal to make a sustained challenge to their supremacy – Manfred Mann and the Animals. The former took their name from the group's South

African-born founder and organist, and developed from a tight-knit jazz outfit to a blues band and then into a pop-cum-R&B group as commercial fashion dictated. Mann himself saw no contradiction in playing red-hot blues at a club gig and appearing on BBC TV's *Top of the Pops* the next day to promote a piece

Below: down from Newcastle and electrifying London club-goers - the Animals at the Flamingo in 1965

of ephemeral pop fluff like 'Do Wah Diddy Diddy' or 'Pretty Flamingo'. His innate pop taste and knack of choosing hit material was the band's great saving grace: alternating superior American pop fare like Goffin and King's 'Oh No, Not My Baby' with weightier songs from the Bob Dylan songbook (most notably 'Mighty Quinn' and 'Just Like a Woman'), his highly commercial approach to single-making was balanced by an apparent desire to encourage a creative appreciation of pop as a form. With lead singer Paul Jones proving a most articulate spokes-man on youth matters – his personality was a blend of Jagger-like bohemianism and McCartney-esque charm – Manfred Mann also won themselves a reputation as a thinking man's pop group, bookish and studious yet with just a hint of collegiate protest about them.

It was the Newcastle-based Animals however, that the Stones themselves regarded as their most serious rivals. This five-man group had travelled down to join a waiting London R&B scene during 1963, with singer Eric Burdon's repu-tation as the best white blues voice in Britain preceding them. Burdon's passionate and committed reproduction of the Ray Charles vocal style contrasted sharply with the mannered parody of black singers that formed the basis of Jagger's style, while the powerhouse organ playing of Alan Price gave the group a drive and intensity unmatched by the predominantly guitar-based London groups. They took over as the number one attraction in the clubs once the Stones had graduated to national package tours, and it was apparently with the Stones' example in mind that they chose to trust their recording career to an independent pop operator, pro-ducer Mickie Most, who leased his pro-ductions to Columbia, one of EMI's subsidiary labels. For a time, the relation-ship worked spectacularly well: their

rugged, four-minute (unusually long and therefore supposedly uncommercial) version of the folk-blues standard 'House of the Rising Sun' topped the British and American charts, while Most was careful to select material for single release that fitted their no-nonsense R&B image – their teeth-clenchingly suspenseful

Top left, above left, left: the Animals, the Kinks and Manfred Mann – three of the most commercially successful bands to emerge from within Britain's thriving R&B scene

treatment of Mann and Weil's cod protest song 'We've Gotta Get Out of This Place' was a perfect example. In common with many R&B-based groups of the time, however, they eventually tired of the commercial strictures placed upon them and demanded to pursue musical paths of their own choosing. Mickie Most lost interest, the hits dwindled, and Burdon disbanded the group late in 1966.

March of the mods

The success of the Animals offered a timely reminder that British R&B was always more than just a London-based phenomenon. Belfast group Them, led by Van Morrison, arrived in London and served a brief apprenticeship in the clubs before signing with Decca and working under visiting American producer Bert Berns. Several hit songs resulted – 'Gloria' and the soul-inflected 'Here Comes the Night' among them – but the group's line-up was forever changing and only Morrison himself seemed to have real R&B promise. After the group broke up in 1967, Morrison moved to New York to record as a solo act for Berns' Bang label. The Birmingham area, meanwhile, produced the Moody Blues, who broke through with a strong, piano-dominated version of a Bessie Banks' R&B classic, 'Go Now', in 1965, and the Spencer Davis Group, who had a precocious singer-organist in 17-year-old Stevie Winwood and a particularly sympathetic and imaginative recording manager in Chris Blackwell. Fresh from producing Britain's first home-made bluebeat hit, 'My Boy Lollipop' by Millie Small (which featured a harmonica break by another R&B unknown, Rod Stewart), Blackwell put his knowledge of West Indian music to work in finding suitably obscure black-originated material for the group; their two 1966 Number Ones, 'Keep On Running' and 'Somebody Help Me', both compositions by Jamaican singer Jackie

Edwards, were by far the best British approximations to the records of Otis Redding, Sam and Dave and other newly-emerging black soul stars.

Despite these successes however, the impact of R&B – in strictly commercial terms – was patchy. The top singles group of 1964 – the Beatles apart – was the Irish singalong trio the Bachelors, with the Rolling Stones and the Animals some way behind; a year later, folksy middle-of-the-roaders the Seekers were the most consistent chart act, closely followed by the ever-popular if far from fashionable Cliff Richard. Chart success eluded most bands on the R&B circuit: lacking the managerial astuteness of an

Faces and figures of mid-Sixties pop: ace record producer Mickie Most (above), who worked with the Animals and Donovan; the Spencer Davis Group (left), the best of a good crop of Birmingham-based R&B bands; Them (below), from Belfast, whose line-up included the young Van Morrison on vocals; and (opposite) Paul Jones, Manfred Mann's lead singer and later a successful solo artist

Andrew Oldham or the sympathetic studio back-up of an innovator like Shel Talmy (who produced the Kinks' releases), such bands as the Artwoods, the Graham Bond Organisation, the Cheynes, Shotgun Express and the Downliners Sect found recognition only among the club cognoscenti and avid readers of the top British music trade paper, *Melody Maker*. Georgie Fame did finally reach the chart with 'Yeh Yeh' in late 1964, and Chuck Berry made a very welcome comeback in the UK on the strength of revived interest in R&B, but the London club scene remained primarily a live phenomenon

Below: Birmingham's Moody Blues, whose 'Go Now' was a 1965 UK Number 1. Their line-up at that time included Denny Laine (centre), later a stalwart of Paul McCartney's Wings

that was very difficult to transfer to disc.

Top Ten hits for the Stones, Animals, Kinks and others could only hint at the music's infiltration of the London club scene and the astonishing rate at which R&B clubs were opening everywhere. In London, the Scene, the Ram Jam Club, Tiles, Klooks Kleek and the Bag O'Nails were some of the most patronised, while similar clubs were started in nearby towns. With such expansion, however, came a distinct change in both the clubs' clientele and the nature of the music played there. College students continued to make up part of the audience, but there were now the mods too, those hip ex-secondary modern school kids with office jobs and a lot of money to spend, whose real passion was not the strung-out R&B of the Fifties that gave the Stones such inspiration, but imported, contemporary American soul. One of the first ways in which the clubs acknowledged this was by holding regular disc sessions: Guy Stevens set the style at the Scene club in Great Windmill Street, playing selections from his formidable soul collection, and his enthusiasm extended to releasing the more obscure imported items on his own independent label, Sue, which he co-owned with Chris Blackwell.

Almost imperceptibly, the R&B scene took on a new identity. Those intent on maintaining the original revivalist and reverential spirit of the movement kept largely to their own venues, and the more experimental of them had their patience and commitment rewarded within a year or two, as guitar-based improvisation on the jazz-blues model formed the basis of 'progressive rock'. Elsewhere, though, the mods were in the ascendant – and it was only a matter of time before they would make their presence felt beyond the clubs and in the pop market at large. From 1965 to 1967, mod taste determined both the look and sound of British pop.

FROM MOD STYLE TO POP ART

Although the media image of mods was one of rampaging, parka-jacketed hordes who smashed up seafronts on bank holiday weekends, the mod cult was characterised more by single-minded narcissism than mindless tribalism. The life of the typical mod revolved around soul music, night-clubbing, scooters, excitability-inducing pep pills and – above all – clothes, the artful purchase and selection of which brought instant peer group credibility. To mods, outward style and appearance signified individual worth, and most favoured clerical or shop jobs that allowed them to keep their fastidiously smart look throughout the working day. Mods were unsettlingly cool, aloof, free-spending and élitist, and as such they presaged those archetypal swinging Sixties figures – the materialistic, arrogantly flamboyant and calculatedly outrageous clothes designers, photographers, models, artists and pop entrepreneurs who formed the capital's new hip aristocracy. Most important for pop, the mods – originally small in number and limited mainly to London – gave a lead not only in the world of fashion but in taste generally that the rest of teenage Britain proved quick to follow.

Right: another Birmingham band, the Move, emerged during 1966 on the coat-tails of the Mod movement. They smashed television sets in the name of pop-art, earned a libel suit from Harold Wilson as a result of their over-the-top promotion for 'Flowers in the Rain' in 1967, yet still made a string of memorable singles. Roy Wood (second from left) later formed the Electric Light Orchestra with drummer Bev Bevan (far right) and fellow Brummie Jeff Lynne

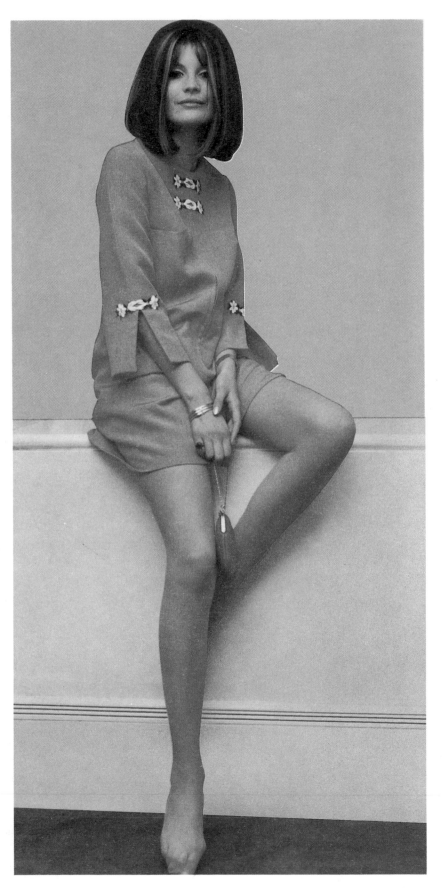

The prime agent in putting mod style and mod music before the public was a television programme – ITV's *Ready Steady Go!* – which attracted an audience approaching ten million at the peak of its popularity. It began in August 1963, ostensibly as a showcase for beat groups, but its London location and the broad musical policy of producer Elkan Allan ensured that many R & B outfits and visiting black American soul acts were featured as well. This in itself gave the show a mod ambience, and it was soon drawing its regular studio audience of dancers from the mod strongholds of south and west London. Recognising this, Allan replaced the professional but increasingly bewildered looking Keith Fordyce as compère with the giggly, gauche but street-wise Cathy Mac-Gowan, who introduced guests with the air of a real fan and turned the show into more of a mod fashion parade than ever. Its influence in introducing new acts and spreading the popularity of Tamla Motown artists in particular was crucial, but on a more general level *RSG!* gave mass youth culture in mid-Sixties Britain a sense of corporate identity that was entirely mod-defined. From being a purely local phenomenon, the mod cult took on a national dimension: soon kids all over the country were calling themselves mods as a matter of course.

Ultimately, the mod cult turned into just another form of teenage consumerism, fed by *RSG!*, by new pop-and-fashion teen magazines like *Rave* and *Valentine*, and of course by the record industry itself. At first, record companies were content simply to drape their artists in the latest Carnaby Street chic and give them musical settings pinched straight from soul music: Pye's Sandie Shaw leaned heavily on the Burt Bacharach-arranged records of Dionne Warwick, while Philips' Dusty Springfield lent her magnificently authentic soul voice to

Cool and fashionable, the long-legged and barefooted Sandie Shaw (opposite) epitomised the look of the mid-Sixties. Her singing rivals included Dusty Springfield (top), who was the nearest Britain had to a female vocalist in the Aretha Franklin class. Both Sandie and Dusty were regulars on TV's Ready Steady Go! *(top right), hosted by the engagingly gauche Cathy MacGowan (above)*

such re-creations of the Motown sound as 'Little by Little' and 'In the Middle of Nowhere'. Otherwise, with the major labels still trying to slot their groups into a Beatles or Stones pigeonhole, it was left to the mavericks of the industry – the independent producers and managers in the Andrew Oldham mould – to take the seemingly obvious course of fashioning specific groups in the mod image. Making full use of the new promotional media open to publicists and record labels – not only programmes like *RSG!* and its chart-oriented BBC competitor, *Top of the Pops*, but the pirate radio stations now operating from off the British coast – such sharpshooters as Kit Lambert, Chris Stamp, Simon Napier-Bell and Tony Secunda generally ignored the mods' original narrow soul focus and instead exaggerated the more aggressive, anti-social aspects of mod style.

Mod myths set to music

The first band to be successfully promoted with a mod image was the Who, a group from Shepherds Bush in London with a strong local following but spurious mod credentials. As the Detours, they had gone through a remarkable number of musical changes since the early Sixties, beginning as Shadows-type instrumentalists, graduating to standard beat repertoire after the Beatles' breakthrough, and then moving on – following guitarist Pete Townshend's entry into art school – to R&B. Self-proclaimed mod Peter Meaden, a clothes designer and former part-time publicist for the Rolling Stones, heard them during 1964 and became their manager; he changed their name to the High Numbers, after the fashion for numbered T-shirts, put them in mod gear and persuaded them to include more soul material in their act. The final touch was their recording debut with a Meaden composition that sounded like a tourist guide to modland – 'I'm a Face', 'face' being mod jargon for an especially stylish dresser. After that disc's failure, Meaden sold his interest in the group to Kit Lambert and Chris Stamp, who developed the mod angle further by encouraging the band to reach new heights of musical violence that supposedly matched the mods' natural aggression. The ruse worked: the sheer force and attack of their television appearances and the destruction of instruments and amplifiers that invariably climaxed their stage act quickly established them as the most difficult to handle group in British pop.

Despite the exploitative nature of this identification with the mods, the Who – their original name restored by Lambert and Stamp – took their new roles as mod figureheads very seriously. Told by Lambert to go away and write songs as 'statements', Townshend responded with a stream of lyrics that revealed both a canny understanding of the mind of the average pill-popping mod and a deep empathy with the mods as a sub-culture:

'Anyway, Anyhow, Anywhere' and 'The Kids Are Alright' celebrated the camaraderie of the mod gang; 'Substitute' hinted at the insecurities and neuroses lurking beneath the typical mod's supercool exterior; and 'My Generation' was a venomous hymn of hate towards the older generation that featured one of the most famous lyric lines in the whole of rock history – 'things they do look awful cold/hope I die before I get old'. On record, too, the latter song was all the more effective for being sung by lead vocalist Roger Daltrey in a mock stammer, thereby simulating the effect of being 'blocked' on amphetamines.

Below: the Who on Brighton beach, the setting for numerous mod vs rocker clashes on mid-Sixties bank holidays and for Pete Townshend's retrospective musical account of mod culture, Quadrophenia, *which was filmed in 1979*

In time, the theatricality of the Who's stage performances took on a life of its own and the group came to be seen less as mod spokesmen and more as exponents of what Kit Lambert liked to describe as the 'pop art' sound. In reality, pop art was a branch of the visual arts that took its subjects from commonplace popular culture and its techniques from commercial art: thus, the Who's music was similarly portrayed as a critique of the mundane, the everyday, in the often violent language of commercial pop music. Their image was certainly pop-art influenced – the Union Jack T-shirts, for instance, screamed out an ironic patriotism – while their destruction of sound equipment was excused in some quarters as a symbolic act of spite against society. Likewise, the feedback effect that Townshend achieved by shoving his guitar at the speaker cabinet was described as a howl of anger and an attempt to transcend the limitations of a machine. All this could be taken with a heavy pinch of salt, yet an uneasy – but always interesting – mix of basic rock energy and grandiose conceptual ideas pervaded much of the Who's recording work. 'A Quick One While He's Away', a miniature 'rock opera' about suburban infidelity that appeared on their 1966 album of this name was a typical Townshend

experiment like his later, more elaborate composition *Tommy*, while *The Who Sells Out* (1967) was a superbly realised lampoon of the advertising world that featured a sleeve extolling in graphic fashion the virtues of Odorono deodorant and Heinz baked beans.

Beyond the pop formula

The Who inspired a glut of copyists, some with more genuine mod connections but few with the wit to develop beyond them. The Action, Creation, the Birds, and the Eyes all came and went, while the Small Faces (from London's East End) – four teenage mods with a solid grounding in soul – made an impressive showing in

The changing face of the Who – offering 'maximum R&B' on a TV show in 1965 (below), smashing up equipment as part of a gratuitously anarchic stage routine in 1966 (below left), and sending up the world of advertising for the cover of the 1967 album The Who Sell Out *(left)*

all the record charts but were initially forced into a conventional beat mould. On transferring to Andrew Oldham's Immediate label from Decca, their individuality began to blossom through such singles as 'Here Comes the Nice' and the Ray Davies-like 'Lazy Sunday'. And as pop art exhibitionism took over from mod style, so Surrey group John's Children (managed by Simon Napier-Bell) enjoyed brief but spectacular notoriety with their smashed instrument routine and extravagant, feedback-dominated experiments in sound. Birmingham band the Move, handled by Tony Secunda, were taking the same route as late as 1967, but making up for their laughably derivative stage act with some cleverly crafted, comically topical singles from the pen of guitarist/singer Roy Wood.

The flirtation with pop art disguised a deeper degree of genuine experimentation going on within British rock, notably that effected by another of Napier-Bell's groups, the Yardbirds. They made their Top Ten debut within a month of the Who's own first entry into the chart (with 'I Can't Explain') in 1965 and were for a time labelled as a mod group, but they had firm roots in the London R & B scene and owed their initial break to Crawdaddy boss Giorgio Gomelsky, who managed their affairs for a while. The undoubted star was Eric Clapton, a blues perfectionist with a technical ability and feel for the music unmatched on the club circuit, but he left the group in protest at the overt commercialism of début hit 'For Your Love' and found a more suitable environment for his skills in John Mayall's Bluesbreakers and, later, Cream. What the Yardbirds lacked was a clear recording identity: handicapped by their inability to write their own material, they relied too heavily on pop songwriters like Graham Gouldman (composer of hits for the Hollies and Herman's Hermits) and found themselves caught

Precursors of the progressive rock era that began in 1967 included R&B masters the Spencer Davis Group (top left), whose lead singer Stevie Winwood quit to form Traffic, and the Yardbirds (below), whose line-up briefly included guitar legend-to-be Eric Clapton. Long after Clapton left, the Yardbirds consolidated their considerable international following with their appearance in the film Blow-up, directed by Michelangelo Antonioni. The film starred those bright young things of the Sixties, David Hemmings (left, in a still from the film) and Vanessa Redgrave

between the demands of the pop audience on the one hand and their R & B following on the other. With Jeff Beck replacing Clapton, the group ended up taking neither direction but moving into a much more experimental mode, improvising in the customary blues fashion but adding new electronic effects and using feedback to the full. In time, they toyed with Indian raga scales and introduced a sitar into their range of instruments, while album tracks like 'Still I'm Sad' (based on a Gregorian chant) marked them as precursors of the progressive rock era – dedicated extemporisers whose minds were open to anything and whose ideas, though unfocused and not always fully developed, helped move British rock decisively beyond the beat and R & B straitjackets.

The Yardbirds never achieved the success in Britain that their trail-blazing warranted, but their ideas influenced both emerging American garage bands and San Francisco Bay area groups to a particularly noticeable degree. Their guitar-smashing appearance in Michelangelo Antonioni's archetypal swinging Sixties film *Blow-Up* added to their international reputation, but that was an uncharacteristic concession to pop fashion (prompted by Napier-Bell) made at a time – late 1966 – when their creative spark was beginning to dwindle. Forgotten by home fans as many of the original R & B bands re-shaped themselves as progressive outfits during 1967 (the year in which Jeff Beck, now solo, hit the UK chart with the Mickie Most-produced flower-power anthem 'Hi Ho Silver Lining'), the Yardbirds failed to capitalise on a trend they did much to create.

Overleaf: progressing into pastures new – John Lennon and George Harrison rehearse in the recording studio for the Beatles' 1966 album, Revolver. *Within a year, the Beatles were embracing flower-power and throwing off the last vestiges of their mop-top image (inset)*

Left: the Small Faces, soul boys from London's East End whose later records – 'Lazy Sunday', 'Itchycoo Park' – were delightfully comic slices of mock-psychedelia. Lead singer Stevie Marriott departed to form Humble Pie in 1969 and the remaining members reformed as the Faces, with Rod Stewart as vocalist

If the success of such groups as the Stones, Kinks, Yardbirds and the Who was the major achievement of the British R&B movement, credit was also due to the Beatles for helping create a climate conducive to musical change. From 1963 onwards, Beatle music was an accurate barometer of the times: not only did they show an exceptional knack for absorbing different elements of current rock styles and making them work in the context of their own music, they legitimised and popularised new pop developments with each successive album or single. They reflected the soul boom, for instance, in tracks like 'Can't Buy Me Love' and 'You Can't Do That' (which John Lennon described as 'my attempt to be Wilson Pickett'), and expanded on the rich, dense guitar sound of the Searchers and American folk-rockers the Byrds on 'Ticket to Ride'. Following the Yardbirds and the Stones, they used a sitar on 'Norwegian Wood' to augment brilliantly a wry tale of Swinging London promiscuity; and they satirised the media and mass culture in general in 'Paperback Writer', combining Ray Davies-style social comment with Beach Boy-type harmonies.

They also set a key precedent by giving up live performances – which had long been mass orgies of adulation, where fans came to scream rather than listen – to concentrate all their music-making energies on studio work. In *Rubber Soul* (1965) and *Revolver* (1966), the subject-matter of their songs broadened markedly, and they began applying their highly professional approach to new areas, producing technically sophisticated songs in a variety of contemporary idioms. 'Eleanor Rigby', the track (from *Revolver*) that apparently confirmed them as artists of the new age, was a stylised piece of Dickensian commentary that expressed concern without commitment – not only was the imagery of the lyrics self-

consciously stark, but George Martin's arrangement in the manner of Haydn accentuated the detachment between singer and subject. Elsewhere on the album, George Harrison highlighted his new proficiency on the sitar on 'Love You To' and created a briefly lauded new genre called 'raga rock', while John Lennon took the lyrics of his LSD-influenced 'Tomorrow Never Knows' almost word for word from Timothy Leary's drug bible, *The Tibetan Book of the Dead*.

In Britain, the Beatles were pop figure-heads, respected by all but not always taken seriously by other musicians. When it came to real, enduring stylistic influence, they were some way behind the Stones, the Who and several other major mid-Sixties names: their greatest skill was to listen diligently to what was going on around them and fashion music that provided a succinct, intelligent and spirited picture of the times. In America, however, their influence was arguably greater – and they dragged US rock screaming into a new and astonishingly productive era.

CHAPTER 5

THE TIMES THEY ARE A-CHANGIN'
Folk-rock and after

The folk singers of Greenwich village adopted rock instrumentation to lead America's response to British beat

Left: the Mamas and Papas, folk-rock harmonisers with a Greenwich Village background. With groups like the Byrds, the Beau Brummels and the Lovin' Spoonful, they spearheaded America's response to the Beatle-led British invasion

Below: the Beau Brummels from San Francisco, the first American band to find major success by imitating the Beatles' sound. Guitarist Ron Elliott (second from left) was a particularly fine songwriter whose compositions were later recorded by the Everly Brothers, Harpers Bizarre, the Young Rascals and others

After the Beatles, American pop music was never quite the same again. The commercial effects of their 1964 breakthrough were obvious enough – the opening up of the US market to British acts, the sudden datedness of conventional teen idols of the Bobby Vee-Bobby Rydell variety, the emergence of countless copycat groups – but on a creative level their impact went far deeper. It was not so much that the Beatles were particularly innovative, for much of their appeal lay in the manner in which they *re-created* basic American rock'n'roll within a beat group context; rather, they were catalysts, reminding American youth of the quality and richness of its rock tradition and inspiring other equally inventive and in some ways more musically accomplished artists to take the music to still greater peaks. Established groups and newcomers alike

responded to the Beatle challenge in ingenious and imaginative ways – and the result was a period of unparalleled creativity within US rock, characterised by barrier-breaking experimentation and cross-fertilisation of sounds and styles.

No musician, songwriter or producer working within the American pop field was unaffected by the Beatles' dramatic surge to pop primacy. For some groups, imitating the Beatle sound and look was just a means of getting noticed, but along the way they absorbed the more significant lesson of the Beatles' success – that pop artists could and should write their own material and take control of their own musical direction. This was especially true in the case of San Francisco group the Beau Brummels, the first of many US bands to be promoted as an American 'answer' to the British invasion. Behind their shaggy dog haircuts, Lennonesque vocals and self-consciously English name lurked the elegant, ethereal composing style of rhythm guitarist Ron Elliott and a range of expansive musical ideas based on the skilful pop application of twelve-string guitar. They had two major national hits before carving out a new, weightier image for themselves as the first rock group to be signed by Warner Brothers (who bought up their contract from Autumn, an independent) in 1966. Another group to build on and eventually outgrow their pseudo-Beatle beginnings were the Sir Douglas Quintet, a Texan five-piece whose very name – connoting Englishness and aristocracy – was chosen to help disguise their temporarily

Above: Texan band the Sir Douglas Quintet took the Beatles' 'She's a Woman' as inspiration for their first US hit, 'She's About a Mover', in 1965. The band's resident creative force was Doug Sahm (left)

unfashionable all-American origins. Their one big international hit, 'She's About a Mover' in 1965, was directly inspired by the Beatles' own 'She's a Woman', but their easy command of Tex-Mex sounds and Chicano rhythms gave their version of UK-style beat an engagingly raw and rugged quality. They too had a resident songwriter and creative all-rounder in Doug Sahm, whose career had previously taken in country music and late Fifties Texas rockabilly. The group's move to San Francisco in 1967 was his decision, following which they became stalwarts of the city's influential acid-rock scene.

If the championing of the Brummels and the Quintet typified the industry's reaction to the Beatle-inspired British onslaught, the emotional impact of the UK groups on American rock's grass roots was immeasurable. Scores of small towns and cities the length and breadth of America experienced an explosion of amateur groups, most taking the British

beat sound as their base but modelling their self-consciously rebellious image on that of the Rolling Stones. Raucous, crude and musically limited, these 'garage bands' – so nicknamed in honour of their favourite rehearsal places – nevertheless represented America's first great flowering of collective rock talent since the rockabilly era. Making extensive use of such new and cheaply obtained inventions as the fuzz-tone guitar distortion box and the portable Vox organ (first popularised by the Sir Douglas Quintet) the bands produced a sound that was tinny and punkish in texture and sounded more dynamic in live performance than on record. Few of the groups found much lasting chart success – the best, like the McCoys, the Cryan Shames, Shadows of Knight and Music Machine, rarely proved more than one-hit wonders – but the garage band boom was responsible for giving many of the most creative figures in late Sixties and Seventies rock their career starts.

FOLK GOES ELECTRIC

Most crucially for the long-term development of rock, the success of the Beatles also sparked the interest of musicians working outside the pop mainstream – especially those with college or university backgrounds, who had left rock'n'roll behind in the late Fifties for the supposedly worthier pastures of folk music. As Bob Dylan later recalled to his biographer Tony Scaduto, 'I had heard the Beatles in New York when they first hit ... they were doing things nobody was doing. Their chords were outrageous, just outrageous, and their harmonies made it all valid. You could only do that with other musicians. I knew they were pointing the direction of where music had to go'. At that time, Dylan was the most enigmatic and influential of America's young breed of folk singers – a man largely unknown to pop audiences, whose chosen musical field took pride in its political awareness and its identification with social issues and generally stood aloof from the supposedly rampant commercialism of pop. His Beatle-inspired conversion to the rock sound was a key moment in the history of rock, not only marking the birth of a new hybrid style – 'folk-rock' – but bringing to the music a whole new range of political, artistic and intellectual concerns.

America's folk music scene had parallels with the R & B movement in England, in that it was dedicated to the conservation of traditional musical idioms and it had a largely middle class and academia-based following and distinct affiliations with radical politics. In the context of the late Fifties, when the mushy sentiment and dubious financial dealings of Philadelphia pop alienated many of the most diehard of original rock fans, the appeal of folk to America's student generation was easy to understand. Folk, after all, was a music of honesty, integrity and intellectual purity; it was the sound, or so it was believed, of the working classes, the poor, the migrant workers and immigrants – the very sections of society with which liberal-minded campus America sought to ally. It also offered young musicians an education in such traditional styles as rural blues, gospel, bluegrass, calypso, and the 'talking blues' (topical protest commentaries) of Woody Guthrie, an itinerant folk singer of the

Great Depression years whose bohemian lifestyle and commitment to worker unionisation made him one of the folk movement's most romantic figures.

Between 1958 and 1964, America enjoyed a major folk revival that even made some inroads into the national chart: the Kingston Trio, Harry Belafonte, the New Christy Minstrels and Peter, Paul and Mary all had hits with folk-style material and helped give the folk scene a cosy campfire image that was a distortion of its true nature. Much truer to folk's political colours were the songs of a handful of young singers and writers, most of them members of the folk community based in New York's Greenwich Village, who took Woody Guthrie's compositions as a model and spoke out in song about the great issues of the day – the demand for black civil rights and the escalating cold war between east and west. Joan Baez, Phil Ochs, Tom Paxton, Eric Andersen, Bob Dylan and Patrick Sky were particularly important figures, lending support whenever they could to marches, peace drives and demonstrations, and providing the various anti-segregation and pro-disarmament organisations with political anthems.

Graduates of the Greenwich Village folk circuit – Phil Ochs (above), Joan Baez (left), and Peter, Paul and Mary (below left). All gave their time freely to liberal and left-wing causes, especially the fight for black civil rights

Dylan breaks out

This faction of folk singers was viewed with some hostility by the folk music establishment, who regarded traditional material as somehow more 'authentic' than topical songs composed in the heat of a political moment. Bob Dylan was singled out for special criticism, not so much because of the content of his deftly constructed 'folk' songs – which ran the gamut of all the social and political subjects with which the folk audience concerned itself – but because of his apparent determination to assume Woody Guthrie's mantle for himself. His cultivated Guthrie-esque disregard for grammar in his songs, his constant use of

Woody Guthrie (above) was a powerful inspiration for Bob Dylan (above right) and many other Sixties folk singers. Guthrie knew the hardship of the Depression and led a freewheeling and energetic life, travelling the continent, singing its old songs and writing new ones in praise of its 'plain folk'. He died of Huntington's chorea in 1967

the highway motif, and the sheer cheek of a lyric like 'A Song To Woody' – in which he appeared to compare the limited experiences of his life to date with the chequered life of his mentor, whom Dylan was then visiting as he lay dying in a New York hospital – all pointed to Dylan's saturation in the Guthrie myth. It was in more polemical songs like 'Masters of War' and the apocalyptic 'A Hard Rain's Gonna Fall' that his originality as a songwriter became obvious, and in 1962 he received national recognition for the first time as the composer of the wistful yet curiously non-committal 'Blowin' in the Wind', which Peter, Paul and Mary took into the US Top Ten.

Dylan's appearance at the 1963 Newport Folk Festival, the most prestigious event in the folk calendar, established him as the guru of the American Left and

a true folk superstar, but he was happy with neither role. His album *The Times They Are A-Changin'*, released early in 1964, was packed with snarling protest songs that were nevertheless a world removed from the detached, forthright anti-Government epics of his friend and rival, Phil Ochs: while Ochs dealt in political certainties, Dylan offered his songs as moods rather than statements and kept the focus of his anger deliberately imprecise and his message elliptical. In fact, Dylan was itching to leave protest behind altogether, and from 1964 onwards he dismayed his folk followers by cutting down noticeably on the number of political songs in his concert repertoire. His next album, appropriately titled *Another Side of Bob Dylan*, confirmed his move into a much more personal mode of songwriting with such tracks as 'It Ain't Me Babe', 'To Ramona', and the reflective 'My Back Pages', which found Dylan railing against 'the lies that life is black and white'. No longer dependent on his folk influences for constant inspiration – not just Guthrie but Ramblin' Jack Elliott, Dave Van Ronk, Bob Gibson and Pete Seeger – he at last seemed to have found his own voice.

At a time when America was becoming more deeply embedded than ever in the Vietnam war, and the assassination of President John F. Kennedy had left a vacuum in young, go-ahead liberal leadership, Dylan's abdication from the political arena was viewed by some as a betrayal. Worse, his astonishing switch to rock'n'roll instrumentation on his *Bringing It All Back Home* album

and his appearance with the Paul Butterfield Blues Band at the 1965 Newport Folk Festival was regarded by many folk fans as a sell-out to commercialism and a misjudged stab at becoming some kind of teen idol. It was a dangerous gamble, but one that the recording of rock versions of his songs by the Byrds, the Animals, Manfred Mann and others – following fast on his first-hand exposure to British music on his 1964 UK tour – had convinced him was worth taking. The Beatles were a symbolic influence, bringing alive again the freshness and vitality of his first love, rock music, while the Animals' R&B version of 'House of the Rising Sun' – a folk standard recorded by Dylan in Van Ronk style early in his career – proved to him beyond all doubt that a

Below: the Byrds, whose ethereal re-working of Dylan's 'Mr Tambourine Man', a worldwide hit in 1965, ushered in the folk-rock era

rock backing could add new dimensions of energy, attack and power to his songs.

Poetry and invective

Bringing It All Back Home and Dylan's second 'rock' album, *Highway 61 Revisited*, featured accompaniments heavily influenced by the Animals and the Rolling Stones and revealed the extent of his own absorption in the rock tradition. 'Subterranean Homesick Blues', the hit single taken from the former album, took the tongue-tripping structure and sceptical stance of Chuck Berry's 'Too Much Monkey Business' and turned them into a fast, funny and acidic commentary on young street culture. 'You don't need a weather man to know which way the wind blows', he sang, as compellingly aphoristic as ever, 'don't follow leaders, watch the parking meters'. With the intense, magisterial organ playing of sideman Al Kooper giving the songs a cutting yet impressionistic quality, Dylan introduced a level of invective to rock that only Jagger and Richard came close to matching. But whereas the concerns of the Stones' songwriting team were narrow, their targets mainly unnamed individuals, and their lyrics calculated to confirm and enhance their anti-social public image, Dylan used the full armoury of folk poetry – allegory, allusion, imagery – to present his own idiosyncratic vision of a chaotic, disordered and fundamentally dishonest world. In the past, he had reworked folk ballads in an attempt to put over this vision – 'A Hard Rain's Gonna Fall', for instance, was based on the traditional lament, 'Lord Randal'. Now, drawing equally on the lessons of French Symbolist poets like Rimbaud and Gautier and the surrealistic tradition of American poetry that stretched from Walt Whitman to Allen Ginsberg, Dylan brought new literacy to rock and incalculably broadened its frame of reference.

Left: Bob Dylan and Joan Baez, who were lovers for a time in the early Sixties

Below: Dylan in the studio with sideman Mike Bloomfield, a noted blues guitarist whose dynamic playing graced the singer's Highway 61 Revisited *album in 1965*

Dylan's impact on rock songwriting was very quickly felt: John Lennon, deeply impressed by Dylan's use of the song as a means of self-expression, began writing in the confessional style with 'Help!' and 'You've Got to Hide Your Love Away', and even arch-professionals Goffin and King were moved to write 'Going Back' (recorded by Dusty Springfield and the Byrds) after hearing 'My Back Pages'. In other key respects, however, Dylan's long-term influence was just as vital. He gave a new realism to rock lyrics, taking social and political comment – however obliquely expressed – into the record charts for the first time. He also changed the nature of the pop song, writing about love from a distinctly *anti*-romantic point of view, questioning the permanency of relationships in 'Don't Think Twice, It's Alright' and 'One Too Many Mornings', and deriding conventional courtship in such songs as 'It Ain't Me Babe' and 'Just Like a Woman'. And he also showed that a rock singer did not necessarily need a good blues or pop voice to succeed, that effective use of intonation and nuance could compensate for the lack of customary vocal strengths.

VILLAGE VOICES AND PROTEST POP

Opposite page, left: Dylan in thoughtful mood, at the Columbia studios in New York during 1965

Opposite page, right: two key albums in Dylan's artistic development – The Freewheelin' Bob Dylan (1963) and Blonde on Blonde (1966)

Dylan was not the first folk musician to see the potential of a folk-rock synthesis, but he was the first to put his career on the line in pursuit of it. By the end of 1964, there was much dissatisfaction within folk circles at the appropriation and prettification of folk music by the slick city night-clubs, who hired middle-of-the-road folk outfits like the Limeliters and Les Baxter's Balladeers while effectively barring any artist with a political reputation. There was a feeling, too, that the folk scene no longer offered any scope for musical or commercial progress, and the increasing popularity of jug bands – aggregations of musicians playing a mixture of blues, jazz and folk repertoire with a good-time flavour – seemed to point one way forward. Even as Dylan was considering his switch to

rock, members of such bands were already toying with electric instrumentation in tentative imitation of the British rock groups. Elsewhere, guitarists like Jim McGuinn and David Crosby – musicians with folk leanings but no great commitment to the folk scene as such – were enthusiastically adopting amplification and looking for drummers and bassists to help them create a sound as close to that of the Beatles as possible.

For McGuinn, as for many others, seeing the Beatles in *A Hard Day's Night* was enough to persuade him that the rock route was worth taking. It was not just Beatle music that so impressed but their status as personalities, their easy wit and obvious intelligence, and their refusal to take themselves too seriously. In short, the Beatles showed that rock was no longer a form of music necessarily dominated by record industry machinations or the requirements of the mass market: it had style and originality, and to move into it meant no loss of credibility. When McGuinn formed the Byrds out of the remnants of two directly derivative Beatle-type bands, the Jet Set and the Beefeaters, he took the courageous step

Right: the Byrds on stage with Bob Dylan in 1965. Their careers were complementary during the mid-Sixties, the Byrds' success with Dylan material prompting Dylan to explore further the possibilities of rock accompaniment

Above: the Byrds (with leader Roger McGuinn in granny glasses) pose for a moody photograph, very much in the style of the first Rolling Stones album cover. The 'British invasion', of which the Stones were such a part, was a crucial point of departure for the UK folk-rock boom. McGuinn changed his first name from Jim to Roger after his 1968 conversion to the Hindu doctrine of Subud

of casting them in a hip, arrogant image that anticipated the Beatles' own move into more intellectual pastures. Musically, too, he broke new ground by clinically matching folk harmonies and material with rock instrumentation, thereby creating what was in effect a folk-rock *sound*, finely textured and graced by some of the most appealing twelve-string guitar work ever heard in the rock idiom.

This Byrds' sound was a recording studio concoction, perfected on their debut hit 'Mr Tambourine Man' through numerous re-takes and the astute production ideas of Jim Dickson. So intent was McGuinn on getting the sound precisely right that he brought in three vastly experienced ex-Phil Spector session

men, Hal Blaine, Leon Russell and Larry Knechtel, to complement his own guitar and vocals, and the result was a dreamlike production that accentuated the melody of the Dylan original and hinted at the kaleidoscopic qualities of an hallucinogenic drug trip. Recorded before Dylan's conversion to rock but released shortly after, it had the effect of turning folk-rock into an overnight craze, but failed to provide the Byrds with a springboard to even greater success. Although they continued to record Dylan songs, McGuinn's thirst for experiment won them further critical plaudits, but it lost them a major part of their audience. Shifting from folk-rock to electronic experimentation on their psychedelia-laced *Fifth Dimension* album, and from there to a seminal blend of country-rock (in 1968), they became very much a musicians' band, consistently pointing to new directions in rock yet never quite receiving the credit they deserved for making possible the successes of other, some considerably less talented, groups.

On the Village beat

McGuinn and fellow Byrds David Crosby, Gene Clark and Chris Hillman were all sometime residents of Greenwich Village, but their particular blend of folk-rock was very much a product of the Californian recording environment. Although many fellow Villagers followed them into folk-rock, surprisingly few of the original folk set benefited from the intense commercialisation that the folk scene underwent in the wake of the Byrds' and Dylan's success. Solo singers tended to fare less well than groups in the beat-obsessed climate of 1965, and the few who did gain important record deals suffered in Dylan's shadow. Tim Hardin, for example, had a distinctively world-weary vocal style borrowed from jazz, and specialised in bitter-sweet love songs even more starkly introspective than Dylan's own, yet he never achieved more than cult status, though such delicately autobiographical songs as 'Reason to Believe', 'If I Were a Carpenter' and 'Misty Roses' were extensively recorded by other artists. For the singer-songwriters who had pioneered folk in its pre-'Mr Tambourine Man' days – names like Richard Farina, Peter LaFarge and Fred Neil – there was rarely even this kind of consolation.

Many of these singers were already tied to small folk-based record labels that lacked both the money and the inclination to give their signings a big push in the pop market. Much luckier were native New Yorkers Paul Simon and Art Garfunkel, who had recorded a handful of folk tracks for the major Columbia label

before going their separate ways in early 1965. A few months later, with Garfunkel at college and Simon playing the provincial folk clubs of England, producer Tom Wilson unearthed their tapes in search of suitable material to promote as 'folk-rock'. Adding a basic rock accompaniment to the most appropriately 'poetic' of the tracks, 'The Sounds of Silence', Columbia found themselves a Number One hit and – as it happened – the most popular and enduringly commercial act to emerge out of the folk-rock era. With Simon's exquisitely-crafted modern folk songs reflecting the vulnerability, tensions, insecurities and liberal concerns of mid-Sixties student America, Simon and Garfunkel appealed to those who found Dylan's rasping, strident delivery and occasionally mind-bendingly complex lyrics hard to take.

Simon and Garfunkel apart, the two unqualified successes of the New York folk scene were the Lovin' Spoonful and the Mamas and Papas, each of whom evolved out of established Greenwich Village jug bands. The Spoonful played jug band music with bass, drums and electric guitar, and their songs – mostly written by lead singer John Sebastian – matched the amiability and romanticism

Below: John Sebastian, lead singer and resident songwriter of the Lovin' Spoonful. His background included a spell in Greenwich Village folk group the Mugwumps with Cass Elliot and Denny Doherty of the Mamas and Papas (bottom)

Below: Art Garfunkel and Paul Simon, America's foremost folk duo, whose career began in high school as Everly Brothers imitators Tom and Jerry. Success finally came when their folk-style recording of Simon's 'The Sounds of Silence' was discovered in the Columbia vault and issued, without their knowledge, as a would-be folk-rock track

of the Beatles' best work with the lazy charm of old-time jazz compositions by the likes of Fats Waller and Hoagy Carmichael. Especially notable were 'Nashville Cats', Sebastian's homage to the southern rockabilly and country musicians who had helped form his tastes in the late Fifties, and the brilliantly atmospheric 'Summer in the City', which captured the sweaty tension of a long hot New York summer. The Mamas and Papas, by contrast, were primarily a vocal group in the Peter, Paul and Mary mould, who had an adroit leader and songwriter in John Phillips, and a bohemian image fashioned in part by their manager, Lou Adler. Their long run of chart hits, beginning with the singularly appropriate 'California Dreamin'' in early 1966, followed their signing with Adler's Hollywood-based Dunhill label and consequent move to the west coast.

Pursuit of the dollar

The full-scale marketing of folk-rock as a craze in fact began on the west coast,

with Adler its principal architect. He had been a songwriting partner of trumpeter and A&M Records boss Herb Alpert and had himself moved from New York to Hollywood in 1960 to set up a west coast division of Don Kirshner's Aldon Music publishing house. A typically shrewd Californian pop operator, his introduction to folk and Dylan in particular came via *Bringing It All Back Home*, in which he saw immediate possibilities. Staff song-writer Phil Sloan was given the album to mull over, as Adler later recalled in a *Melody Maker* interview: 'I gave Phil a pair of boots and a hat and a copy of the album, and a week later he came back with ten songs, including 'Eve of De-struction'. It was a natural feel for him – he was a great mimic. Anyway, I was afraid of the song – I didn't know if we could get it played. But the next night I went to Ciro's, where the Byrds were playing. It was the beginning of the freak period ... the place was jam-packed, spilling out on to the street. In the middle of it was this guy in furs, with long hair, and dancing; I thought he looked like a leader of a movement'. The guy was Barry McGuire, former singer with the New Christy Minstrels. Adler gave him 'Eve of Destruction' to record, and by September 1965 it was Number One.

The disc was little more than an un-subtle, awkwardly constructed barrage of complaints against authority. It had just the kind of all-purpose protest lyric – its targets including everything from segregation to the Bomb, religion to Indo-China – to send shudders through the US radio networks and inspire irate letters to newspapers. It was ersatz Dylan, cleverly capitalising on the pub-lic's confusion of folk-rock with a more generalised folk-based form of protest music, and its success precipitated a brief boom in similarly castigatory records. By the autumn of 1965, there were so many so-called folk-rock or pro-test discs in the chart that the industry's trade magazine *Variety* ran the headline, 'Folk + Rock + Protest = Dollars' on the

One of the most important backroom figures in California pop, Lou Adler (above left) helped plot the successful chart careers of Jan and Dean, the Mamas and Papas, Johnny Rivers and ex-New Christy Minstrel Barry McGuire. McGuire's publicity shots for Eve of Destruction (1965) pictured the singer emerging from a nuclear fall-out shelter (above)

front page, and under it an article claiming that the new sound was American pop's first proper response to the British beat domination.

In reality, the fad signalled little more than the California record industry finally coming into its own after years in the shadow of the big New York-based companies. For much of the late Fifties and early Sixties, the west coast record scene had lacked a real identity, with interest concentrated mainly on acts like the Beach Boys and Jan and Dean, who eulogised the joys of surfing, hot-rod riding and the laid-back California lifestyle in hits that were basically white vocal group interpretations of the Chuck Berry sound. Los Angeles did, nevertheless, become the home of many fine ex-rockabilly musicians who gathered there to seek work on film scores, in the lucrative night-clubs, and in session work for people like Frank Sinatra and Dean Martin. Such session men as Hal Blaine, Glen Campbell, David Gates, Leon Russell, Jim Gordon and Joe Osborne were astonishingly versatile, providing accompaniment on countless middle-of-the-road albums and many of the one-off hits produced during the surfing craze.

Los Angeles' pop identity emerged first through the production work of Phil Spector, which taxed the skills of his session crews to the full and spawned many imitations. Brian Wilson of the Beach Boys was a particularly willing pupil, adding Spector-style batteries of percussion instruments and countless vocal overdubs to creations like 'California Girls', 'Wouldn't It Be Nice' and the classically-flavoured 'God Only Knows'. Yet Spector's influence was felt most on those Hollywood-produced discs that passed for folk-rock, notably the Turtles' bombastic version of Dylan's 'It Ain't Me Babe' and the run of hits recorded by Sonny and Cher between 1965 and 1966.

This duo consisted of former Spector arranger Sonny Bono and his wife, herself a one-time Spector backing singer, who were marketed by the Atco label as the personification of hip, modern, fun-seeking youth – the harmless face of protest, in fact, whose chief complaints concerned the unwillingness of parents to tolerate long hair. In their oversize sheepskin coats, fancy striped trousers, flowery shirts and pointed boots, Sonny and Cher were taken briefly for Greenwich Village refugees, but their brand of musical besottedness soon took on a hollow ring and they ultimately settled for the security of cabaret appearances and a national television show. Against the likes of the Byrds and the Beach Boys, their music quickly sounded dated.

CALIFORNIA DREAMIN'

The folk-rock boom changed the Greenwich Village scene for good, and by the end of 1965 many of its most illustrious residents had migrated to California, enticed by the promise of a freer musical climate – one less hidebound by the folk music establishment – and better record deals. Guitarists Steve Stills and Richie Furay were just two who made the journey, teaming up in Los Angeles with drummer Dewey Martin – an ex-member of bluegrass group the Dillards – and a former folkie from Toronto named Neil Young. Calling themselves Buffalo Springfield, they developed into a highly innovative rock band, using their unusual line-up of a three-man vocal team (Stills, Young and Furay) and two lead guitarists to explore a variety of styles from straight folk-rock ('Nowadays Clancy Can't Even Sing') and hard rock'n'roll ('Rock'n'Roll Woman') to a disciplined form of 'acid-rock', elaborated on stage through long instrumental jam sessions and on record through shorter but equally evocative sound collages like 'Broken Arrow'. Like the Byrds, they were slightly ahead of their time, comparatively uninterested in commercial success and riddled by internal dissension; as with the Byrds, lesser groups purloined their ideas, and it was not until the re-emergence of the twin creative forces of Stills and Young in the late Sixties supergroup Crosby, Stills, Nash and Young that their influence on post-1967 American rock was fully acknowledged.

Buffalo Springfield had one major American hit – the coolly impressionistic

'For What It's Worth', written by Stills after witnessing an anti-police riot on Hollywood's Sunset Strip, and recorded in Los Angeles for Atlantic, the biggest east-coast independent. Atlantic were one of several important New York-based companies to explore the burgeoning California scene during the mid-Sixties – some in fact moved their whole base of operation to Los Angeles after 1967 – while on the west coast itself, television and film companies like Warner Brothers and Screen Gems-Columbia consolidated their financial interest in the rock recording scene by either setting up record subsidiaries or buying into music publishing houses. Screen Gems made the boldest move by taking a controlling stake in Don Kirshner's Aldon Music and bringing over dozens of the biggest names in New York songwriting – Goffin and King, Neil Sedaka and Neil Diamond among them. Once ensconced in Los Angeles, Aldon's workforce were given the task of providing music for Screen Gems' ingenious new pop television series, *The Monkees*, which centred on the lives of a mythical pop group. Borrowing heavily from the visual humour and madcap antics of the two Beatles films, the venture was a huge international success and made its four hand-picked actor/musicians – Micky Dolenz, Davy Jones, Mike Nesmith and ex-folknik Peter Tork – into overnight stars.

In many ways, the Monkees were the ultimate California response to the Beatles – a group deliberately fashioned in the Beatle image, promoted and merchandised through television, and using

Below: the Monkees, a pop group manufactured for television exposure and intensive merchandising, were the pet hates of rock critics during 1967 but recorded a string of decent and highly memorable teen-oriented hit singles

all the splendid resources of Los Angeles pop, right down to the familiar session team of Blaine, Russell, Gates, Campbell et al who gave Monkee hits like 'I'm a Believer' and 'Last Train to Clarksville' such a professional veneer. Television was responsible too for the national success of two other California-based Beatle soundalikes in Gary Lewis and the Playboys and Paul Revere and the Raiders, who were ever-present on syndicated shows like *Shindig* and Dick Clark's *Where the Action Is!* The Raiders, to be fair, had real originality; coming from Oregon, they had been a working unit since well before the British invasion and mixed the best qualities of pre-Beatle vocal group pop with the storming beat of early period Beatles, Kinks and Rolling Stones records. Curiously, other Los Angeles groups, equivalents of the garage bands but with marked folk-rock leanings, suffered because of the city industry's new preoccupation with serving the national market. With local followings whose tendency to freakish behaviour and psychedelic excess had been known to frighten off key A&R men, such bands as the Seeds, the Grass Roots, the Standells, the Chocolate Watch Band and Love rarely reached the television screens.

Acid dreams and hippie trails

Nevertheless, despite record company indifference, it was groups such as the Seeds and Love who were most in tune with the changes going on within California rock at a basic level. Elsewhere in California, in the musically isolated city of San Francisco, a quite different version of the folk-rock hybrid had evolved that betrayed the unmistakeable influence of a new hallucinogenic drug – lysergic acid diethylamide-25 (LSD). The drug had been in common use by the city's beatnik community since the early Sixties, their bible a book by Harvard professor

Timothy Leary – *The Politics of Ecstasy* – that depicted LSD as a means of not only achieving a kind of personal Nirvana but of changing the very nature of society itself. Another important proselytiser was Ken Kesey, author of *One Flew Over the Cuckoo's Nest*. He gathered around him an entourage of followers called the Merry Pranksters who travelled around California in a brightly painted bus, spreading the promise of mind-expanding acid trips and cerebral liberation as they went. Giant LSD parties known as Trips Festivals were organised by Kesey, attracting a whole new hippie subculture peopled by beatific-looking, beads and bangles bedecked acid-heads from the University of Berkeley, many of whom set up camp in the Haight-Ashbury district of the city.

LSD was not illegal at this time so its use spread unchecked. As the expanding hippie community developed its own acid-based lifestyle, drawing on all kinds of mystical and counter-cultural influences from Zen Buddhism and astrology to revolutionary politics, so the musicians within its ranks assumed a special importance, providing suitably freakish accompaniment at community dances, fund-raising events and multi-media 'happenings'. What they played was

From top left, clockwise: some of the key personalities of the '67 scene – the Seeds, who were originally known as Sky Saxon's Blues Band; Love, pictured on a 1967 record sleeve; and the messiah of LSD, Dr Timothy Leary, pictured with 'Yippie' activists Abbie Hoffman and Jerry Rubin

Top: the Haight-Ashbury intersection in San Francisco, the spiritual centre of the hippie movement

Above: the Beach Boys' Pet Sounds, *one of the very first albums to betray a distinct LSD influence*

generally an anarchic, deliberately unstructured blend of folk, blues and British beat, heavily improvised but placing little importance on musical ability. At its best, 'acid-rock' was a peculiarly democratic, free-form style, eschewing any hint of professionalism and valuing music-making as primarily an expression of personality. Yet it was also very much a community music, echoing and articulating the zonked-out egalitarianism of the Haight-Ashbury set in a gesture of commitment to, and solidarity with, a section of San Franciscan youth increasingly persecuted by the city's authorities.

The record industry's complete lack of interest in the city's rock and folk scenes meant that both could thrive and develop at their own pace, unhindered by the expectations of the record-buying audience and free of media attention, but the acid-rock gospel spread quickly within the rock cognoscenti. Even before a single San Francisco hippie band became nationally known, signs of LSD use could be detected on tracks by the Beatles – 'Tomorrow Never Knows' and 'She Said She Said' on *Revolver* – and on Dylan's mystically-flavoured *Blonde on Blonde* double album, a multi-faceted affair imbued with an air of stoned relaxation and more than a hint of his developing fascination with Zen teachings. Dylan appeared to be taking rock on to a higher metaphysical plane *and* divorcing it from its commercial roots. Likewise, the eye-opening utilisation of studio technology on *Revolver* and the LSD-befuddled single 'Strawberry Fields Forever' at the start of 1967 pointed to the Beatles' desire to work in a free-form mode of their own devising.

But the many changes in American rock since the onset of Beatlemania were best epitomised by the two major 1966 releases of California pop's elder statesmen, the Beach Boys. They had enjoyed creative and commercial control of their recordings since their early surf music days, so they were free to follow whichever direction they – or their leader Brian Wilson – wished. Hankering after the intellectual acceptance given the Beatles, Wilson hitched his Spectorish ambitions to self-written songs that embodied the California myth of sunshine, surf, and the unencumbered pursuit of pleasure and excitement. Hits like 'I Get Around' and 'Fun Fun Fun' had a hedonistic stance not so different from the live-for-kicks spirit celebrated by the San Francisco groups, while such album tracks as 'In My Room' and 'Caroline No' struck a vein of introspection that echoed John Lennon's 'In My Life' and 'Girl' on *Rubber Soul*. Like Jim McGuinn of the Byrds, Wilson was most interested in sound textures and a rich interplay of vocal harmonies; exposure to LSD during 1966 unlocked the most complex and daringly bizarre of aural fantasies, resulting in the majestic *Pet Sounds* album and one of the most influential rock singles ever, 'Good Vibrations'. The latter's suggestion of personal liberation through spiritual awakening, its lyric brilliantly couched in hip vocabulary, captured the mood of the moment precisely.

The success of 'Good Vibrations' was one of the factors in establishing the rather nebulous concept of a west coast 'sound', an amalgam of solar-powered vocal group pop, folk-rock message and instrumentation, Spector-style production and acid-rock free-for-all. All the fuss had the effect of distracting attention from the variety and richness of the east coast scene, of which Greenwich Village folk music was just one facet. In New York, Long Island group the Young Rascals donned pseudo-English Little Lord Fauntleroy suits and had their arrival advertised on the Shea Stadium scoreboard on the night the Beatles played there. One of the first white groups to be signed by Atlantic, they played swirling, streetwise blue-eyed soul and inspired their own batch of imitators – the Vagrants, Vanilla Fudge, the Rich Kids, the Hassles and others. In Manhattan, on the Lower East Side, poets Ed Saunders and Tuli Kupferberg formed the politically uncompromising and often outrageously offensive rock-cum-poetry band the Fugs, while the Velvet Underground emerged from under pop art figure-head Andy Warhol's wing to assault the ears with ambivalent songs about the heroin-tortured underside of New York life. Elsewhere in the city, Al Kooper, Steve Katz and others came together as the Blues Project, New York's first native electric blues band and the forerunner of numerous such jazz/rock/blues ensembles in the late Sixties.

In terms of emotional and commercial impact, however, none of these names quite matched their Californian counterparts. The point was that the west coast had more going for it than just its musical eclecticism: the transformation in musical attitudes that the Beatles and Dylan had started found a natural home there, while its creations came to reflect not only the increasing intellectualisation of rock but the growing politicisation of its audience. This had less to do with party politics or the adoption of specific left-wing causes than with American youth's rejection of materialist values and its alarming acceptance of Timothy Leary's acid-induced advice to 'tune in, turn on and drop out'. By 1967, rock – and west coast rock in particular – seemed no longer just the voice of youth but a prime weapon in a cultural revolution.

The Velvet Underground (top) offered a dark, cynical antidote to the naïve west coast optimism of their California contemporaries. Like the Fugs (above), the Velvets grew out of an alternative street culture that was markedly different in style and expression to that emerging in San Francisco in 1967

CHAPTER 6

LOVE IS ALL YOU NEED
From flower-power to Altamont

America's youth tuned in, turned on, dropped out – and pop lost its innocence on the road from San Francisco

Opposite page: Janis Joplin, simultaneously the voice and symbol of late Sixties hippie culture

Below: the years 1967 to 1970 saw the heyday of the giant open-air rock festival. Britain's biggest was held on the Isle of Wight in August 1970, when around 250,000 rock lovers invaded the small holiday island to witness what turned out to be Jimi Hendrix' final UK appearance

For better or worse – and the merits of it have been argued ever since – 1967 was the year in which rock music came of age. The events of that year precipitated major changes not only in the way the music was produced – with musicians rejecting tried and trusted pop formulae in pursuit of artistic excellence – but in the manner in which it was marketed, promoted and consequently consumed. It was during 1967 that albums began taking over from singles as the most important rock commodities; that the industry moved decisively from monaural sound to the brave new world of stereo; and that ballrooms were superseded by concert halls and open-air festivals as prime venues for live music, symbolising the transformation of rock from a participative dance form into something requiring passive appreciation – music to be *listened* to, thought about, pontificated on, intellectualised.

The talk on everyone's lips was of a new maturity in rock, manifested by the emergence of the 18 to 24 age group – and students in particular – as the music's largest and most profitable market. Equally, the self-consciously adult themes of post-1967 rock, its celebration of sexuality, its political awareness, and its open endorsement of drug-taking as a means to self-discovery, indicated a fundamental switch in the way the music was perceived (and in the values placed upon it), by both musician and listener. Perhaps, as some optimistic souls suggested, rock music actually could change minds and revolutionise not only American society but the world at large: if the unquestioned leaders of youth culture, the singers and groups, could proselytise the hippie lifestyle as a realistic alternative to the 'straight' way of life, then anything was possible.

None of these changes happened suddenly: they were all logical consequences of the direction in which the Beatles, Dylan, the Rolling Stones and others had taken rock since 1964. But 1967 was the watershed year when, in effect, musicians were obliged to take sides – to choose the implicitly anti-commercial, high-art stance favoured by the emerging west coast rock culture, or remain stuck in the same old pop groove, catering for teenyboppers or the easy-listeners on the cabaret circuit, making money but no musical progress. To fail to take the former course meant banishment to an artistic wilderness and identification with the reactionary elements in pop, yet it soon became clear that anti-commercialism could itself be a selling point and that the new rock was every bit as lucrative as the old pop – in fact more so, because sales of *Sergeant Pepper*-type 'concept' albums brought in far greater revenue than a run of single releases ever could. Contrary to all expectations, the record companies learned to live with this new wave of anti-establishment rock very quickly, to the point of investing millions in its expansion. Their own abandonment of the young teenage market – the high school kids who had long made up pop music's bed-rock audience – was one of the less fortunate aspects of an era that offered extraordinary innovation and unparalleled self-indulgence in almost equal measure.

1967 saw the birth of the multi-media rock event. Jefferson Airplane (above, pictured at the Monterey festival) employed psychedelic lighting, slide shows and film to reinforce the mesmeric nature of their music, while the Beatles (left) used their appearance before millions on the 'Our World' TV extravaganza to unveil the ultimate in peace-and-love anthems, 'All You Need is Love'

HIPPIE DREAMS BOUGHT AND SOLD

As the Sixties progressed, the image of Californian youth changed; suntans and beach buggies gave way to long hair and psychedelically-painted trucks. Drugs had long been a part of San Francisco's jazz scene, but by 1967 teenagers were experimenting too. A new lifestyle, with its own music, was born

The place to be in 1967 was San Francisco, home of the hippies and an acid-drenched philosophy of living that the media christened 'flower-power'. Hippies were joke features of many a news bulletin from early '67 onwards, their genuine commitment to mutual aid and community co-operation overlooked in favour of the weird paraphernalia with which they surrounded themselves – the Indian jewellery, daffodils, kaftans, open-toed sandals, incense sticks, and colourful placards bearing slogans like 'make love not war'. But attempts to trivialise the San Francisco scene on television and in the press had the reverse effect, and the city soon had to cope with a vast influx of visitors and would-be settlers from all over America. Two events were crucial in turning hippiedom into myth – the giant Human Be-In, an LSD and music festival held at Golden Gate Park in January 1967, and the release of folk singer-turned-hippie spokesman Scott McKenzie's elegiac 'San Francisco (Be Sure to Wear Flowers in Your Hair)' just a few months later. The former showed the

FROM FLOWER-POWER TO ALTAMONT

'San Francisco (Be Sure to Wear Flowers in Your Hair)', sung by one-hit wonder Scott McKenzie (above), caught the mood of 1967 in highly commercial fashion. The song's composer, John Phillips of the Mamas and Papas, was one of the chief organisers of that summer's Monterey International Pop Festival (right), the first rock event of its kind, to which a whole host of rock personalities were attracted as both participants and spectators. Pictured here (below right) is Brian Jones of the Rolling Stones

world the sheer size and scale of the hippie phenomenon; the latter amounted to an open invitation to young America to pack its rucksacks and join the hippie trail, to become part of 'a whole generation with a new explanation'.

McKenzie's record was in fact the first real indication of any record industry interest in the goings on in San Francisco. McKenzie was yet another refugee from the New York folk scene, a former singing buddy of John Phillips of the Mamas and Papas; 'San Francisco' was a Phillips composition and production, cut in a Los Angeles recording studio for Lou Adler's newly formed Ode label, his first venture into ownership since selling his Dunhill company to the huge ABC Corporation in 1966. In every respect, the record was a typical Los Angeles product – topical, professional, beautifully arranged and sung – but it passed momentarily for a 'Frisco creation and certainly inspired other, bigger Hollywood-based companies to look deeper into what was by now a fully fledged and pleasingly diverse music scene. The same month that saw the McKenzie disc enter the US Top Ten, Adler and Phillips helped organise a massive event designed in part with the industry in mind – the First Annual International Monterey Pop Festival, held at a small coastal town halfway between the two cities. The idea was to re-create the stoned atmosphere of the Human Be-In without the engaging anarchy that had been one facet of the event's success: Monterey acts were kept to a tight schedule, rock stars from Britain and America were invited to attend and lend credibility to the occasion, record company bosses were asked along and entertained behind the scenes, the television and film rights were sold in advance, and Beatles publicist Derek Taylor was brought in to handle all the media liaison. Every San Francisco-based act who had performed

at the Human Be-In was invited to Monterey, although the Grateful Dead – distrusting big-money involvement in exploiting SF music – camped outside the grounds and performed for free.

Monterey was universally acclaimed not just as a success in its own right but as the dawn of a new era, the symbolic birth of a new kind of relationship between performers and their audience. It was, or so its admirers believed, a successful translation of San Francisco hippie values to a larger stage: when the

Beatles appeared on the internationally networked *Our World* television show just a few weeks later, dressed in hippie gear and singing the ultimate hippie anthem 'All You Need is Love', it did indeed seem that the message of Monterey could find a place in the hearts of millions. What all the talk of love, peace and 'good vibes' concealed, however, was commercialisation on the grand scale, as the companies – frightened at the prospect of losing out on a spectacularly popular new trend they themselves barely understood – fought among themselves to sign up every San Francisco band going. As a

photographer present at Monterey throughout its three days commented, 'You think the action was out on the stage and in the audience? No way! The action was at the bar, where the record executives and the managers were'.

The moguls move in

Prior to Monterey, the only major San Francisco bands signed to big contracts were Jefferson Airplane and their offshoot, Moby Grape. The Airplane dated back to 1965, when they played a form of Lovin' Spoonful-influenced folk-rock, but their conversion to LSD and the replacement of original singer Signe Anderson by Grace Slick – from another early SF band, the Great Society – turned them into one of the first multi-media bands, with Glenn McKay's Headlights light

show a distinctive attraction of their live performances. Signing with RCA, they became well-known for their recalcitrance and refusal to play the normal pop game, but their two major singles of 1967 – 'Somebody to Love' and 'White Rabbit' – were perfect commercial encapsulations of the San Francisco experience. More typical Airplane tracks were the obliquely titled and mesmeric 'The Ballad of You, Me and Pooneil' and '3/5 of a Mile in 10 Seconds', appropriate showcases for the group's electronic experimentation and Slick's powerhouse vocals. Of all the San Francisco groups, they proved the most influential and enduring; they were fortunate, too, in being discovered some time before the 'Frisco scene broke. By contrast, Moby Grape – formed by ex-Airplane drummer Skip Spence – suffered

In spite of the vast publicity accorded the San Francisco groups, only a handful made any great commercial impact. The launch of Moby Grape (above) was badly misjudged by their record company, and the band never lived down the overdone hype that surrounded it. The group from which Moby Grape was originally an offshoot, Jefferson Airplane (left), enjoyed a run of hit singles and albums before splintering in the early Seventies

Below: a spectator at Monterey, June 1967

FROM FLOWER-POWER TO ALTAMONT

from one of the worst forms of company hype, their 1967 signing by Columbia heralded by the simultaneous release of five singles and an album and a wave of promotional overkill. Record buyers were unimpressed, the hippies disowned them, and the group became the first casualties of the burgeoning scene.

Columbia soon showed itself to be the most aware of the major companies, however, by signing the biggest new name to emerge at Monterey – Big Brother and the Holding Company, an instrumentally undistinguished four-piece whose great asset was their tigerish lead singer Janis Joplin. She had possibly the best female blues voice yet heard in rock and an earthy sexuality that she played up to the full; in rejecting the pop stereotype of the demure female singer, she became a symbol of and for hippie womanhood and turned what on paper were stock anti-male blues laments – 'Ball and Chain', 'Piece of My Heart' – into joyous feminist assertions. Her elevation to superstar status (following her break with Big Brother in 1968) was a personal triumph for Columbia boss Clive Davis, who entered the post-1967 rock minefield with skill and insight and secured his company's fortune by hand-picking the most original (and not always obviously commercial) new acts on the west *and* east coasts. Joplin and Big Brother aside, his most imaginative signings were the Electric Flag, a new-wave blues band formed by ex-Paul Butterfield stalwart Mike Bloomfield; New York-based jazz-rock fusion exponents Blood, Sweat and Tears, founded by Al Kooper; their Chicago-rooted counterparts the Chicago Transit Authority, their name later abbreviated to Chicago; and two San Francisco bands who were careful to distance themselves from acid-rock, latin-rock expansionists Santana and soft-rock specialists It's a Beautiful Day.

Capitol, meanwhile, gave A&R head Nik Venet full rein to sign countless local bands, his wisest signings being the 1965-formed Quicksilver Messenger Service and one of many bands from outside California to move base to San Francisco during 1966/67, the Steve Miller Band. Quicksilver played archetypal SF acid-rock, built around the tremeloed guitar sound of John Cipollina, while Steve Miller – who almost singlehandedly changed rock economics by insisting on

rambling, loosely improvised sets for free – in San Francisco and elsewhere – well into the Seventies.

The artists call the tune

The record companies paid a high price for their involvement in the new rock, and not just in financial terms. Their willingness to offer big signing-on fees and high royalty payments to virtually untried acts left their established artists understandably disgruntled and demanding similar treatment: as a consequence, contractual wrangles and company/artist disputes became very much a feature of the late Sixties scene. The labels also found they had to surrender artistic control to their groups or singers – a radical break with pop tradition – and treat their acts less as employees and more as artists in the true sense, enjoying patronage in the style of 18th-century court composers. The post-1967 bands were given unlimited studio time and fantastic album budgets, the aim being to create an atmosphere in which a second *Sergeant Pepper* could take shape. To this end, producers assumed a greater importance within individual company hierarchies: Warner Brothers had a whole team of

Superstars of the new rock: Left: would-be jazz-rockers Blood, Sweat and Tears, who quickly became trapped in an easy-listening/Las Vegas mould

Below: white soul starlet Janis Joplin, who left Big Brother and the Holding Company for a tragically short solo career in 1968

Bottom: the Grateful Dead, the most defiantly anti-commercial band of the San Francisco era

an unprecedented 75,000 dollar advance payment for his band's first Capitol release – played straight Chicago blues with acid-rock leanings. Warner Brothers, meanwhile, failed to resurrect the career of one of the very first, pre-acid San Francisco bands, the Beau Brummels, but took a calculated risk by contracting arguably the most difficult to handle and least marketable SF band of all, the Grateful Dead. As the Warlocks, they had been the resident band in Ken Kesey's Merry Pranksters set-up, and their manager was electronics wizard and renowned LSD chemist Owsley Stanley, who not only kept them and their huge communal 'family' of followers supplied with acid, but built them the most elaborate sound system yet seen or heard in rock. Always suspicious of other bands who 'sold out' by making big recording deals, the Dead kept their music unstructured and took delight in incurring debts of over 100,000 dollars during the making of their first three Warners albums. Essentially a live band, they maintained the acid-rock faith longer than most of their SF contemporaries and were still playing long,

them, each seconded to a particular act and expected to build up a special relationship, the fruits of which would repay company investment in the long- rather than short-term.

Financing the new rock also meant a change of image for many of America's most established labels. Columbia led the way, running a series of promotion campaigns in the rock press that attempted to identify the company with new radical thinking: in one advertisement, a group of hippies in a police cell were pictured below a headline that read 'But the man can't bust our music . . .', while another tried to persuade the hip readership that 'the revolutionaries are on Columbia'. Warners mounted similar campaigns for some of their more esoteric signings, selling Van Morrison with the copy line 'last night this man scored' and offering one of the most expensively produced albums in rock history, Van

Dyke Parks' acid-soaked *Song Cycle*, for just five cents as part of a very involved loss-leader scheme. Columbia and Warners in particular set great store by their closeness to the street, even hiring kids from the communes or universities to act as 'house hippies', advising the labels on who was currently hot, who was worth signing, and what the latest trends were likely to be. As Danny Fields, resident hippie at Atlantic, later recalled, '(I was) a kept hippie, mediating between the turtle-necked Titans of the record industry and the unpunctual, crazy monsters called musicians'.

For the companies, the risks involved in associating themselves with the new rock were high, but the rewards potentially great. Their task was made easier by the parallel emergence of new media – FM radio and the underground press in particular, both with San Francisco origins – which provided ready vehicles for their promotions and lent that elusive quality of credibility to their efforts. The FM radio stations, created when America's broadcasting networks were ordered to provide different services on their AM and FM frequencies, saw album-oriented rock as ideal programming and a key means of capturing that free-spending student market. Run mostly by ex-Top 40 radio disc jockeys to whom commercial chart pop was now anathema, these stations favoured a low-key, cool and thoughtful style of presentation in deliberate contrast to the freneticism of AM radio. Similarly 'alternative' in approach were magazines like *Rolling Stone* (run on a co-operative basis by enthusiasts and young rock radicals), which set themselves apart from the established rock press by carrying long, discursive articles on political as well as musical matters and set many of the critical canons by which late Sixties music – British as well as American – came to be judged.

ART-ROCK AND ALL SORTS

Below: like Lennon, McCartney, Harrison and Starr, Donovan Leitch proved himself a sharply observant and frequently wickedly funny commentator on the trappings of flower-power

I n Britain, 1967's events had equally far-reaching consequences for the country's musicians, record companies and consumers. Flower-power was taken up briefly by London's hip circles, where LSD had been freely available since the middle of 1966, although nowhere in Britain was there a real counterpart to Haight-Ashbury, a community built on naive notions of love and peace and dedicated to the drop-out ethic. British musicians and songwriters were intrigued mostly by the *trappings* of flower-power – hippie clothing and vocabulary, the cult's cute mysticism and anything-goes approach to creativity – and the best British-produced 'acid-rock' records of 1967 were for the most part wonderfully comic commentaries on it all: the Small Faces' 'Itchycoo Park', Donovan's 'Mellow Yellow', the Move's 'Flowers in the Rain', and the Troggs' 'Love is All Around'. Artists who expressed too much enthusiasm for the flower-power cause threw themselves open to ridicule, and this unfortunate fate befell the once hard-nosed Eric Burdon, who re-emerged early in 1967 with a re-shaped Animals line-up and a string of aggressively pro-hippie singles packed with half-pint profundities about the new youth consciousness.

Nevertheless, UK musicians were showing clear signs of wanting to shrug off commercial restrictions and create artistic music for an intelligent audience. The prime motivators here, as always, were the Beatles – now no longer a working pop group in the old sense of the term, but in effect a musical workshop, with the ever-dependable George Martin acting as their factotum. *Sergeant Pepper's Lonely Hearts Club Band*, released bang in the middle of that flower-power summer, was their claim to creative immortality – a gargantuan, multi-faceted commentary on the times that was replete with musical allusions to everything from music-hall ('When I'm 64', 'Lovely Rita') to Indian ragas ('Within You, Without You'). The lyrics hinted merrily at drug excursions ('Lucy in the Sky with Diamonds'), drew on random newspaper stories ('She's Leaving Home', 'A Day in the Life'), and dwelt

with curious nostalgia on the mundaneness of suburban life ('Fixing a Hole', 'When I'm 64' again). Collectively, the songs in *Sergeant Pepper* offered a superficially optimistic but faintly paranoid vision of youth obsessions circa 1967. Its qualities were inevitably overstated at the time, but there was no doubt that the album found the Beatles at their imaginative best, demonstrating their unmatched ability to fashion something accessible, even mainstream, out of the more avant-garde trends in British and American rock.

Sergeant Pepper was fundamentally a gloriously self-indulgent 'concept' album, the first of its kind, which was permeated throughout by a retrospective mood and an ironic view of show business rituals. The band of the title were the Beatles' alter egos and the album was in effect their 'show', a public statement

of their abilities. If the album's music was ornate, grandiose and adorned with orchestral and psychedelic trappings, this was precisely because of the circumstances in which the Beatles now found themselves. Kings of the EMI castle, they now had the time, the money and – most importantly – almost unlimited musical and technological resources to be as idiosyncratic as they liked. Tales of how George Martin had thrown together tapes to create the swirling effect on 'Mr Kite', and how a full orchestra was hired just to create the climactic note on 'A Day in the Life', soon became part of pop music legend, and it was their breathtakingly expansive use of the recording studio – and especially stereophonic sound – that proved most immediately influential. The album set a technical standard that producers in particular were hard put to match; west coast producer David Anderle commented, 'it took a lot of producers many years to find out that they could not all make *Sergeant Peppers*. They all tried. God knows we had a year and a half of some of the weirdest sounds on record. Everybody trying to make *Sergeant Pepper*'.

Progression and pretension

With *Sergeant Pepper*, the Beatles brought credence and respectability to a developing genre – progressive rock. Progression meant musical maturity, and there were countless bands with solid pop or R&B beginnings who shunned the teenybopper limelight during and after 1967 and found a welcome audience among sixth-formers and students. As in America, the record industry was quick to appreciate the change: several of the major labels set up their own progressive subsidiaries, each with a suitably hip-sounding name like Dawn (owned by Pye), Harvest (EMI), and Deram (Decca), the intention being to co-opt for themselves the hip credentials of genuine

Below: Alvin Lee of Ten Years After was one of numerous 'guitar heroes' to emerge out of the blossoming progressive rock scene of the late Sixties. The band found particular favour in the US, where their reputation was sealed by a spectacular if histrionic performance at Woodstock

independents like Blue Horizon and Island, whose chief signings were Fleetwood Mac and Traffic respectively. Changes in British radio, too, sharpened the teenybopper/student split, as the pirate stations were closed down by Government legislation and their place was taken by a national pop network, Radio One, that kept to a strict chart format by day and switched to FM-type programming at night. Progressive rock lovers complained of mistreatment and neglect by Radio One, but in reality the new station – through key programmes like John Peel's *Top Gear* – gave identity to the new music and helped immeasurably in the dissemination of new bands like Ten Years After, Tyrannosaurus Rex, Deep Purple and the Nice.

Progressive rock was not so much a style as a rather sombre-faced crusade, its chief characteristics an inordinate reverence for instrumental and technical virtuosity, a disdain for commercialism, and a belief that bands should change and develop with each successive

Below: the Nice at the first Isle of Wight festival in 1969. Originally singer P.P. Arnold's backing group, their line-up included the classically-trained Keith Emerson (extreme left). Their albums contained clever but soulless reworkings of classical pieces like Sibelius' Karelia Suite and Bach's Brandenburg Concerto

FROM FLOWER-POWER TO ALTAMONT

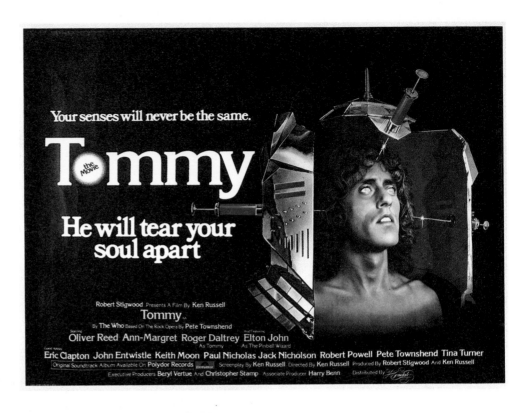

album. Established bands were affected by these notions – the Who, despite Pete Townshend's professed dislike for hippies, produced *Tommy* as a concept album-cum-'rock opera', and Ray Davies of the Kinks came up with a similar work in *Arthur (Or The Decline and Fall of the British Empire)* – but progressive rock was mainly the province of a vast array of new groups from a variety of backgrounds, most of whom fell into one of three main categories. Of greatest importance was something vaguely called 'art-rock' that took in grand musical statements, meaningful lyrics and all the decorative ingredients – arty album covers, gatefold sleeves, sound effects – that the Beatles had pioneered on *Sergeant Pepper*. The Moody Blues, miraculously transformed from a run-of-the-mill R&B band into avatars of the progressive age, set the pattern with *Days of Future Passed* in late 1967. The addition of a mellotron keyboard to their instrumentation gave their sound greater body, but it was their lyrics about spiritual journeys and the pain of self-doubt that inspired their almost evangelical following, especially in America.

If their publicity was to be believed, the Moody Blues were the first to bring the complexity of classical music to rock, but there were other bands who created a far more plausible rock/classics fusion. King Crimson was one such, its baroque

extravagances – mainly the work of mellotron wizard Robert Fripp and his lyricist partner Pete Sinfield – paving the way for the more lauded creations of Yes and Emerson, Lake and Palmer. These two bands featured classically trained musicians Rick Wakeman and Keith Emerson respectively, both of whom developed a mastery of the Moog synthesiser – that most ubiquitous of progressive rock instruments – and were worshipped for their keyboard pyrotechnics and flashy showmanship. Less concerned with spectacle but equally preoccupied with rococo lyrics and the appropriation of classical phrases were Procol Harum, who evolved out of Essex R & B outfit the Paramounts. Their multi-million selling debut release, 'A Whiter Shade of Pale' (1967), was typically based on a Bach cantata and featured a Keith Reid lyric packed with images drawn from English literature. Engagingly mysterious and disturbingly ethereal to some, the song struck others as rock at its most purposelessly obscure and pretentious.

Going underground

A second strand of progressive rock appeared via the nearest thing Britain had to an alternative arts and music movement on the San Francisco model – the London-based underground scene, which had its own select events, bands and clubs, and even its own radically-oriented newspaper in the shape of *International Times*. The scene dated from 1966, when visiting American avant-gardist Steve Stollman organised a series of 'Spontaneous Underground' happenings at the Marquee club, and this experiment was repeated at venues all over London before one particular club – the UFO in Tottenham Court Road – became established as the home of the city's self-styled hippie culture. The club's house band was the Pink Floyd, formed by art school drop-out Syd Barrett in 1966 as an R & B outfit, but quickly expanded into a vehicle for his avant-garde ideas. Their mixture of unsettling and goonishly oddball songs, studied musicianship and stage spectacle – especially their pioneering use of light shows, then completely new to Britain – won them a cult following and a recording contract with EMI that produced two quirky slices of English psychedelia, 'Arnold Layne'

Kingpins of the art-rock vogue included King Crimson and Procol Harum, who made notable album debuts with In the Court of the Crimson King *and* Procol Harum *respectively. Crimson was the brainchild of guitarist and Mellotron player Robert Fripp (pictured left, with fellow band member Boz Burrell), who later recorded solo and with the likes of Brian Eno, David Bowie and Peter Gabriel. The mainstays of Procol Harum (below, captured at the Fillmore East in New York during 1968) were vocalist Gary Brooker and his songwriting partner Keith Reid, whose lyrics were among the most sombre and mind-bendingly cryptic of the post* Sgt Pepper *era*

FROM FLOWER-POWER TO ALTAMONT

and 'See Emily Play', both 1967 hits. With the departure of Barrett, the Floyd lost their eccentric bent but found a growing audience for their abstract improvisations and tightly executed sound collages, painstakingly created over months of studio effort, then diligently reproduced and often elaborated upon in their ever-more spectacular stage performances. Other bands worked in a similar vein – notably Soft Machine, one of several jazz-rock experimental bands based in the university city of Canterbury – but the Floyd were really leaders in a field of one, aural architects who broke new ground by treating music-making as a design process.

The third and most widely adopted strain of progressive rock developed directly out of the mid-Sixties R&B scene, with blues bands adopting a new range of influences – particularly the jazz-

laced playing of Chicago guitarists B.B. King and Freddie King – and creating a sound high on technique but generally low on substance. Towering above all others in this category were Cream, founded in 1966 as a showcase for the skills of ace R&B instrumentalists Eric Clapton, Jack Bruce and Ginger Baker. Everything about Cream broke the accepted pop rules: they dazzled the R&B intelligentsia from their inception, ignoring the rock convention of restricting improvisation to pre-planned solo breaks, and instead building their whole performances around long, exploratory free-form solos. Trusting the outcome of each performance to some innate internal chemistry between the three members, Cream produced the most instrumentally advanced music of the mid to late Sixties and encouraged countless other groups to parade their technical prowess in similar fashion. Their use of guitar distortion, the insular, self-absorbed pose of the group on stage, their apparent lack of interest in structure and form, and their wild success in America all left an indelible mark on the musicians who followed. Clapton in particular was the first in a long line of late Sixties guitar heroes, though he eschewed the overbearing macho stance of many of his successors, among them tight-trousered egotists like Alvin Lee of Ten Years After and Ritchie Blackmore of Deep Purple, who fondled and flaunted their guitars in phallic fashion.

THE DREAM GOES SOUR

British progressive acts found a ready market in America, where great individualists like ex-Yardbird Jeff Beck – now fronting his own group, with Rod Stewart as featured vocalist – could find even greater fame than at home. The UK was also responsible for uncovering and nurturing the talent of the greatest guitar *personality* of all – expatriate black American Jimi Hendrix, who was brought to London from New York in September 1966 by ex-Animals bassist Chas Chandler. Noel Redding (bass) and Mitch Mitchell (drums) joined him to form the Jimi Hendrix Experience, whose first album *Are You Experienced* was a masterpiece of controlled musical invention, shot through with a slinky, faintly dangerous sexuality that set the particular Hendrix brand of progressive blues apart from the more clinical approach favoured by Cream. His appearance at the Monterey Festival – where he was added to the bill at Paul McCartney's personal insistence – caused a sensation and his reputation spread with his first American tour as support band to the Monkees, from which he was sacked after just a few days on the insistence of America's Mothers Union. That incident brought him instant hip acceptance, but his penchant for wild on-stage histrionics and the critics' attempt to portray him as some kind of new age rock Messiah eventually left him emotionally and creatively drained. By 1968, without the now-defunct Experience, he began playing dates in an absolutely straight fashion, without the gimmicks – playing his guitar with his teeth, setting fire and stamping on it – that his followers had come to expect. He was booed, and only his formation of a new band in 1969 – Band of Gypsies – restored his audience's faith. He died just a year later, an apparent victim of the pressures of rock stardom and a symbol of the largely unfulfilled promise at the heart of much late Sixties rock.

Others in the Hendrix mould coped better with their success, thanks usually to a ruthless devotion to professionalism and the high-powered financial backing of committed record companies. The biggest long-term commercial success of UK progressive rock was Led Zeppelin, conceived and brought together specifically with the big-money American market in mind by ex-Yardbird guitarist Jimmy Page and manager Peter Grant. Recruiting singer Robert Plant, bassist John Paul Jones and drummer John Bonham, Page and Grant created the ultimate heavy rock band – impossibly loud, technically perfect, a well-oiled noise machine whose music drew variously on electric blues, acoustic folk and fuzzed, feedback-saturated versions of riffs and lyrics previously used by blues pioneers like Howlin' Wolf and Albert King. The Atlantic label signed them without even seeing them perform and granted the group the largest advance ever given to a new act, together with the promise of total control over everything from production to marketing. In return, Led Zeppelin delivered consistent album sales and helped push Atlantic to major label status by 1970.

Retreats and realities

America produced its own crop of progressive blues specialists, not all of them necessarily influenced by their British counterparts. Johnny Winter, Harvey Mandel and Taj Mahal played in various aggregations and were generally far closer, musically and physically, to the black sources that inspired the UK groups than these groups were themselves. Taken overall, however, there were major differences in approach between the UK and US progressive bands, not so much in form or style as in what might vaguely be called cultural commitment. With a

few notable exceptions, the UK bands had an insular, even conservative streak: far from identifying with particular causes or even reflecting on the world outside, the progressive groups generally offered songs soaked in an airy-fairy romanticism, replete with allusions to J.R. Tolkien's hobbit world, medieval mythology, eastern mysticism, astrology and black magic. In this sense, progressive rock seemed to symbolise a retreat

Opposite: Jimi Hendrix, inarguably the most gifted and original guitarist in rock history

Below: Led Zeppelin, whose powerhouse sound was ideally suited to the outdoor venues of the US stadium circuit

FROM FLOWER-POWER TO ALTAMONT

from political realities, a refusal to face many of the implications of the events of 1967. Britain's underground press expanded to include such newspapers as *Oz, Frendz* and *Ink*, festivals and free concerts were held on the American pattern, and violent demonstrations at the London School of Economics and the American Embassy in Grosvenor Square proved that the spirit of rebellion was not entirely dormant, but the country's student population was passive by comparison with its overseas contemporaries and paid little more than lip service to the counter-cultural values propounded across the Atlantic.

In the US itself, rock momentarily became more political than ever, especially following the traumatic events of 1968. That year saw the assassinations of the two political leaders with whom American youth most identified, Martin Luther King and Robert Kennedy; riots in black ghettoes throughout America; vicious police action against anti-war demonstrators during the Democratic Party Convention in Chicago; and the election of Richard Nixon, symbol of middle-American conservatism and a hate figure for young people since his opposition to John Kennedy in the 1959 campaign, as US President. The country was in deep social turmoil, added to which the Vietnam war was steadily intensifying and

American rock at its most political, c. 1968: Country Joe and the Fish (above right) satirised US involvement in Vietnam in 'Feel I'm Fixin' to Die Rag', in which American parenthood was invited to be 'the first on your block to have your son come home in a box'. The MC5 (below), from Detroit, struck a still more aggressive note in 'Kick Out the Jams' and climaxed their stage shows by tearing the Stars and Stripes to pieces in anti-establishment defiance

impinging directly on the consciousness of the nation's youth; quite apart from their moral antipathy to the war, every young man over the age of 18 now faced the threat of conscription. The counter-culture, born in San Francisco and now spreading its influence to every American campus, became a focal point for protest – and 'dropping out' from society was increasingly seen as perhaps the only sure way of staying alive.

The American rock fraternity responded to all this with alacrity. Country Joe and the Fish, San Francisco's most polemical band, produced a brilliant anti-war satire in 'Feel I'm Fixin' To Die Rag'; the Young Rascals recorded a soaring and dynamic plea for harmony, 'People Got to Be Free', the day after Bobby Kennedy was shot; and Los Angeles band The Doors released 'The Unknown Soldier' and promoted it with a film of lead singer and self-confessed death cultist Jim Morrison spewing blood. Heavy metal heroes Steppenwolf and the MC5 came up with two classic anti-establishment anthems in 'Born to Be Wild' and 'Kick Out the Jams'. Rock festivals developed into vehicles for anti-war rhetoric, besides giving both musicians and audiences a chance to marvel at their mutual solidarity against Nixonian oppression, and small budget, high-grossing films like Peter Fonda's *Easy*

Rider (1968) made plain the conflict between 'straight' and alternative society by using rock numbers on their soundtracks. The Rolling Stones, revitalised after the disaster of the *Satanic Majesties* album, pledged their support with a track that everyone interpreted as a call for revolution – 'Street Fighting Man' – and the newly politicised John Lennon launched the Plastic Ono Band with Yoko Ono, his new songs (written without McCartney) taking the form of simple slogans set to music that left the listener in no doubt as to where he stood.

End of an era

In the end, however, the counter-culture could not sustain itself. American youth did not bring the Vietnam war to a close, nor did they unseat Nixon. Drugs were not the key to either self-salvation or the setting up of a new society, but rather a fatal irrelevance – the late Sixties saw too many young minds destroyed by psychedelic excess, and by the early Seventies even Timothy Leary was recanting his teachings. What lingered among young people was a certain sense of failure or at least anti-climax, which the success of the giant Woodstock Festival in August 1969 only partly assuaged. Woodstock was the biggest outdoor rock event ever and attracted over 300,000 people; it featured dozens of top international rock acts and was remarkable for its genuinely harmonious atmosphere, both on stage and off it, yet rumours of the colossal fees paid to particular acts and the profits made by selling the film and album rights drew attention to the constant commercial pressures that threatened to undermine hippie idealism.

Below: top New York band the Rascals dropped the 'Young' from their name in 1968, in keeping with their desire for musical maturity. Their most outstanding single of the year was the heartfelt 'People Got to Be Free', dedicated to the memory of assassinated presidential candidate Bobby Kennedy

FROM FLOWER-POWER TO ALTAMONT

Above: Charles Manson, leader of the band of hippie killers responsible for the brutal deaths of Sharon Tate and four friends in August 1969. He was already well-known within rock circles as an associate of the Beach Boys, and it was claimed at his trial that he took murderous inspiration from a warped interpretation of Beatle lyrics

Above right: the fatal stabbing of a spectator at the Rolling Stones' Altamont concert in December 1969 was captured by a camera crew hired to shoot footage for a forthcoming Stones film. The scene was cynically used as one of the selling points of Gimme Shelter, *given its cinema release during 1970*

Such issues preoccupied the underground press – the self-appointed guardians of hippie ideology – during the summer of 1969, but much greater shocks were waiting just around the corner. First came the horrific murder of actress Sharon Tate and four others in a Hollywood suburb, for which self-styled hippie evangelist Charles Manson and members of his 'family' of followers were arrested during December 1969. Also in late 1969, the Stones returned to the US for a tour of large-capacity venues that was exploitative in the extreme and apparently undertaken to clear large debts accumulated since their signing to Decca in 1963. Ticket prices for the concerts were ridiculously high, and Mick Jagger in particular was accused by *Rolling Stone* and others of betraying the anti-capitalist cause he seemed to endorse so enthusiastically on 'Street Fighting Man' and the *Beggar's Banquet* album from which it came. Partly as a penance, but also to give the tour's film recordists a chance to shoot some extra footage, the Stones agreed to play a free concert at the Altamont racetrack in San Francisco. In an awesomely naive move, the tour management agreed to let the city's notorious Hell's Angel fraternity police the event – with predictably violent results. As Jagger started to perform his self-aggrandising 'Sympathy for the Devil', a young black named Meredith Hunter was stabbed to death by Angels in front of the stage. It was one of rock music's blackest moments, a symbolic shattering of the love and peace ethos in which the American young had placed their faith. The inquests were many, but the universal conclusion was that the tragic events at Altamont represented the end of an era.

Above left: a still from the film Woodstock, which was promoted during 1970 as a documentary record of 'three days of peace and love'. Although she did not appear there, Joni Mitchell (above) helped cement her own reputation as a singer-songwriter by romanticising the festival in a song of the same name

The events of 1970 hammered further nails into the coffin of the youth culture – and the death metaphor is entirely apposite. In quick succession came the deaths of Hendrix and Joplin, the killing of four unarmed student protesters by the military at a Kent State University anti-war demonstration, and the trial of ex-Beach Boys hanger-on Charles Manson and his 'family' of hippies for the brutal murder of actress Sharon Tate – an act inspired (it was claimed) by the Beatles' song 'Helter Skelter'. By the time the film of the Woodstock festival appeared in late 1970, to do roaring business in cinemas all over the world, hippiedom was already a focus for nostalgia, and attention in the rock world was switching to new singer-songwriters like James Taylor and Joni Mitchell whose intensely personal songs were held to articulate a new mood of introspection among disaffected youth.

Yet all this hippie heart-searching obscured much more interesting developments in rock – the rise of soul music and the tendency of musicians to turn their backs on experimentation for its own sake and rediscover and explore the pre-1967 rock tradition. The Beatles' follow-up album to *Sergeant Pepper* was one example of the latter, the plain title and packaging (*The Beatles*, presented in a pure white double sleeve) indicating their wish to return to rock'n'roll basics. Bob Dylan's *John Wesley Harding* was another, a country-flavoured album packed with direct and simple statements that marked his return to recording after a year-long recuperation from a serious motorcycle accident. Both albums looked back to look forward, implicitly rejecting utopian notions. In this, they set the whole tone for the coming decade.

CHAPTER 7

DANCING IN THE STREET
From soul to disco

The sacred sound of gospel mixed with R & B to blaze the trail for a new black consciousness and a new black music

Opposite: the Supremes – Mary Wilson, Diana Ross (centre) and Florence Ballard – on the 1965 Motown tour of Britain. Their brand of sophisticated Northern soul contrasted with the emotional Southern version exemplified by Otis Redding (below), who died in an air crash in 1968

In 1967, just as white American rock was entering its pseudo-revolutionary phase, black singer Aretha Franklin topped the national chart with 'Respect', a song ostensibly aimed at some surly lover but interpreted by many as an attack on white disrespect for the black race. It was perhaps the most impassioned and implicitly political single of that year, and it underlined just how far black music had come since the rock'n'roll years of the Fifties, when the realities of the marketplace had dictated that only a diluted or sweetened version of the black R & B sound would impinge upon the national consciousness. The particular black idiom in which Franklin specialised was 'soul', born of a marriage of R & B with gospel music and largely free from the degree of white exploitation and appropriation that had characterised the earlier era. Although vastly popular among whites, soul was primarily the music of young black America, and a form brilliantly expressive – as hits like the Four Tops' 'Reach Out, I'll Be There', the Impressions' 'People Get Ready', and James Brown's 'Say It Loud, I'm Black and I'm Proud' further demonstrated – of the solidarity, pride and defiance of black society at a time of acute social change.

Soul had its roots in the Fifties, and it grew out of the interaction of different musical forms, different musicians and different commercial pressures. The term 'soul' first gained currency in late Fifties jazz circles, when black musicians like Cannonball Adderley and Charlie Mingus began to dispense with the increasingly complex chord sequences of modern jazz and use simpler, more basic and therefore more 'soulful' blues and gospel patterns. Most influential of all was multi-instrumentalist and singer Ray Charles, whose recordings for New York's Atlantic label included one of the very first gospel-R & B syntheses, 'I Got a Woman' (1954), and the appropriately titled *Soul*

137

Brothers album (1957), made with the Modern Jazz Quartet's ace vibraphonist Milt Jackson. It was Jackson who provided one of the earliest and most succinct descriptions of soul as something that 'comes from within; it's what happens when the inner part of you comes out. It's the part of playing you can't get out of books and studies. In my case, I believe that what I heard and felt in the music of my church . . . was the most powerful influence on my musical career. Everyone wants to know where I got that funky style. Well, it came from the church. The music I heard was open, relaxed, impromptu – soul music'.

To some, however, mixing gospel and blues was morally unacceptable. Among the Church establishment, the brazenness with which Ray Charles took favourite gospel songs and expunged their lyrics of all spiritual references caused particular offence: 'I Got a Woman' was a straight rewrite of 'When I'm Lonely I Talk to Jesus'; 'This Little Girl Of Mine' took 'This Little Light Of Mine' as its base, and 'Nobody But You, Lord' became 'Nobody But You'. More fundamentally, blues was by tradition a

secular music, belonging to the theatres, clubs, drinking dens and brothels, and concerns of the flesh – sexuality, the next meal, hitting the road in search of work – provided its main subject matter. Gospel, by contrast, was God's music, and its concerns were spiritual and communal rather than profane and personal. In some black areas, gospel and blues records were not even sold over the same counter, while even those with an interest in both musical camps kept their involvements entirely separate. Big Bill Broonzy, both a bluesman *and* a preacher, spoke for many when he said of Ray Charles, 'He's got the blues, he's cryin' sanctified . . . he's mixing the blues and spirituals and I know that's wrong'. Against this kind of opposition, and despite the massive commercial success of Ray Charles' storming gospel rocker 'What'd I Say' in 1959, the gospel-R&B match had little future as anything more than a branch of jazz, appreciated mainly by aficionados. Parallel developments, notably within the pop world itself, nevertheless ensured that 'soul' would grow beyond its original élitist connotations.

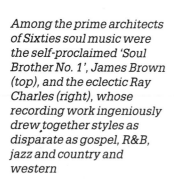

Among the prime architects of Sixties soul music were the self-proclaimed 'Soul Brother No. 1', James Brown (top), and the eclectic Ray Charles (right), whose recording work ingeniously drew together styles as disparate as gospel, R&B, jazz and country and western

THE GODFATHERS OF SOUL

One factor above all others precipitated the emergence of soul as a distinct *commercial* style during the early Sixties – the increasing presence in the record charts of groups and singers with obvious gospel leanings. The vast majority of black vocal acts who enjoyed brief fame in the Fifties – the Ravens, Larks, Crows, Flamingos, Penguins, Moonglows and scores of others – had personnel who learned their vocal skills in the neighbourhood church choir and whose early mentors included the likes of the Soul Stirrers and the Dixie Hummingbirds, giants of the small but lucrative gospel recording scene. While gospel in its purest sense was never a feature of Fifties popular music, aspects of the gospel style became very commonplace indeed – particularly the ability of a

Below: black vocal groups enjoyed a great vogue in the Fifties, though few survived as major acts into the following decade. The Moonglows, pictured here, woro lod by Harvcy Fuqua (far right), whose own Tri Phi record label became part of Berry Gordy's Motown empire in 1960. Later in the Sixties, Fuqua – who married Gordy's sister Gwen – was appointed head of Motown's famous Artist Development Department

singer to bend and twist a note around a single syllable, and the fine interplay of bass and tenor voices, calling and answering each other in apparently spontaneous sequences.

Two singers in particular built on their group training to become major precursors of and influences on the coming soul era. Both Clyde McPhatter and Jackie Wilson were one-time members of the Dominoes, a quartet formed in 1950 by noted New York vocal coach Billy Ward, and both perfected a pleading vocal style that carried obvious echoes of the devotional attitudes of gospel singing. McPhatter's background was classic gospel – the son of a Baptist minister, he was a keenly admired boy soprano by the age of ten and matured into a fearsome gospel shouter after his voice broke. After leaving the Dominoes, he brought together the original Drifters and subsequently enjoyed sporadic success as a solo artist, notably with 'A Lover's Question' (1958) and 'Lover Please' (1962). His meagre run of hits belied his impact on the generation of soul singers that followed: he was the first of the great soul exhibitionists, a performer whose bodily contortions, knee-drops, air-punching and general all-round pentecostal verve could raise the emotions of an audience to fever-pitch. Jackie Wilson was cast in the same mould, but – despite his twenty US Top 40 entries between 1958 and 1966 – he was another singer whose electrifying stage presence could never be properly captured on disc.

McPhatter and Wilson were both caught in the vacuum left by rock'n'roll towards the end of the Fifties: too soon on the scene to be classified as soul artists and so enjoy the musical freedom granted to such later stars as Otis Redding and Wilson Pickett, they were often obliged to record so-so pop material dressed up in formulaic, soulless arrangements. Neither was ever totally in

R&B stars Jackie Wilson (above) and Clyde McPhatter (right) had a gigantic influence on the soul singers who followed them. Wilson's patronage of songwriter Berry Gordy resulted in a string of hits for the singer in the late Fifties and helped give Gordy the financial security on which to build his Motown enterprise

control of his creative or commercial destiny, and it was this that set them apart from a figure like James Brown, a Fifties contemporary and fellow gospel shouter whose unwavering self-belief and refusal to follow pop convention became as symbolically significant to the growth of soul as any of his recording achievements. Born near Augusta, Georgia and heavily influenced by the example of Little Willie John – creator of two Fifties R&B classics, 'Fever' and 'Need Your Love So Bad' – Brown brought a Southern perspective to his brand of R&B-laced gospel. The style and tone of his career was set as early as 1956 by his first regional hit, 'Please, Please, Please', which he recorded for the King label in Cincinnati: the disc was an exercise in fraught vocalising, with pauses in the accompaniment adding a

melodramatic dimension to his half-sobbing, half-defiant delivery. Building his reputation by shrewd, single-minded career planning and sheer hard work, he toured tirelessly and turned his travelling revue-like stage show into a shameless act of self-celebration, embellishing his performances with dance routines of impossible athleticism and selecting a wardrobe of stage clothes as dazzling as anything Little Richard had worn.

Symbols and sermonisers

By 1962, Brown was proclaiming himself 'Soul Brother No. 1' and plotting his next move. With his own capital, he recorded one of his shows and released the results on the *Live at the Apollo* album, which went on to sell over a million copies and reach Number 2 in the pop album charts. This was an unprecedented achievement for a black star from the R&B field and it presaged a string of national pop hits – 'Prisoner of Love', 'Oh Baby Don't You Weep', and 'Out of Sight' among them – that put Brown right at the forefront of American black music. At a time when black singers were still having to make major compromises with the demands of the white market and trust their careers to the marketing nous of producers or money men, Brown stood out as an individualist and no mean businessman in his own right. He formed his own production company in 1964 and negotiated his own switch from the independent King to the much larger Mercury label; by the time 'Papa's Got a Brand New Bag' was released a year later, he had assumed complete control over both the commercial and artistic sides of his career, providing his fellow artists with a model and giving a symbolic boost to the black struggle for economic and cultural independence.

Sam Cooke, too, became a figurehead of early Sixties black music for much the same reason, though stylistically he and Brown stood some way apart. Brown was all extravagance and sweat, his distinct vocal style built around extemporising ballads in tortured sermon-like fashion. Cooke, however, was the epitome of black cool, his voice crystalline and supple and his phrasing and stage manner always measured, controlled and smooth. He was a star of the gospel field long before he turned his attention to the pop market, initially making his mark in the Soul Stirrers, America's premier black gospel group, which he joined in 1950 as the replacement for their legendary lead tenor R. H. Harris. The group recorded for the Specialty label's gospel division in Los Angeles and their recordings with Cooke singing lead – notably 'Pilgrim of Sorrow', 'I'm Gonna Build On That Shore', and 'Touch the Hem of His Garment' – are universally regarded as

James Brown (above) and Sam Cooke (right) had sharply contrasting backgrounds but became both pivotal figures in the new soul music and embodiments of the growing enterprise and confidence of American blacks

among the finest expositions of gospel ever heard, Cooke's vocals a breathtaking combination of technical skill and spiritual feeling. By the mid-Fifties, he was the biggest attraction on America's black gospel circuit and, thanks to his striking good looks and smooth sexuality, a heart-throb to thousands of young female fans.

Cooke crossed over from the gospel field to the pop market in 1957, though his first recordings in a pop style were made in rather furtive fashion: 'Lovable' was issued on Specialty under the name of Dale Cooke, partly to test the market but mostly because of Sam's own apprehension about leaving his hard-core religious audience behind. Any thought that he could sustain dual careers in gospel *and* pop was dispelled by the negative reactions within gospel circles, and by the chart-topping success in early

white listeners while keeping secular black audiences enthralled. Hits like 'I'll Come Running Back To You', 'Only Sixteen', and 'Wonderful World' were unashamedly aimed at the mixed race pop mainstream, while on his albums he tackled jazz numbers and popular standards with the large and lucrative adult market in mind.

The holy trinity

Cooke joined RCA in 1959, negotiating the terms himself, and he immediately began writing songs of his own for single release – 'Chain Gang', 'Cupid', and 'Twistin' the Night Away' among them. His ballad compositions retained devotional characteristics, but his lingering commitment to his gospel roots showed itself most in his founding, in 1961, of a record label dedicated to the discovery and promotion of gospel-oriented acts.

Both Sam Cooke (below left) and Ray Charles (below) made important inroads into the white pop market between 1957 and 1964, their greatest commercial successes following their signings with major companies RCA and ABC respectively. The development of the R&B – gospel synthesis into a distinct style was, however, largely the achievement of two independent labels, Stax in Memphis and Motown in Detroit

December 1957 of 'You Send Me', his début release under his real name. The break with gospel seemed final and irreparable, but the distinguishing feature of his subsequent pop material was his unerring, gospel-derived ability to invest the most sentimental and lightweight of lyrics with an ethereal quality. This, coupled with the easy charm of his delivery and the clarity of his diction, made Cooke an instant favourite with

Called SAR, the label's roster included the Sims Twins, Mel Carter and the Valentinos, whose line-up included Cooke's long-time guitarist Bobby Womack. This foray into the world of label and artist management also had the effect of enhancing his image as a sharp, sophisticated, super-cool man-about-town, and for many young blacks he was the personification of upwardly mobile black style – living proof, in fact, that blacks could make it in the white entertainment world without compromising their integrity. His death in December 1964, in a bizarre shooting incident at a Los Angeles motel, was an event as shattering to many black Americans as the assassination of President Kennedy had been a year earlier.

In his last recordings – notably the soaring revivalist paean that was 'A Change is Gonna Come', released posthumously on the flipside of 'Shake' in 1965 – Cooke seemed to be moving quite consciously into the soul idiom, digging back into his gospel beginnings and testifying to his faith in the new dawn then being declared by Rev. Martin Luther King. 'I was born by the river in a little tent/and just like the river I been running ever since', he sang, 'It's been a long time coming but I know a change is gonna come!'. Anticipating the classic Memphis soul sound still further were tracks like 'Shake' itself, the imploring 'Bring It on Home to Me', and 'Yeah Man', which used horn patterns later emulated by legendary soul accompanists Booker T. and the MGs and became the model for Arthur Conley's celebratory 1967 hit, 'Sweet Soul Music'. The virtual creator of the soul ballad tradition subsequently followed by Smokey Robinson, Otis Redding, Marvin Gaye and Johnny Nash, Sam Cooke all but defined soul music in its original inspirational sense, and his example encouraged dozens of other young gospel performers – Aretha

Franklin among them – to forsake the church for more commercial pastures.

Ray Charles, James Brown and Sam Cooke were soul's holy trinity, seminal figures whose impact on white as well as black popular music was enormous. Charles influenced a whole generation of British blues vocalists, from Stevie Winwood and Eric Burdon to Elton John and Joe Cocker, while legend has it that Mick Jagger learned all he knows about on-stage movement from watching Brown at first hand during rehearsals for the film *The TAMI Show* in 1965. In the UK particularly, the repertoire of all three singers was raided regularly by up-and-coming bands seeking to establish their credibility with fans of black music. On a broader level however, the trio were important because they destroyed the prevailing white stereotype of the black entertainer as the eye-rolling, clownish Uncle Tom of tradition – a stereotype even great jazzmen like Louis Armstrong had been obliged to follow. As the commercial boom in soul music began around 1964, serviced by the hit-making machines of Detroit's Motown label and Stax in Memphis, so the true face and voice of black America came to be seen and heard regularly in a chart context.

The multi-racial group Booker T. and the MGs (top) provided the backbone of the Stax sound: guitarist Steve Cropper (second from right) produced numerous Stax sessions with label boss Jim Stewart (centre page). Stewart's partner was his sister, Estelle Axton (above): their surnames provided the label's name

MOTOWN AND MEMPHIS

Numerous record companies, almost all of them minor-league independents, sought to capitalise on the new gospel-R&B synthesis in the early Sixties, but the trend was initially reflected – despite the occasional crossover hit like the Isley Brothers' 'Twist and Shout' (1962) on Wand – more in the R&B charts than in the mainstream pop listings. No labels matched the achievements of Motown and Stax, who took very distinct approaches to the soul sound that in some ways exemplified the differing musical spirits of their respective locations – Motown specialising in sophisticated, tightly-crafted urban soul aimed firmly at the dance floor, Stax producing hard-edged, individualistic southern soul that followed no obvious commercial formula.

Motown's dramatic rise to prominence – from a mere six Top 20 US hits in 1962 to 22 during 1966 – was very much the product of the marketing genius of Berry Gordy Jr, who combined a brilliant understanding of gospel and R&B basics with unmatched skills as a business administrator and as a judge of performing and backroom talent. The familiar Motown sound of bedrock bass lines underpinning call-and-response vocals, with the beat accentuated by tambourines and a fluid rhythm section, emerged quickly through the production efforts of Gordy's hand-picked team of Eddie and Brian Holland and Lamont Dozier, who worked with the Marvelettes, Marvin Gaye and Martha and the Vandellas before achieving their biggest successes writing and producing for the Four Tops and the Supremes. Varying the mix of musical elements in the basic sound to suit particular artists, Holland, Dozier and Holland created a flexible 'house

Below: stars of the Gordy stable, the Supremes, confer with Lamont Dozier and Brian and Eddie Holland, writers and producers of many of the group's hits during Motown's golden years of the mid-Sixties

style' that was developed further by in-house producers Mickey Stevenson (whose work included Martha and the Vandellas' 'Dancing in the Street', Jimmy Ruffin's 'What Becomes of the Broken-hearted', 'Marvin Gaye's 'Stubborn Kind of Fellow', and the Marvin Gaye-Kim Weston duet, 'It Takes Two') and the legendary Norman Whitfield.

Gordy maintained Motown's high standards through diligent 'quality control', vetting the label's product with ruthless efficiency and releasing only those discs he was *sure* would make the mainstream chart. While other labels chose to release a scatter of singles hoping some would succeed, Gordy could claim a consistent two-in-three success rate; he was also known to insist on refinement and reworking of particular recordings if he was dissatisfied with the final mix, and he encouraged cut-throat competition between producers, arrangers and artists, to the point of giving them the same song to work on. Gordy sought to establish a corporate identity for Motown in other ways, too – by giving particularly favoured artists like Smokey Robinson positions of responsibility within the Motown organisation, by promoting all his acts under the slogan 'The Sound of Young America', by creating a travelling roadshow entitled the Motortown Revue as a showcase for them, and – most curiously – by insisting that the company song be sung before each and every business meeting. A wily combination of incentives and fear encouraged loyalty, the principal reward for toeing the company line being the promise of not only sustained chart success but of a genuine showbusiness career, plotted and fostered by Gordy's Artists Development Department. Headed by Gordy's long-time business associate Harvey Fuqua, with roadshow musical director Maurice King and choreographer Cholly Atkins, the Department (which

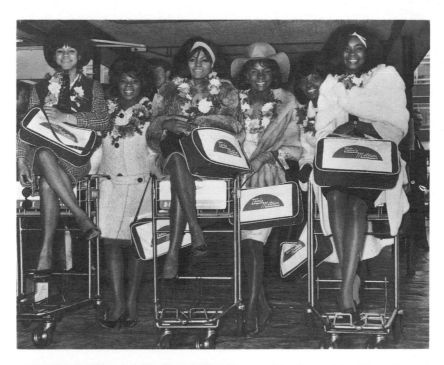

Martha and the Vandellas (above) pose for airport photographers as the travelling Motortown Revue arrives in the UK in March 1965. Their biggest hit, 'Dancing in the Street' (1964), was co-written by Marvin Gaye (left), whose own momentous chart career included such transatlantic hits as 'How Sweet It Is' (1964), 'I Heard It Through the Grapevine' (1968) and 'What's Going On' (1971)

was widely known as the 'kick, turn, smile' school) trained its charges in on-stage professionalism and all-round performing skills, devising everything from the celebrated hand gestures of the Supremes to the ostensibly ad-lib stage patter in which the groups indulged between songs. Gordy believed his discoveries should be as at home on the stages of Caesar's Palace or the Copacabana, the playgrounds of middle-class white America, as before the cameras of a teen-aimed pop show like *Shindig*. In the long term, as several of Motown's key acts made the transition to night-club work and even – in the case of Diana Ross – to film roles, Gordy's much-criticised policy of gradually expanding Motown's horizons beyond soul music appeared vindicated.

Despite all the behind-the-scenes planning of Motown's creative team however, the success of the label finally depended on the artistry of the singers themselves – most of whom were Detroit based and had church choir backgrounds. Marvin Gaye, son of a church minister and (with Harvey Fuqua) once a member of the Moonglows, began his Motown career with heavily gospel-flavoured material like 'Can I Get a Witness' and 'Pride of Joy' before finding his own style with sleekly sexual, compulsive dance records like 'Ain't That Peculiar' and 'I Heard it Through the Grapevine'. Smokey Robinson of the Miracles had a pleading falsetto particularly well-suited to self-written romantic ballads like 'I Gotta Dance to Keep From Crying', 'The Tracks of My Tears' and 'I Second That Emotion', each graced by impeccably sweet turns of phrase and appealingly simple imagery. The Four Tops could boast the proud, booming voice of Levi Stubbs and a ten year run of hits that included the magnificent 'Reach Out, I'll Be There', a brilliant example of how a traditional, timeless gospel message – that of 'holding on' to faith and hope – could be incorporated into a soul-style love song. Of comparable greatness were such Motown stalwarts as the Temptations, Stevie Wonder, Gladys Knight and the Isley Brothers – all of them major hit-makers in the middle years of the Sixties but destined to produce much of their most creative and successful recording work from the early years of the Seventies onwards.

Soul down south

Next to Motown, the single most successful record label dealing in soul music during the Sixties was Stax, founded in Memphis in 1959 by former bank-teller Jim Stewart and his sister Estelle Axton. Unlike Motown, Stax was no monument to commercial black enterprise – its owners were white – and its sudden rise out of southern obscurity had everything to do with its affiliation to Atlantic, the New York R&B independent, and the direct interest that Atlantic's top A&R man-cum-producer Jerry Wexler took in the Stax output. The success down south of ''Cause I Love You'', by father and daughter duo Rufus and Carla Thomas, one of the very first Stax releases, first caught Wexler's attention, and Carla's solo single 'Gee Whiz', the Mar-Keys' 'Last Night', and William Bell's 'You Don't Miss Your Water' all became national hits via the Stax-Atlantic distribution deal. All were unmistakable products of the richly cosmopolitan yet

Above: Motown boss Berry Gordy long regarded Diana Ross as the pearl of his roster. The personification of black sophistication and glamour, she was groomed for solo stardom by Gordy while a member of the Supremes and took the lead role of Billie Holiday in the Motown-financed biopic, Lady Sings the Blues, *in 1972*

musically independent Memphis environment, chunks of hard-hitting R&B laced with gospel and white country influences in equal measure – a natural hybrid as startling to mainstream audiences as that other Memphis hybrid, Sun rockabilly, had been little more than a decade earlier.

There were some parallels with the Sun operation, in that the distinctive company 'sound' was originated and developed by a tight-knit creative team of producers and musicians working informally and instinctively, initially with only the needs of a local market in mind. The backbone of the sound was provided by house band Booker T. and the MGs, who scored nationally with 'Green Onions' in 1962 (released on Stax's Volt subsidiary) before contributing lithe, raw yet free-flowing accompaniment to virtually every hit created in the Stax studios during the Sixties. Guitarist Steve Cropper and bassist Donald 'Duck' Dunn (both white) gave the tracks a rhythmic, country-sharp anchor, while drummer Al Jackson Jr contributed tight, emphatic percussive fills and organist Booker T. Jones added a gospel texture with his imaginative, extemporised but never over-fancy playing. Their whole approach was a revelation to a hardened northern record man like Wexler, who later recalled to Gerri Hirshey (author of the definitive soul history, *Nowhere to Run*), 'It was different down there – a total departure from anything we'd known in New York, since it veered away from formal, written arrangements and back to head arrangements . . . it put the creative burden back on the rhythm section, to a symbiosis between the producer and the rhythm section. It's instinctual. You don't know why they're doing it – maybe some of it comes from subconscious memory. But it's southern, very southern. Which is to say extremely ad-lib'.

Bass player Donald 'Duck' Dunn (left) and drummer Al Jackson Jr (above) were the twin pillars of the Stax sound. Their contribution to the success of records by artists like Sam and Dave – pictured below, flanked by Atlantic producer Jerry Wexler (far left), Stax vice-president Al Bell (second from right) and Ahmet Ertegun (far right) – was incalculable

Wexler's own early attempts to emulate the soul sound at Atlantic were ingenious mélanges of gospel feeling and country melody, typified by former gospeller Solomon Burke's 1961 reading of a familiar Nashville tearjerker, 'Just Out of Reach'. A little later, just as Stax was hitting its stride, he made a brilliant move in sending new signing Wilson Pickett – Alabama-born but now resident in Detroit – south to work with Cropper and company on a series of sessions. Pickett's talent was duly ignited, and the

results included recordings of unprecedented sweat and sass that introduced a new mythology to soul music, picturing the singer as a superstud in mohair, a night owl ready to come alive on the stroke of midnight. 'In the Midnight Hour' (1965) was quintessential Pickett, oozing sexual confidence and power, but its very success made the Stax management nervous of further competition and Atlantic was subsequently barred from using the studio again. Undaunted, Wexler took Pickett deeper south to the studios of the small Fame label in Muscle Shoals, Alabama, where a regular unit of black and white musicians, marshalled by producer Rick Hall, proved well able to replicate the spirit and style of Stax soul at its best. Other Wexler signings also recorded there, including Clarence Carter, Joe Tex and Percy Sledge, whose emotion-wrenching lament 'When a Man Loves a Woman' (1966) was one of the first of the southern soul recordings that was conceived, written and performed in a reflective, non-macho vein.

While Atlantic continued to extend its own formidable soul roster and relations with Stax became strained, Stax itself enjoyed massive international success

with such hits as Rufus Thomas' 'Walkin' the Dog', Sam and Dave's 'Soul Man', Eddie Floyd's 'Knock on Wood', and the Bar-Kays' 'Soul Finger'. Even these achievements, however, were dwarfed by the consistent mainstream chart success of Otis Redding, yet another preacher's son who could claim early exposure to both gospel and the rip-roaring R&B of Little Richard and Roy Brown. His other influences included a strong dose of white country, particularly the blues-inflected ballads of Hank Williams, and his voice had the hesitant, vulnerable quality of some of the better white country singers of the Fifties. Joining Stax in 1962, after a performing apprenticeship on the southern club circuit, he established himself almost

immediately as a master of the yearning, soul-searching ballad with hits like 'These Arms of Mine', 'Mr Pitiful', and 'Pain in My Heart', before branching out into writing and production work for other artists. His plain, sincere and unadorned style made him easily the most accessible of soul singers to white audiences, a fact Redding seemed to acknowledge during 1967, when he accepted an invitation to appear at the Monterey Festival – Jimi Hendrix was the only other black musician to be so 'honoured' – and became one of the event's unqualified successes. When he died in an air crash on December 10, 1967, he was on the threshold of becoming the first true black superstar of the new progressive era.

Soul music's greatest extrovert, Wilson Pickett (opposite left), was signed to Atlantic but achieved his long-awaited chart breakthrough in 1965 after his first sessions at Stax's Memphis studios. Rufus Thomas (opposite right), by contrast, was one of Southern soul's earliest successes, his hits including the much-covered 'Walking the Dog' (1963). But for many mid-Sixties soul fans the most abiding memory is that of Otis Redding's emotional, almost histrionic, live performances in front of a blazing horn section (above)

149

FUNK, PHILADELPHIA AND THE DISCO DIMENSION

Below: 'Lady Soul', the great Aretha Franklin. Her career to date has had two peaks: in the late Sixties when she reached the chart with Otis Redding's 'Respect' and Jagger-Richards' 'Satisfaction', and in the mid-Eighties, when recording with Eurythmics put her back in the limelight

Redding's death proved to be a turning point in the fortunes of Stax and in the development of soul music itself: although posthumous interest in the singer and a bank of hitherto unreleased material kept Stax more than financially secure, his loss was a psychological blow to the label that coincided with the ending of its distribution link with Atlantic and the beginning of a disastrous period under the control of the Gulf and Western big business conglomerate. Atlantic, meanwhile, assumed greater prominence in the soul world than ever with the signing of Aretha Franklin, the mighty-voiced daughter of Rev. C. L. Franklin, who was one of the most powerful figures within gospel music and a preacher of devastating bombasticity. Aretha had been contracted to Columbia for some years but had never been allowed to perform in a gospel or soul mode; at Atlantic, under the supervision of Jerry Wexler, her extraordinary vocal skills were matched to the sympathetic accompaniments of the Muscle Shoals session men, resulting in such power-house outpourings of emotion and ecstasy as 'I Never Loved a Man (The Way I Love You)', 'Natural Woman' and 'Chain of Fools'. Perhaps her greatest triumph was her 1968 recording of 'Think', which fairly shook with gospel fervour and fury: recorded shortly after Martin Luther King's assassination, it seemed aimed squarely – like 'Respect' – at the white establishment, generating its power from the unbearably intense repetition of the phrase 'think about it . . . ' and the word 'freedom'.

Not all soul performers were so keen to bring such a political dimension to their music, but during 1968 it was increasingly difficult for black performers of any ilk to distance themselves from the events on the streets. Rioting in black ghettoes, the rise of the Black Panther movement, the growing militancy of Black Muslims made any failure to acknowledge 'black consciousness' seem like fence-sitting, and Motown in particular was criticised by old guard civil rights campaigners and black power activists alike for sticking to its policy of producing formula dance music for whites. For some, the most positive response came from James Brown, who followed his anthem-like 'Say It Loud, I'm Black and I'm Proud' – a Number 10 hit in the US in September 1968 – with further calls to black unity and organisation like 'Get Up, Get Into It, Get Involved' and 'I Don't Want Nobody to Give Me Nothing (Open Up the Door, I'll Get It Myself)'. His stance was that self-help and solidarity alone would bring change, and his influence was such that his appearance in a television concert marathon – hurriedly arranged by the Lyndon Johnson administration – was credited with defusing the atmosphere and keeping people off the streets at the height of black rioting in Boston and Washington D.C. in 1968.

Brown's music at this time also took on a harder instrumental edge and introduced a new word into the soul vocabulary – funk. The term was again of jazz origin, but in the context of the late Sixties it came to mean the meaty, harsh, grubby sound of the inner city ghetto – a sound that rejected the sweetening tendencies of Motown and crossed the staccato horn breaks of Memphis and Muscle Shoals soul with newer rock influences like the grinding, electrically-charged, blues-locked guitar playing of Jimi Hendrix. Brown used the sound but others developed it further, notably Sly and the Family Stone in San Francisco, whose acid-rock leanings prompted the unveiling of yet another new generic term – psychedelic funk. Led by former independent label boss and disc jockey Sly Stone – who, as Sylvester Stewart, had produced the first records by the Beau Brummels in the mid-Sixties – they were the only all-black band to make any impact on 'progressive' white audiences in the post-1967 years, and their ingenious pot-pourri of screaming saxophones, wah-wah guitars, undulating bass rhythms and chanted vocal exhortations was much copied.

Their influence could immediately be

Left: Eddie Kendricks of the Temptations, whose brand of Norman Whitfield-produced 'psychedelic soul' created major hits in 'Cloud Nine' (1968), 'Psychedelic Shack' and 'Ball of Confusion' (1970)

seen on the music of the Temptations, for long one of Motown's most charismatic vocal groups, who entered a mystical, expansive phase under the guidance of producer Norman Whitfield. Their change of direction was one sign of Motown's acceptance that the market for black music was changing, though both the self-conscious complexity and the

Above: Sly and the Family Stone, led by Sylvester Stewart (on keyboards), won a large following among 'progressive'-minded white rock fans and were one of the few black acts to appear at Woodstock.

The music of ex-Impressions leader Curtis Mayfield (above) had a political directness that was echoed in such albums as There's a Riot Goin' On *by Sly and the Family Stone and Marvin Gaye's* What's Going On?

hope for their spiritual resolution ('Beautiful Brothers of Mine', 'Move On Up'). He was also one of several soul musicians to contribute soundtrack scores to the spate of black-financed, black-oriented films that appeared in the early Seventies. His score for *Superfly* (1972) was a *tour de force* of sweetly textured rhythms and looping melodies, though the film itself had the air of an exploitation movie, romanticising the ghetto environment and creating a new black stereotype in the medallion-sporting, jewellery-laden, fur-coated macho man of the film's title.

New directions

As well as carrying the funk formula into the Seventies, Mayfield was an important example to artists like Marvin Gaye and Stevie Wonder at Motown, who saw him exercise the kind of creative freedom and musical independence that Berry Gordy had always discouraged, supposedly for the company good. Gaye lost some of his drive and creative spark after the death of his long-time singing partner Tammi Terrell in 1970 and set off on a more personal musical direction with the heavily introspective album *What's Going On?*, which was recorded and released against much opposition from the Motown board. Two years later came the libidinous *Let's Get it On*, with its low moans and sighs and explicit sexual references – a meandering, sultry, sophisticated work whose sales more than justified his fight with Gordy for artistic control of his own releases. Stevie Wonder, meanwhile, battled against Gordy's preconception of him as an artist best suited to piling up huge album sales in the middle-of-the-road market and topping the bill at Las Vegas. He finally broke free in 1971 with *Where I'm Coming From*, which contained philosophical lyrics in the then popular vogue and featured extensive use of moog synthesiser, and on the strength of the

hallucinogenic references of 'Cloud Nine' (1968) suggested an eagerness to ape the studio excesses of late Sixties white rock. Much surer in touch was their 1972 million-seller, 'Papa Was a Rollin' Stone, a brooding and atmospheric account of ghetto life that marked a return to the confident attack of earlier classics like 'Get Ready', 'My Girl' and 'Ain't Too Proud to Beg'. Elsewhere, the former leader of the Impressions, Curtis Mayfield, began working in a somewhat lighter funk vein and writing black-consciousness songs that keenly projected ghetto tensions ('If There's a Hell Below', 'Stone Junkie') while holding out

While Motown built its continuing success in the Seventies on such established artists as Stevie Wonder (left, pictured early in his career), other ex-Gordy signings like Gladys Knight and the Pips (top) found greater musical and commercial freedom with other labels. Among the most notable departures were ace production team Holland, Dozier and Holland, who in 1970 set up their own Invictus label and released hits by Chairmen of the Board and Freda Payne (above)

resulting sales was able to renegotiate his financial and personal terms for staying with Motown. Left entirely to himself on his subsequent recordings – including *Music of My Mind* (1972), on which he played all the instruments – he became Motown's biggest seller of the Seventies and re-signed with the company in 1975 for $13 million, at that time the biggest advance in US record industry history.

Internal disagreements were in fact characteristic of Motown in the early Seventies, with popular stars like Gladys Knight and Martha Reeves departing for other labels and the Holland/Dozier/Holland team leaving to set up their own

rival company, Invictus, to write and produce highly Motown-like hits for Chairmen of the Board, Freda Payne, and others. Losing interest in the singles market, Gordy gave most of his attention to grooming ex-Supreme Diana Ross as a movie star in the classic Hollywood mould and he was repaid when she won an Oscar nomination for her portrayal of jazz singer Billie Holiday in the Motown-financed film *Lady Sings the Blues* (1973). Ross, like Wonder and Gaye, continued to sell across both black and white markets, but the company's predominance as *the* premier black label was threatened from 1971 onwards by the

success of Kenny Gamble and Leon Huff's Philadelphia International label, which developed its own 'Philly Sound' on the Motown model and made the names of Harold Melvin and the Blue Notes, the Three Degrees, the O'Jays and Billy Paul internationally famous. Wrapping their productions in plush orchestrations (supplied by the outstanding Mother, Father, Sister, Brother session band), Gamble and Huff hit on an easy formula that was also used by acts on other Philadelphia labels – the Delfonics, the Stylistics, jazz singer-turned-soul brother Johnny Mathis and Ronnie Dyson among them. Another Philadelphia-based producer, Barry White, signed himself and his protégées, all-girl trio Love Unlimited, to 20th Century Records and recorded a string of massive selling sub Marvin Gaye-like calls to copulation with titles like 'Can't Get Enough of Your Love Babe' and 'I'm Qualified to Satisfy'. With such vivid descriptions of his sexual appetites, he seemed a gross parody of the Superfly figure that Curtis Mayfield was enshrining in song.

Later commentators would mark the arrival of the Philadelphia acts, and Barry White in particular, as a key point in the 'decline' of soul, and the reasons were understandable: Philly records were pure formula, contrived by very professional

arrangers and producers with the adult easy-listening market firmly in mind. There was no sense of the groups having any of the political or racial awareness of a Stevie Wonder, who took deliberate advantage of his mainstream appeal to hammer home social or ecological messages in hits like 'Living for the City' and 'Higher Ground'. But the Philly sound also marked a revived appreciation on the part of arrangers and producers of soul as *dance* music – and this had a direct bearing on the growth of discothèques as places of entertainment in the US and on the ensuing emergence

Top left: Leon Huff and Kenny Gamble – father figures of the Philadelphia International label. Philly-based soul acts to grace the charts between 1971 and 1975 included the Stylistics (top), Harold Melvin and the Blue Notes (above), and Barry White (opposite bottom). The orchestral approach of the Philadelphia producers was poles apart from that of Seventies funksters Parliament (opposite top), whose line-up included members of James Brown's band the JBs

of 'disco' music as a category in its own right. Slowly and subtly, soul came to be re-defined not as a music of political struggle or spiritual salvation but as a hedonistic, escapist body music.

The disco scene

The disco craze began in a major way around 1974, when discothèque owners and disc jockeys in New York started asking record labels and individual producers for longer, remixed versions of soul records for use at their venues. Demand grew, and with it the realisation not only that discothèques could be a powerful promotional medium – as important as radio in putting product before a prospective customer – but that dance-floor remixes (called 'disco mixes', and often released in 12in form for maximum sound quality) could sell as well as three-minute radio versions. Certain independent labels built their fortunes on catering for the growing disco market – T.K. in Florida, for instance, produced two giant disco hits in George McCrae's 'Rock Your Baby' and Anita Ward's 'Ring My Bell' – and some specialised in feeding dance crazes with tailor-made instrumental tracks. Avco, for example, gave free rein to Stylistics producer Van McCoy and were rewarded with 'The Hustle', which in turn inspired numerous follow-ups and imitations on the lines of 'Do the Latin Hustle' and 'Spanish Hustle'. And as disco-going became a national phenomenon, so black funk acts like Earth, Wind and Fire and Parliament were obliged to acknowledge the new market and adapt their music accordingly. A whole batch of established soul stars – James Brown, Wilson Pickett and Joe Tex included – did the same, and old-timer Johnnie Taylor, the man who took over from Sam Cooke in the Soul Stirrers nearly twenty years earlier, recorded one of the biggest selling disco records ever in 'Disco Lady' in 1976.

The film Saturday Night Fever *put disco before an international public and made fortunes for its star John Travolta (above) and the creators of its soundtrack score, the Bee Gees (top, pictured with their manager and* Fever *producer Robert Stigwood). Meanwhile, Donna Summer (centre right) drew on the genius of German producer Giorgio Moroder to become one of the genre's biggest recording stars. Although the disco craze had petered out by the close of the Seventies, the flag of quality soul was kept flying well into the new decade by such hugely popular names as Michael Jackson (far right) and ex-Commodore Lionel Richie (opposite, inset). The success of the Reverend Al Green (opposite) proved that black music was still in touch with its gospel roots*

With white dance bands like K.C. and the Sunshine Band also carving a career in disco, the genre's links with black soul came to seem less and less relevant – a tendency confirmed by the worldwide success of German-produced 'Euro-disco' records between 1976 and 1979. The catalyst was Donna Summer's 17-minute 'Love to Love You Baby', an erotic litany set to a mesmeric synthesised beat, which was produced in Munich by Giorgio Moroder. A seminal track, it established the synthesiser as the primary 'instrument' in disco and opened up the US market to European disco imports like Silver Convention and Boney M. In 1977, a different European connection was revealed as *Saturday Night*

Fever packed cinemas across America: the first of several disco films, its soundtrack highlighted the immaculate falsettoes of Britain's Bee Gees, who ever since their UK chart début a decade earlier had specialised in absorbing and re-packaging the topical sounds of the day – from Beatle pop in 1967 to middle-of-the-road country in 1970, from sweet harmony AOR (adult-oriented rock) in 1972 to soul-cum-disco in the mid-Seventies. The resulting album sold in millions throughout the world, yet it was difficult to disagree with those who saw the whole flashy, super-hyped venture as the ultimate white distortion of a once-thriving, meaningful, deep-rooted black American style.

Disco, of course, did not spell the end of soul: bands like Brass Construction, Kool and the Gang, Slave and the Ohio Players flirted briefly with the disco charts but quickly returned to the business of making good, hard funk. In 1977, guitarist Nile Rodgers and bassist Bernard Edwards came together to found the Chic Organisation, a partnership that went a long way towards reshaping the sound of disco by reasserting the primacy of the guitar/bass coupling. They also helped revitalise the career of Diana Ross, who left Motown for RCA in 1981, and produced tracks by a wealth of other soul, disco and pop artists, among them Sister Sledge, Debbie Harry and Carly Simon. There were still some great soul voices to be heard, too, in newly-emerging stars like Deniece Williams, Brenda Russell, Randy Crawford and Angela Bofill, while Michael Jackson and ex-Commodore Lionel Richie kept funk-flavoured R & B and romantic soul balladry at the top of the international chart during the first half of the Eighties. And finally, as if to symbolise soul music's continuing links with its church past, there was the magnificent spectacle of the Reverend Al Green – one of soul music's brightest stars and most accomplished vocal stylists in the Seventies and, a decade later, a born-again preacher renewing his roots and treating audiences to a vibrant, electrifying brand of red-hot gospel. Of all the soul stars of the Eighties, he seemed simultaneously a symbol of black music's past, of its living present, and of its likely future.

AFTER THE GOLDRUSH
Sounds of the Seventies

Back-to-basics music making and glam-rock flamboyance formed the contrasting faces of a new decade in rock

Right: a psychedelic wall mural adorned the Beatles' Apple boutique in London – one of several ill-thought out ventures into which the group put their money and some of their energies during the late Sixties

Opposite: David Bowie as Ziggy Stardust, on stage in 1972

For the world of rock, the Seventies began on an inauspiciously low note – with the break-up of the Beatles – the group who had long personified the youth culture's sense of unity and optimism. Their split had in fact been looming for some years, possibly since as far back as 1966, when they stopped touring and control of their affairs began to slip out of Brian Epstein's hands. His death a year later, their involvement with the Maharishi Mahesh Yogi, Lennon's relationship with Yoko Ono and McCartney's marriage to Linda Eastman all contributed to personal rifts that nobody in the group seemed particularly interested in healing. The last straw was the messy failure of their idealistically-inspired Apple Corps enterprise, set up early in 1968 as an exercise in what McCartney called 'western communism'. Intended to be an outlet for the talents of unknown musicians, writers and artists – those denied a fair hearing by the arts and entertainment establishments – Apple rapidly deteriorated into a freeloader's paradise, administered by profligate Beatle associates and hangers-on with neither business experience nor true hippie-style commitment. The Apple débâcle and the consequent acrimony over the Beatles' finances typified in many ways the general sourness of the period and the rock culture's inability to realise its brave ambitions. 'The dream is over', John Lennon commented with characteristic bluntness, 'and it's time to get down to so-called reality'.

To the end, Beatle music reflected the

mood of its time: *Abbey Road* (1969) and *Let it Be* (1970) were low-key albums, musically basic and lyrically downbeat, while the first solo recordings of each member mirrored several of the key themes and tendencies in early Seventies rock. McCartney became the living embodiment of one of the decade's most enduring clichés – the rock musician escaping to the country to seek artistic renewal – when he retreated with wife and son to his Scottish farm to write *McCartney* and *Ram*, two albums heavy on back-to-nature sentiments and simplistic love songs. The intense self-analysis of Lennon's eponymous solo album, recorded after he underwent primal therapy in California, was echoed in the work of many newly emerging (and mostly American) singer-songwriters.

All four ex-Beatles recorded solo albums during 1970, but it was George Harrison (above) who earned the greatest critical acclaim and the largest sales with All Things Must Pass. A triple album set, it was produced by a re-emerging Phil Spector, who also worked with John Lennon between 1970 and 1975

But it was George Harrison, for so long in the creative shadow of Lennon and McCartney, who enjoyed the greatest commercial and critical success with *All Things Must Pass*, which explored the same implicitly spiritual territory touched on by that other multi-million selling album of 1970 – Simon and Garfunkel's *Bridge Over Troubled Water*. The perspectives were different – Paul Simon's songs were questioning, uncommitted, yet straining for spiritual *rapprochement*, while Harrison's love songs to God and Krishna were unequivocally celebratory and affirmative – but a post-hippie era search for personal inner peace formed the thematic core of both.

Quasi-religious questing, obsessive self-examination, back-to-the-country simplicity – each could be seen as a reaction against all the high-minded cant and naïve utopianism of the previous years. The very sound of early Seventies rock – cooler, folksier, more countrified – seemed symptomatic of a cooling of radical fervour, and all the fashionable talk was of 'getting back to the roots', which in musical terms meant rediscovering the seminal rock idioms of country and blues. For the superstar names of the Sixties, the start of the new decade was a time for retrenchment and reassessment, with some decamping to Europe to plot new musical strategies – the Beach Boys to Holland, the Rolling Stones to southern France (for much publicised tax reasons), acid-rock hero Jim Morrison of the Doors to the Parisian Left Bank – and others joining the exodus to the new musicians' communities of Laurel Canyon in California and Woodstock in upstate New York. The signs everywhere – even in Britain, centre of a major revival in teenage pop from 1970 onwards – were of a refreshing if ultimately transitory return to the basic strengths that rock music had in the days before 1967.

TROUBADOURS AND TRADITIONALISTS

At the forefront of the general softening in US rock around 1970 were relative newcomers like Joni Mitchell, Carly Simon, John Denver and Melanie (Safka) – latter-day troubadours with a pleasant if limited line in deeply confessional lyrics, homespun melodies and sparse guitar or piano accompaniments. As part of a growing singer-songwriter trend, such artists tended to be depicted in the pages of magazines like *Time*, *Newsweek* and *Rolling Stone* as the true voices of the post-Woodstock generation, the angst they articulated so eloquently in their songs supposedly symbolic of the wider political malaise. James Taylor, a lanky Bostonian who had once been on Apple's books, was the first to suffer this treatment: his former heroin addiction and his spells in mental hospitals during the Sixties were assumed to make him an expert on his generation's ills, though only one song on his best-selling 1970 album *Sweet Baby James* – the much covered 'Fire and Rain' – drew directly on such experiences. Hyped unmercifully by his record label, Warners, and savaged by the critics when his follow-up release *Mud Slide Slim and the Blue Horizon* failed to meet their expectations, he proved singularly ill-equipped for the pressures of Seventies stardom and became a semi-recluse.

Many of the singer-songwriters to emerge in Taylor's wake had been around the rock and folk scenes for years, either in groups or as songwriting professionals. Neil Young and Steve Stills (ex-leaders of Buffalo Springfield), David Crosby (ex-Byrds) and Graham Nash (ex-Hollies) made solo albums and also recorded corporately under the precarious 'supergroup' set-up of Crosby, Stills, Nash and Young; former Lovin' Spoonful leader John Sebastian and Youngbloods singer Jesse Colin Young drew heavily on their folk-rock roots in embarking on solo careers; and ex-Them singer Van Morrison, now resident in Woodstock, made

one of the most outstanding solo débuts of all with *Astral Weeks*, in which he eschewed familiar folk-style backings for a rich instrumental mixture of jazz and R & B stylings. Meanwhile, the former songwriting superstar of New York's Brill Building, Carole King, renewed a recording career that had lapsed in the early Sixties with the ten-million selling *Tapestry* (1971), packed with homely love songs in the James Taylor mould. She and Taylor in fact played regularly on each other's albums, and his version of her 'You've Got a Friend' gave him his biggest US hit.

King was an arch-professional and, despite the contemporary gloss of songs like 'You've Got a Friend' and 'Tapestry' itself, her new music differed from her early Sixties material only in a superficial maturity and the simple accompaniments used. In effect, she was producing a kind of hip easy-listening music – pop music for adults, the old songs updated for the same audience that had loved her music some ten years beforehand. Her recordings lacked any sense of challenge and in this she compared unfavourably with a performer like Joni Mitchell, who was never afraid to chart the ups and downs of her love life in sharply conceived explorations of sexual politics, and began experimenting with jazz settings – in her albums from *For the Roses* (1973) onwards – long before it became fashionable to do so. King was nevertheless influential, in that her success inspired other one-time pop songsmiths to resurrect their careers in the new singer-songwriter guise – Barry Mann, Neil Sedaka, Ellie Greenwich, Kenny Young and Jimmy Webb all cut albums of highly subjective material. Neil Diamond, one of Carole's Brill Building colleagues and a pop performer since 1967, also turned his back on teen music to record a string of huge selling albums in the prevailing introspective mode.

Formerly one half (with husband Gerry Goffin) of one of America's greatest-ever songwriting teams, Carole King (above) resurfaced in 1971 with Tapestry, *a selection of songs that celebrated the simple joys of friendship, the home and one-man love. Her professionalism was as admirable as ever, but Carole's songs had little of the insight or challenge of the best work of Joni Mitchell (left)*

Above: Crosby, Stills and Nash – ex-members of the Byrds, Buffalo Springfield and the Hollies respectively – came together in a mood of optimism and idealism in 1969. Within months, they were joined by Stills' ex-Springfield colleague Neil Young. For many, CSN&Y were the musical personification of the Woodstock generation, their music reflecting the naivety of the time yet also capturing – as in 'Ohio', recorded immediately after the Kent State shootings in 1970 – moments of pure, heartfelt anger

Literally hundreds of singer-songwriters were launched between 1970 and 1973, many of them by the three labels affiliated to the giant Kinney leisure corporation, Warner Brothers, Elektra and Atlantic, whose releases were collectively marketed under the WEA banner. With a reputation for looking after its artists and an administration in the careful hands of producers and A&R men – some of them former artists themselves – who understood the new youth market from the inside, WEA became the big record industry success story of the early Seventies. Its signings, too, became strongly identified with a new rock 'jet set' based in chic Laurel Canyon, and the gossip columns followed their activities avidly. While Joni Mitchell wrote of her love affairs with fellow singer-songwriters James Taylor and Graham Nash in such songs as 'See You Sometime' and 'Willy', it was also very common for these new hip superstars to guest on each other's albums. The presence of Crosby, Stills, Nash and Young (who were signed to Atlantic) on Joni Mitchell's records, James Taylor on those by wife-to-be Carly Simon (and vice versa), John Sebastian on Judy Collins' albums, and so on, underlined the incestuous nature of the Laurel Canyon recording scene and its increasingly élitist stance.

All-American vistas

The singer-songwriter cult was in part a throwback to the Sixties folk boom from which many of its leading lights were

The early Seventies was a period for musical re-evaluation and much heart-searching on the part of America's singer-songwriters. Bob Dylan's Self Portrait *(below right) was a sentimental selection of his own favourite songs that smacked of self-indulgence after the quiet nobility and charm of* Nashville Skyline *(bottom right). The solo work of Neil Young (below), meanwhile, far out-stripped anything he produced as a member of CSN&Y: his* After the Goldrush *album in 1970 had the air of a personal political statement*

born, with press and record companies alike intent on portraying their latest finds as 'new Dylans' – the *old* Dylan having lost considerable respect after following his majestic *John Wesley Harding* and *Nashville Skyline* albums with the cynically titled *Self-Portrait*, a self-indulgent and sugary collection of songs by other writers. Many of the new performers seemed to borrow their whole vocabulary and subject-matter from traditional folk music, singing of finding solace in the arms of a highway Madonna, but a few pushed their horizons further to comment quizzically on the American scene and produce songs of often genuinely poetic insight. Neil Young's 'After the Goldrush', the Garfunkel-less Paul Simon's 'American

Tune', David Ackles' 'American Gothic', John Prine's 'Paradise', and folkie Don McLean's magnificent seven-minute resumé of rock history, 'American Pie', were all epic musical statements implicitly critical of Nixonian America and openly nostalgic for lost innocence.

The rich sense of Americana in these songs was matched elsewhere, notably in the music of a handful of bands whose approach to rock could be defined as neo-traditionalist. These bands had diverse geographical roots – the Band from Canada, the reconstituted Byrds from Los Angeles, Creedence Clearwater Revival from San Francisco – but the spiritual home of each was the deep South, birthplace of blues, rockabilly and soul, all rebel styles nurtured outside the

music business establishment and identified with the needs and values of the dispossessed. The South as portrayed by such bands was to some extent romanticised, with rockers like John Fogerty of Creedence seeking their roots in a Memphis or New Orleans of their own idealised imagination, but it did seem to offer a symbolic refuge from the urbanised, over-complicated musical scenario of the late Sixties.

The first to make the musical journey south were the Byrds, whose *Sweetheart of the Rodeo* album (released in 1968) virtually created the genre known as country-rock. Under the guidance of new recruit Gram Parsons – born in Florida and brought up in Georgia and New Orleans, and a country music fanatic since childhood – the group wholeheartedly embraced country instrumentation and harmony and even played Nashville's Grand Ole Opry, this at a time when rock audiences most associated the South with redneck politics and the victimisation of long-haired youth depicted in the film *Easy Rider*. Their efforts, together with Dylan's parallel

incursion into country music from *John Wesley Harding* onwards, helped re-accommodate the country sound within rock, although it was Parsons – breaking away to form the Flying Burrito Brothers with fellow Byrd Chris Hillman – who continued to explore the dynamics of country-rock fusion with the greater originality and commitment. He was a particular influence on singers like Emmy Lou Harris and Linda Ronstadt, young country performers eager for recognition in the rock field, and he helped lay the ground for Nashville's assault on the mainstream pop charts during the Seventies and the consequent 'crossover' success of Dolly Parton, Crystal Gayle, Kenny Rogers and others.

The Band, too, played music awash with country allusions, although the

Don McLean (above left) emerged in 1972 with the extraordinary 'American Pie', a cryptic and venomous account of the state of rock music from the death of Buddy Holly to the events at Altamont. Also taking a retrospective stance, though digging back deeper into rock's country roots, was the ultimately tragic figure of Gram Parsons (above), who died in September 1973 after plotting new directions for the Byrds and forming the Flying Burrito Brothers

As well as being the home of the most famous festival in rock history, the township of Woodstock in Upstate New York also housed a community of musicians whose talents blossomed during the early Seventies. Bob Dylan, Tim Buckley, Van Morrison and the Band (above) were all residents

The almost studied Americanism of the Band's approach – and their honouring of rock's country and blues roots – was paralleled elsewhere. Creedence Clearwater Revival (right) played no-nonsense rockabilly, the songs of John Fogerty (opposite top) conjuring romantic images of swamps and riverboats. Specialising in a new country-rock, meanwhile, were artists like Rita Coolidge and Kris Kristofferson (opposite below) who found success within the country market itself

great strength of their albums from 1968 to 1977 – notably *Music From Big Pink*, their debut, and *Stage Fright* (1970) – was their kaleidoscopic synthesis of folk, soul, rock'n'roll, Baptist hymn *and* country influences. Formerly the backing band of Toronto-based rock'n'roller Ronnie Hawkins and, from 1965, Bob Dylan's regular studio and stage accompanists, they were consummate upholders of America's rock tradition – five Woodstock-resident musicians with a decade of playing together already behind them, whose very choice of name suggested straight, uncluttered musicianship. They also had in leader Robbie Robertson a songwriter with some of Dylan's gift for metaphor and imagery and a historical perspective unmatched in rock. Whether digging back into Civil War history for 'The Night They Drove Old Dixie Down' – written from the point of view of a southern partisan – or articulating a Thirties sharecropper's hopes for better times ahead in 'King Harvest Has Surely Come', he invested his songs with an almost tangible sense of time and place, in the manner of a master storyteller. Musically and lyrically, the Band's objective was the same – to stress, in Greil Marcus' words, 'the continuity of generations', the historical links with the past that the late Sixties youth culture had tended to ignore in its breathless demand for change.

Covering similar ground but drawing on somewhat narrower musical roots were Creedence Clearwater Revival, a four-man group formed by brothers John and Tom Fogerty at the height of the Beatle-led British invasion in the Sixties. Totally out of sympathy with the acid-rock preoccupations of the music scene of their native San Francisco, they resolutely stuck to an updated version of Fifties-style rockabilly, taking their inspiration from both the original Memphis rockers and the black and white musicians latterly creating the soul music blueprint in the city's Stax studios. Recording for an independent label, Fantasy, their approach was unashamedly revivalistic, with John Fogerty-composed hits like 'Proud Mary', 'Down on the Corner', 'Travelin' Band' and 'Up Around the Bend' matching clean, rolling guitar riffs to lyrics that not only explored the traditional rock'n'roll themes of Saturday night revelry and highway cruising but evoked powerful images of a mythicised South – a world of riverboat gamblers, alligator-filled swamps and sweet home cooking. In a word, Creedence music spelt nostalgia, and it came as no surprise to find the temporarily rejuvenated Elvis Presley – fresh from his triumphant return to recording in Memphis – dipping regularly into the Fogerty songbook.

The public's new found taste for southern-style rock also boosted the careers of artists with genuine roots in the region, among them singer-writers Tony Joe White, Joe South and Kris Kristofferson, New Orleans piano wizard Dr John the Night Tripper (actually veteran session man Mac Rebennack in a new guise), white gospel-rock duo Delaney and Bonnie Bramlett and Oklahoma guitarist J. J. Cale. Both the Bramletts and Cale found fame through their association with Leon Russell, producer and arranger of countless Top 40 hits in the early and mid-Sixties, who moved from Los Angeles to his native Oklahoma to set up his own Shelter label as a showcase for his particular brand of fiery, gospel-flavoured country-rock. Touring with English blues singer Joe Cocker and a massive entourage of backing musicians and singers – Delaney and Bonnie and Rita Coolidge included – he achieved instant superstardom, though his own recording success tended to pale beside that of those whose careers he encouraged.

ADULT MARKETS, TEEN SCENES

T he rise of rock traditionalism had a lasting effect on the US music scene in the Seventies, although not in a manner that pioneers like the Byrds and the Band could have anticipated. On the one hand, new wave southern-based outfits like Lynyrd Skynyrd and the Marshall Tucker Band became massive box office draws, filling concert halls and sports arenas with a greasy, loud, heavily electrified form of Confederate rock. Theirs was an unsubtle and distorted version of the sound first established by the Allman Brothers Band, for whom guitarists Duane Allman – one-time session man at Rick Hall's famous Muscle Shoals studio – and Richard Betts effected a seminal fusion of improvised blues and bar-room

Richard Betts (left) and Gregg Allman (above) attempted to take the Allman Brothers to still greater heights after the death of Duane Allman in a motorcycle accident in October 1971. The Allmans' approach was followed more bombastically by southern-based stadium bands like Lynyrd Skynyrd (below left)

country that was widely and succinctly described and marketed as 'southern fried boogie'.

On the other hand, taking the opposite direction to the Allmans and their comparatively small-fry successors, were California bands like the Eagles, the Souther-Furey-Hillman Band, the Doobie Brothers and America – Los Angeles professionals who performed in an increasingly vapid style, tailoring their country-laced harmonies and soft, unchallenging ballads to the requirements of an FM radio network that had long since forgotten its radical beginnings. With FM radio now as tightly programmed as its AM counterpart and aimed squarely at the 25+ age group, record company bosses like Mo Ostin and Lenny Waronker at Warners and David Geffen at Asylum talked bravely of 'adult-oriented rock' (AOR) as the true music of the Seventies and built up their new signings – Bonnie Raitt, Linda Ronstadt, Stephen Bishop, Andrew Gold – as stars of the same. The Eagles, featuring ex-Burrito Brother Bernie Leadon on guitar, represented the

archetypal AOR band, their output including immaculately-crafted highway sounds like the Jackson Browne composed 'Take It Easy' and more grandiose concepts like *Desperado*, an album equivalent of a Hollywood western. Released in 1973, its songs were soaked in romantic frontier images picked from the pages of American history and the conventions of country songwriting – desert winds, lonesome railroad journeys, macho outlaw in-fighting and predatory females, invariably portrayed as 'devils' posing as 'angels'. Such well-made fantasy fare seemed a populist answer to the rather weightier examinations of the American past in which the Band specialised. At their most original when probing the Californian superstar lifestyle in songs like 'My Man' (dedicated to Gram Parsons, who died in 1973) and 'Hotel California', their records in themselves typified the peculiar languor of west coast rock in the first half of the decade.

The growth of AOR was just one symptom of the way in which a new kind of musical conservatism – governed mainly

A more laid-back version of the country-rock sound was adopted by such FM radio-oriented acts as the Doobie Brothers (featuring ex-Steely Dan guitarist Jeff Baxter, pictured bottom left), America (bottom) and Linda Ronstadt (below), whose regular backing musicians included members of the Eagles

by marketing and sales considerations – gradually came to subvert and supersede the traditionalism of the early Seventies. Another symptom was the stereotyping of new acts by A & R departments, who tried to fit their discoveries into often wholly inappropriate country-rock or singer-songwriter pigeonholes: Bruce Springsteen, signed by Columbia in 1973, was just one artist obliged to suffer acoustic accompaniments and a 'new Dylan' billing at the expense of his rock'n'roll instincts, while Steely Dan were promoted as a west coast boogie band despite the tough, jazz-inflected New York street culture ambience of their *Can't Buy a Thrill* and *Pretzel Logic* albums. Even that much-fêted new trend 'jazz-rock' quickly took on a fossilised look, as it became clear that outfits like Blood, Sweat and Tears and Chicago – whose idea of innovation seemed to end at adding brass and reed sections to a conventional rock band line-up – were simply using it as a vehicle for their showbusiness ambitions. Playing the cabaret centres of Las Vegas, New York, Paris and London, such bands chalked up sales by the million while the genuine experimentalists – Miles Davis, John McLaughlin, Weather Report and others – remained appreciated only by the jazz *cognoscenti*.

Above: the Eagles on tour in 1976 to promote their Hotel California *album. More than any other rock group, they embodied the sun-drenched, luxurious yet potentially enervating California lifestyle*

Left: Steely Dan, musically and lyrically one of the Seventies' most sophisticated bands, pictured during a rare concert appearance in 1974

Junior highs

Despite the efforts of a handful of exceptional, idiosyncratic talents – slide guitarist Ry Cooder, pop jack-of-all-trades Todd Rundgren, arch-satirist Randy Newman among them – mainstream US rock retained its air of predictability and blandness well into the Seventies. The blame lay with the strait-jacket that radio imposed on the kind of music produced and heard, and with the industry's growing preoccupation with the adult market, which meant a decreasing commitment to the teenage consumer. In fact, the industry had started to lose sight of its teenage audience as early as 1967, when FM radio and the twin onslaughts of *Sgt Pepper* and San Francisco rock switched the commercial focus to the nation's college population. The success of the Monkees that year showed that young teenagers, especially girls, were as willing as ever to embrace the whole panoply of fan worship, but the result of that success was that teen pop came to be seen solely in that manipulative light – as the musical equivalent of a pin-up or a love story magazine, peddling pubescent fantasy in the shape of some fresh-faced, well-trained young teen idol. This limited vision had a detrimental effect on Top 40 pop, as the chart became cluttered with so-called 'bubblegum' hits – records with a punk-rock inspired Vox organ sound and nursery rhyme lyrics, aimed at children as well as young teens – and revivals of late Fifties hit songs by the latest television-groomed sensations. Most successful of all were David Cassidy, launched by Monkees originators Screen Gems-Columbia in their early Seventies television series *The Partridge Family*, and 12-year old Donny Osmond, junior member of Mormon family entertainment troupe the Osmond Brothers and a familiar television face through appearances on *The Andy Williams*

Show. Both recorded for labels – Bell and MGM – that had little interest in the older rock market, and with producers – Wes Farrell and Mike Curb – who were veterans of early Sixties teen idol pop.

The Osmond-Cassidy heyday lasted barely three years, their lack of longevity echoing that of the *American Bandstand* era idols – Frankie Avalon, Fabian, Bobby Rydell and others – from whom they took much of their repertoire. Much more durable, because their Motown label took great care to develop their individual talents and expand their appeal across several markets, were contemporaries the Jackson Five, whose youngest member Michael had not only teenybopper charisma but one of the finest soul voices of the Seventies. Television, meanwhile, continued to produce good-looking, sweet-voiced stars with teen appeal, among them David Soul – a chart-topper with 'Don't Give Up On Us' following his starring role in *Starsky and Hutch* – and John Travolta, who went from *Welcome Back, Kotter* to pop hits and the films *Saturday Night Fever* and *Grease*.

David Cassidy (top) and Donny Osmond (inset) were both marketed as clean-living American boys-next-door, each the perfect son, brother or boyfriend. The closing years of the decade brought another teen idol to the fore, actor-turned-dancer John Travolta (above), depicted here in the famous 'Summer Nights' sequence from the film Grease

If there was anything approaching a genuine American teenage music, however, in the early to mid-Seventies, it was British-style heavy metal – a loud, lumbering, mind-numbing version of the sound popularised by Led Zeppelin, Deep Purple and others, with almost exclusively *male* appeal. Taking up where late Sixties hard rock bands like Iron Butterfly and Steppenwolf had left off, outfits such as Grand Funk Railroad, Montrose, Black Oak Arkansas and Mountain played to a formula of repetitive, thudding bass riffs, ear-piercing feedback and orgasmic guitar solos. 'If it's too loud, you're too old' was the war cry of Ted Nugent, leader of the Amboy Dukes and the sound's self-appointed chief lieutenant. Others like Alice Cooper, named after their (male) lead singer, embellished their stage acts with visual gimmickry: simulating baby killing, self-mutilation and death by hanging, Cooper turned the band's shows into tacky rock theatre while aiming at the Top 40 with neo-punk adolescent laments like 'I'm Eighteen' and 'School's Out'.

Specific heavy metal influences apart, Cooper's chief mentor was Californian rock avant gardist Frank Zappa, founder of the outrageously decadent Mothers of Invention and perpetrator of vicious and vulgar satires on suburban morals and

the pretensions of the rock culture. Cooper recorded for Zappa's Bizarre label – also the home of such wildly left-field artists as the GTOs (Girls Together Outrageously, each of them a groupie), Wild Man Fischer and Captain Beefheart – before becoming Warners' only significant teen star. Any credibility he may once have had as a rock subversive was lost, however, when appearances on Hollywood talk shows and even in pro-celebrity golfing tournaments revealed him in his true colours – as a wise-cracking, knowing trouper of the old school, updating his act for a blood-hungry new generation. He did nevertheless give a hint of how a later core of Seventies artists – drawing on Zappa's lessons or those of his east coast counterparts – would attempt to assault the pop mainstream with punk-type protest and/or a music and image that revelled in low-life sleaze.

Alice Cooper (opposite, top left and above) exemplified young America's new thirst for loud, pseudo-decadent shock-rock, though he had little of the cynical, satirical stance of his mentor Frank Zappa (left). Taking heavy metal to new heights (or depths, depending on your point of view) were new guitar heroes Mark Farner (opposite, top right) of Grand Funk Railroad and Ted Nugent (opposite, below) of the Amboy Dukes

DAYS OF GLAM AND GLITTER

Launched by his record company, DJM, as Britain's answer to the moody, introspective singer-songwriters from across the water, Elton John (below) quickly contradicted this image by adopting eccentric spectacles and glittering stage suits. A showman at heart, he fitted easily into the glam-rock mould yet had the talent and personality to stay at the top in pop for the next decade and beyond

Across the ocean in Britain, major US names like James Taylor and the Eagles all enjoyed respectable sales, but the early part of the decade belonged to a mainly new set of performers whose success in many ways contradicted and challenged the prevailing trends in US rock. While the UK produced its own string of appealingly introspective singer-songwriters in Cat Stevens, Elton John and others, and the skilful resuscitation of British folk styles by neo-folk-rockers Fairport Convention and Roy Harper suggested parallels with Band-

like traditionalism, the UK's own version of a 'back-to-basics' movement mostly took the unpredicted form of a revival in traditional pop values. Two factors in particular encouraged it – the dissatisfaction of certain key 'progressive' musicians with both the direction and musical philosophy of British rock circa 1970, and the emergence of a new market of young teenage record buyers who demanded just the same qualities of fun, thrills and three-minute teen fantasy that progressive rock protagonists so strongly and snootily spurned.

The point was that progressive rock, for all its money-spinning potential, lacked a truly broad-based appeal: in drawing its audience from the grammar schools and universities, it alienated both younger fans and those from more working class backgrounds, many of whom turned to strongly dance-based sounds like Motown, Stax soul and West Indian reggae. Some joined the latest and most intimidating in Britain's long line of urban youth tribes by becoming 'skinheads', whose uniform of close-cropped hair and steel-capped 'bovver' boots carried an explicit threat of anti-middle class violence. An important task faced by UK rock in the early Seventies was therefore to heal the rifts, to unite the audience in pre-1967 fashion, to render the class distinctions meaningless. Appropriately, the artists who came closest to achieving just this were those with backgrounds in both the mid-Sixties rock scene and the mod movement, that initially select band of working class teenagers whose taste in music and fashion briefly gave mass youth a sense of corporate style and identity. Exaggerating the innate effeminacy of the mods and reviving their narcissistic delight in dressing up, performers like Marc Bolan and David Bowie defined early Seventies UK pop as a larger-than-life version of the sounds and styles that had gone before.

Above and above right: Marc Bolan at the height of what the Daily Mirror called 'T. Rextasy'. Bolan's pre-eminence in the glam-rock world was such that he became the catalyst for a whole new wave of teen appeal singers and groups who were similarly preoccupied with ambivalent sexual posing and narcissistic image-making

In transforming himself from underground progressive hero to teenybopper star, it was Bolan who became the catalyst for the new pop boom. A former male model and one-time member of pseudo-mod demolitionists John's Children, he formed the acoustic duo Tyrannosaurus Rex with percussionist Steve Peregrine Took in 1967, as a vehicle for his strange, quavering voice and Tolkien-inspired mystical lyrics. Three years later, with some modest album sales behind him, he appalled former fans and colleagues by making what seemed a deliberate bid for commercial success: he dropped his acoustic guitar in favour of a Chuck Berry-influenced electric sound, fell out with Took and brought in Mickey Finn, shortened the duo's name to T. Rex and replaced the denims and shaggy hair look with a tight-fitting

sequined suit and a frizzed, glitter-sprinkled haircut. Worse still, he began concentrating on making singles – anathema to progressive thinkers – and his concerts started attracting contingents of screaming girls. John Peel, cult disc jockey and the first to play Tyrannosaurus Rex records on the radio back in 1967, now refused to play them. Bolan remained unrepentant: 'I'm probably more ethnic now than I ever was', he explained, 'because I'm more involved with the art of producing good funky energy rock music. I'm very aware of the people that I'm playing for now'. Yet he was also just a little *too* aware, too calculating and manipulative in his stage act and far too garrulous on the subject of his own fame.

Bolan's records ranged from the kookily atmospheric ('Ride a White Swan', 'Hot Love') to the simply asinine, typified by lyrics like 'I like a Roll's Royce 'cos it's good for my voice/you won't fool the children of the revolution'. His attempt to build a myth around himself as an 'electric warrior' or 'metal guru' of the new age was doomed to failure because of his very lack of mystery, and he became distinctly unfashionable as other, wiser heads moved in to cater for the young teen audience he had done much to uncover. Far more acceptable in the long term, as a spectacular run of cheerfully self-deprecating hits showed between 1972 and 1974, was a character like Gary Glitter – a would-be pop star as far back as the early Sixties but now finally finding fame with an act (and stage name) that gloriously lampooned the gaudiest aspects of Fifties rock'n'roll. It was Gary Glitter, too, who in company with another pop veteran, songwriter/arranger Mike Leander, created one of the most distinctive and extensively copied pop formulae of the early Seventies – the placing of a sparse, reverberating guitar sound over a heavy, stomping, hand-clap enforced beat.

Good-time glam

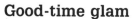

Glitter and Leander were just two of a number of faded, forgotten or never-was stars and backroom boys who found the pop climate of the new decade particularly favourable. In seeking to exploit the newly-emergent teen scene, the artists and the record industry as a whole could look back on their own past and put the lessons – both musical and promotional – that they had learned into practice. So Mickie Most, Britain's most successful independent record producer in the Sixties, returned to the production limelight as head of RAK Records, whose red-hot glam-rock roster included Mud, Smokie, Hot Chocolate and expatriate Detroit rock'n'roller Suzi Quatro. Another independently-owned label, Magnet, re-launched the Larry Parnes-era rocker Shane Fenton in the new guise of Alvin Stardust, while American early Sixties stars Neil Sedaka and Duane Eddy made chart comebacks with new material recorded in England. Roy Wood of the Move formed the Electric Light Orchestra with Jeff Lynne and then broke away to record solo and with Wizzard, whose discs were a joyful pastiche of massed

Behind the stars of the glam-rock era lay some very substantial pop talents. Suzi Quatro (left) came to the UK from Detroit and benefited from the expertise of legendary Sixties producer Mickie Most and the songwriting team of Nicky Chinn and Mike Chapman. Gary Glitter (below) wrote all his own material in collaboration with veteran arranger-producer Mike Leander, whose previous credits included the scoring of 'She's Leaving Home' on the Beatles' Sgt Pepper album

Among the relatively unsung heroes of Sixties rock to emerge triumphant in the early Seventies were Roy Wood (above) who formed Wizzard after founding the Move and the Electric Light Orchestra, and ex-Jeff Beck Group singer Rod Stewart (above right), who between 1970 and 1976 enjoyed parallel careers with the Faces and as a solo artist

cellos, children's choirs, blaring Fats Domino-type horns and a Phil Spector wall of sound. The ingenious pilfering of old sounds and styles continued with Mud apeing Elvis Presley on 'The Secrets That You Keep' and 'Lonely This Christmas', 10cc (with ace Sixties songwriter Graham Gouldman in their line-up) evoking everything from doo-wop to the Beach Boys in 'Donna', 'The Dean and I' and 'Rubber Bullets', and Elton John – having thrown off his moody singer-songwriter pose – cavorting onstage like a space age Jerry Lee Lewis to the catchy Paul Anka-Pat Boone inspired number 'Crocodile Rock'.

Elton's own professional roots were in mid-Sixties London R&B: as plain Reg Dwight, he had backed soul stars Major Lance and Patti LaBelle on live dates and was a member of Bluesology alongside the two men from whom he concocted his stage name – Elton Dean and Long John Baldry. Boasting a very similar rock apprenticeship was Rod Stewart, who became a cult figure in the late Sixties through his work with Steampacket and the Jeff Beck Group but found worldwide fame after joining one-time mod contemporaries the Faces – formerly the Small Faces – as lead singer. Called in to replace the departing Stevie Marriott, who formed progressive supergroup Humble Pie with Peter Frampton of the Herd, Stewart helped the Faces to win a fine live reputation: coming on like a less dangerous version of the Stones, a bunch of boozy mates out for a wild time, their pleasingly extrovert approach to performing and continuous touring caught the changing pop mood precisely. Stewart, meanwhile, set off on a parallel solo recording career, carving out his particular niche with self-composed songs like 'Maggie May' and 'You Wear It Well' that depicted him in the role of a besotted, cuckolded, exhausted lover.

Opposite: the chameleon-like David Bowie began shedding his cult status after the initially modest sales success of Hunky Dory *in 1971. The album that sealed his international reputation was* The Rise and Fall of Ziggy Stardust and the Spiders from Mars *a year later, for which Bowie conceived a spectacular stage act*

Below: Slade had an uninterrupted run of hits in the UK between 1971 and 1975 but, like so many contemporaries, failed to make an impression in America. The late Seventies found them dazzling a new audience of heavy metal fans at events like the Reading Festival, but by the mid-Eighties they had returned as an important chart act

Although frequently compared to Mick Jagger, whose bottom-grinding and microphone histrionics he certainly copied, Stewart was by far the more expressive vocalist and cultivated an image that was very much more down to earth: gangly, slightly fey but eschewing the campness of Bolan and Bowie, he took the stage like a street urchin in soccer tartans and indeed enjoyed a football crowd-like camaraderie with the group's – and his own – dedicated live following.

This kind of approach was also the hallmark of Wolverhampton band Slade, who had flirted briefly with the progressive scene before allowing manager Chas Chandler (former Animal and manager of Jimi Hendrix) to promote them as a 'skinhead' group. The image worked against them at first because of the skinheads' violent reputation, but it wasn't entirely misplaced: the band

identified strongly with the more positive aspects of the sub-culture, its view of pop music as *dance* music, its tribal loyalties, its sense of teenage solidarity, its anti-intellectual stance. Their music came to express all these qualities, though it was not so much the skinheads as their younger brothers and sisters, working class youngsters fresh into their teens, who made up Slade's main body of fans. Dropping the skinhead look and adopting costumes that could have been borrowed from the set of cult film *A Clockwork Orange*, they came to represent the 'good-time' aspect of glam-rock, winning the sympathy of every put-upon schoolkid with their deliberately mis-spelled record titles – 'Gudbuy T'Jane', 'Look Wot You Dun', 'Take Me Bak 'Ome' – and providing the glitter generation with its one great anthem in 'Mama Weer All Crazee Now', a deafening boot-stomper that was just as expressive of

teenage exclusivity as the Who's 'My Generation' had been a few years earlier.

The Bowie dimension

One figure, however, towered over Seventies rock – British and American – in a manner matched by none of his contemporaries: David Bowie. On a superficial level, his influence could be seen clearly in the camp posturings of a group like Sweet – whose hit 'Blockbuster' also echoed Bowie's 'Jean Genie' – and in the spiked hair, make-up and platform boots look that was so prevalent at the time, but his real importance went far deeper. In undermining the macho ethos so intrinsic to rock, in bringing to rock a host of hitherto untapped influences – notably the cold back-street vision of Lou Reed and the Velvet Underground – and in fully realising the theatrical possibilities of rock, he was unquestionably a true rock radical. Enigmatic, eclectic, experimental, he started to rewrite the rules of rock just as the retrospective tendencies in Seventies music were beginning to have an inhibiting effect on creativity.

From his first recordings for Decca in the late Sixties, Bowie refused to be bound by rock conventions – the notion, for instance, that creative musicians should avoid involvement with the star-making process, that flirting with any kind of image-building was a betrayal of artistic integrity and a selling out to commercialism. Bowie *was* interested in becoming a star, and one of the recurrent themes in his work was his fascination with the pressures and obligations that stardom placed upon the individual. Another convention was that songwriters should always write from personal experience, as self-expression; Bowie, by contrast, role-played constantly, changing his persona from album to album, using his songs to explore different viewpoints, to get inside many

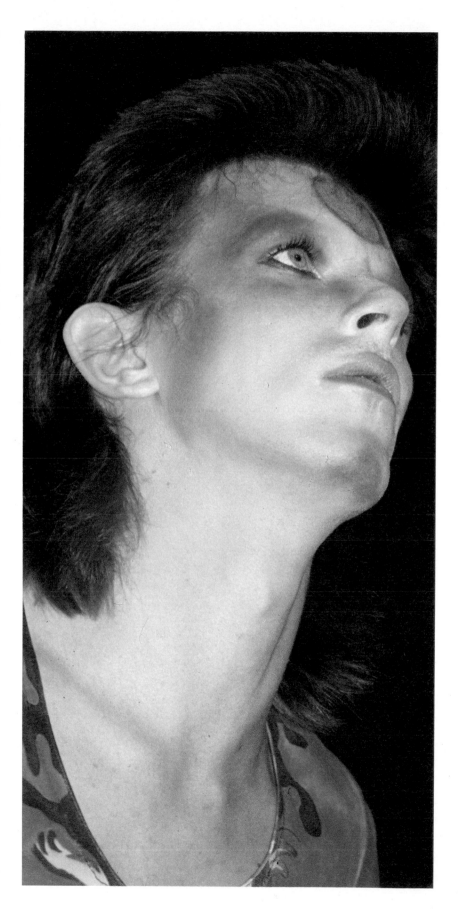

other personalities and sketch out new scenarios. There was, of course, a personal element in his work – the character of Aladdin Sane (a-lad-insane) was, for instance, apparently based on his brother Terry, who was committed to a mental institution when Bowie was in his mid-teens – but, as he frequently explained, he was fundamentally an actor-cum-dramatist who had chosen the rock album and the rock stage as his platform. He was playing at being the eponymous heroes of *The Rise and Fall of Ziggy Stardust* (1972) and *Aladdin Sane* (1973), just as at the beginning of his career he had quite deliberately fashioned himself and his songs in the style of Anthony Newley – interestingly, another actor-turned-singer who had jumped from pop stardom in the early Sixties to writing and performing in his own innovative stage musicals.

Bowie's interest in the theatrical aspects of rock – and his stage shows, especially that created around the *Ziggy Stardust* album, were dazzlingly spectacular – could be traced back to his admiration for Newley and his spell with the Lindsay Kemp mime troupe, while the musical and thematic strands in his work developed out of a number of diverse influences and associations. The pop-art experiments of Andy Warhol, Bowie's own training in commercial art, his experience in running an arts laboratory in Beckenham, and the records of proto-punk stars Iggy Pop and the Stooges and New York hard rock nihilists the Velvet Underground all left a major mark on Bowie's creative outlook, and he acknowledged and repaid the particular influence of these bands by producing solo albums for Iggy Pop and Lou Reed during 1972. Reed's preoccupation with sexual ambivalence was regularly echoed by Bowie, though with considerably less cynicism: for Bowie, bisexuality was a personal cause, and several of

the songs on *Hunky Dory* (1971) made explicit his vision of a future in which, to quote 'Oh You Pretty Things', 'homo sapiens have outgrown their use' and the pretty things themselves evolve into 'homo superiors'.

The high points of Bowie's early Seventies career were *Ziggy Stardust*, *Aladdin Sane* and *Diamond Dogs* (1974), each apocalyptic in tone and message, each tracing the decline of a culture in the face of an unspecified threat. *Ziggy Stardust* was arguably the most accomplished and original, its alternately optimistic and foreboding songs charting the fate of a space-age Messiah who becomes a rock'n'roll star, while *Diamond Dogs* was the most ambitious, a project initially planned as an album treatment of George Orwell's *1984* but radically altered after the novelist's estate refused to grant permission. The promotional tour that followed the album's release also found Bowie undertaking his most elaborate stage presentation yet, the key feature of which was an enormous set with moving sections that elevated the performer to breathtaking heights and angles. Accused by some of taking his ideas way over the top, he responded by

Bowie (top), although the single most important creative force in Seventies rock, drew inspiration from many diverse sources – including the outrageous Iggy Pop (above) whose Raw Power *album Bowie produced in 1972*

making the first of his notorious changes of pace, abruptly dropping his Velvets-inspired hard rock base and futuristic stance to record *Young Americans* (1975). An exercise in what he called 'plastic soul', it gave notice of his new-found interest in dance rhythms and marked a break with his glam-rock past. Bowie's move into the disco field presaged a new phase in rock that found the Bee Gees, Giorgio Moroder and other white performers and producers looking afresh at what had hitherto been a black-dominated sound. His motives, however, were more academic than commercial, the prospect of exploring disco's potential – and particularly the application to it

of new synthesiser technology – appealing to the avant-gardist, experimentalist instincts that had first sparked his interest in rock back in the late Sixties. Given this, it was logical that he should move beyond the simple reproduction of black styles that was the chief feature of *Young Americans* and the subsequent *Station to Station* (1976) to experiment with the uses of sound patterns and rhythmic repetitions within a dance music context. *Low* and *'Heroes'* (both 1977) confirmed this new direction, each the result of Bowie's collaboration with Brian Eno, former keyboard player with Roxy Music and latterly a keen exponent of electronic minimalism.

Below left: Bowie in 1976 and in 1978 (below), changing his image in line with his musical experimentalism

Bottom left: Lou Reed was another influence that Bowie freely acknowledged – he produced Reed's Transformer *album in 1972, thereby bringing the former Velvet Underground leader out of the shadows*

Roxy Music themselves were one of several bands to benefit directly from Bowie's commercial breakthrough around 1972, when the way suddenly became clear for groups with conventional 'progressive' appeal to blend their electronic, synthesiser-based wizardry with the visual style of glam-rock. Like many of the leading lights of the progressive era – and of the British R&B boom that preceded it – Roxy founder Bryan Ferry was an art school student well grounded in pop-art and avant-gardism, and the group was very much a reflection of his rococo tastes and his own sense of Hollywood style. Their music was pure flash, all metallic sound and elegant fury, while their image – following Ferry's conception – combined fashionable futurism with more than a hint of Twenties decadence. Musically they were brilliant, alluding to everything from movie soundtracks and latin American rhythms to unstructured jazz improvisations, but their air of emotional detachment, Ferry's dispassionately icy vocal delivery and their all-round clinicism alienated those looking for a degree

Roxy Music (left) was born of the brilliance of former art teacher Bryan Ferry but became rather too much his vehicle after the departure of Brian Eno in 1973. Independently of the group, Ferry began a solo career, grooming himself in the image of a Thirties lounge lizard and recording languid, world-weary songs of love among the cocktail set (far left)

of warmth in their music. When Eno left in 1973 after a clash with Ferry, the band lost something of its adventurism.

Bowie and Roxy Music apart, the early Seventies were, from a British point of view, light on big-league names who could last: the whole glam-rock era was better seen as a welcome, cheerful and modestly productive pause between two peak periods of pop creativity. Looking beyond the made-up faces, pretty clothes and regurgitated Sixties sounds, it was still possible to find the major progressive names consolidating their popularity – Pink Floyd producing their biggest selling album yet, *The Dark Side of the Moon*, and finally reaching the US market, while Eric Clapton returned to uncluttered, no-nonsense blues guitar as leader of the newly-formed Derek and the Dominoes. In the end, however, what characterised both the chart pop of the glam-rockers and the grand-scale musical outpourings of the more album-based groups was an air of safety, a lack of basic interest (the honourable Bowie excluded) in challenging any preconceptions. By 1976, the time was again ripe for change.

THIS IS THE MODERN WORLD
From punk-rock to new wave

Emerging from the punk venues of London, the rebel class of '76 threatened the fat-cat complacency of establishment rock

The UK singles chart for the first week of December, 1976, gave an accurate indication of the staid, ponderous state of mid-Seventies mainstream pop. At the top were Showaddywaddy, a bunch of doo-wop revivalists dressed in drapes, blue suede shoes and dark glasses, with a slick update of Curtis Lee's minor early Sixties hit, 'Under the Moon of Love'; lower down were two solidly professional exponents of US AOR music, Chicago and Dr Hook, whose UK success was due in no small measure to the opening and expansion (since 1973) of new commercial radio stations on the American model. Hits by Wild Cherry, Barry White and Yvonne Elliman underlined disco music's continuing strength, while glam-rock lingered on uncertainly in the form of 'Somebody to Love' by Queen, a heavy metal band with art school overtones, led

Bryan Ferry-style by former graphic designer Freddie ('I always knew I was a star and now the rest of the world seems to agree with me') Mercury. The burning question of the week was whether the Electric Light Orchestra, America's favourite UK band according to the latest sales figures, or Swedish supergroup hit machine Abba – their style somewhere between disco and high-tech AOR – would reach Number 1 in time for Christmas.

By the end of that week, however, the pop world had a new and – by Seventies standards – uncharacteristically controversial talking point: the sudden intrusion into all this safe, respectable music-making and money-spinning of the ugly face and sound of something called 'punk-rock'. The focus of the uproar was the appearance on prime-time television of the unsettlingly named Sex Pistols, a four-man punk band of calculated disrepute whose rise to cult fame had been steadily raising comment in the music press. Following just five minutes of airtime, they became national bêtes noires, their interview with professional cynic Bill Grundy ending in a shambles of swearing and gesticulating. Switchboards were jammed with calls of protest, and screaming headlines the next day told of London politicians' plans to ban this and any other would-be punk group from every venue in the city – on the grounds, it was said, of possible risks to public health and safety. As the furore grew and heads rolled at the television station involved, the Pistols' first single for EMI – with whom they had signed two months earlier, in return for a £40,000 advance – began picking up sales and staff in the company's pressing plant threatened to strike if they had to make more copies. Yet established rock venues were refusing to book them and, in January, EMI – intensely embarrassed by the controversy – revoked their contract.

At first, the Pistols seemed like an elaborate joke, a parody of the popular image of a rock band as violent, depraved, decadent and unmusical, and it was easy to believe the story – later documented in his film *The Great Rock'n'Roll Swindle* – that manager Malcolm McLaren had brought them together as part of a giant scam at the music industry's expense. But they were also part of a much wider, if somewhat ill-defined, punk sub-culture with its own network of meeting places, clothes shops, makeshift clubs and 'fanzines' – photocopied sheets put together on the cut-and-stick principle and filled with gig information, inside news and vitriolic editorials. It was through magazines like *Sniffin' Glue, Vortex* and *Live Wire* that the punk ideology was disseminated, its basis being a contempt for any kind of establishment values, a delight in confrontation and excess, a cultivation of a kind of gutter individualism, and a curiously noble belief in pure amateurism. Unlike mods and skinheads, punks were not simply 'alienated', they appeared to cut themselves off from society completely, wearing fashions calculated to give any prospective employer the horrors – ripped shirts, bin-liner dresses, Nazi regalia, bondage accessories, black and white make-up, nose studs, safety pin earrings. Similarly, punk music was a sound of savage, untutored, apparently unmarketable primitivism, so basic that the usual sense of distance between performer and audience was destroyed: as McLaren said, 'The Pistols don't play great and, as such, a kid in the audience can relate to that ... he can visualise himself being up there on stage'. It was this anyone-can-do-it spirit that in the end proved punk-rock's most significant legacy, with young people all over Britain following the advice offered by *Sniffin' Glue:* 'This is a chord. This is another. This is a third. *Now form a band'*.

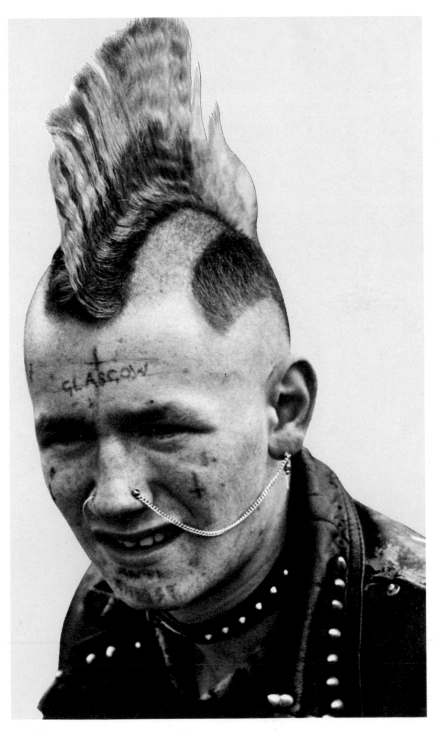

Below: punk fashion became ever more elaborate between 1976 and the end of the decade, developing beyond torn T-shirts and safety pins to incorporate bondage gear, black leathers, nose chains and Mohican haircuts

THE PUNK PLATFORM

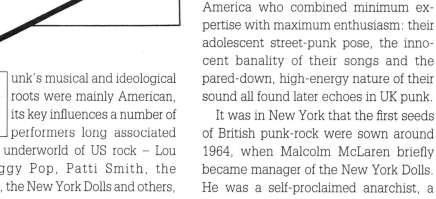

Punk's musical and ideological roots were mainly American, its key influences a number of performers long associated with the underworld of US rock – Lou Reed, Iggy Pop, Patti Smith, the Ramones, the New York Dolls and others, all of whom were renowned for a stark adhesion to rock'n'roll basics and an obsession with the twilight world of the urban outsider. Equally important as

Below: the man responsible for setting the punk style back in '76 was the redoubtable Malcolm McLaren (below) proprietor of Sex on London's Kings Road and creator/manager of the Sex Pistols

spiritual forerunners of the UK punk groups were the original rock do-it-yourselfers, the small-town and city suburb garage bands of mid-Sixties America who combined minimum expertise with maximum enthusiasm: their adolescent street-punk pose, the innocent banality of their songs and the pared-down, high-energy nature of their sound all found later echoes in UK punk.

It was in New York that the first seeds of British punk-rock were sown around 1964, when Malcolm McLaren briefly became manager of the New York Dolls. He was a self-proclaimed anarchist, a follower of the 'situationist' school of confrontation artists and the owner of a fashionably deviant clothing store on London's King's Road; the group were the kingpins of a highly exclusive Manhattan rock scene based around the Mercer Arts Center, a bizarre assemblage of performance spaces where arts academy dropouts, Dadaist intellectuals, Andy Warhol acolytes, street freaks, gays and bisexuals gathered to form bands and listen to others. Decadence was the scene's keynote, with bands like the Dolls, Teenage Lust, the Harlots and Ruby and the Rednecks dedicating themselves to the trash aesthetic propounded by Warhol since the mid-Sixties and articulated with some style by the Velvet Underground until their break-up in 1969. The Dolls, despite some minor commercial success, were already falling apart in a haze of heroin when McLaren followed them to New York after a particularly gross London appearance, but his six months of dressing them in red leather and re-launching them as pseudo-revolutionaries set fire to his entrepreneurial imagination.

Back in Britain, McLaren resumed his partnership with clothes designer Vivienne Westwood and, inspired by his American experience, changed the name of his shop to *Sex* and began packing the

187

FROM PUNK ROCK TO NEW WAVE

Above: clothes designer Vivienne Westwood (right) hangs out in Sex, the punk boutique she ran with Malcolm McLaren; punky friends include Steve Jones of the Sex Pistols (left) and future Pretender Chrissie Hynde (gesticulating with finger)

Below: Siouxsie of Banshees fame struts in S-M gear and Nazi armband

racks with the latest in New York punk fashion – rubberwear, bondage gear, multi-studded leathers, and torn T-shirts in the style popularised there by Richard Hell, bass player with the band Television. With a cult growing in London around the latest wave of bands from New York's underground clubland – Television, the Ramones and the Patti Smith Group among them – *Sex* became a key centre and source of neo-punk style. It also began to attract young dissolutes like Paul Cook and Steve Jones, whose talk of forming a rock band inspired McLaren to set a masterplan in motion: adding part-time *Sex* assistant Glen Matlock on bass and shifting Jones from his assumed role of singer to lead guitar, he started shaping the Sex Pistols as the ultimate statement in rock subversion. By late 1975, he had found a front-man of promising repulsiveness in occasional customer John Lydon, who was rechristened Johnny Rotten after the

state of his teeth. Green-haired, scrawny, dressed perpetually in a T-shirt that read 'I HATE', with his pallid and spotty face locked in an oily grimace, Lydon was a born punk who needed no tutoring from Malcolm McLaren.

Situations vacant

The Pistols' first gig, at St Martin's College of Art in November 1975, set the standard for things to come: an orgy of spitting, swearing and haranguing, it ended with bottles being thrown and the organisers pulling out the amplifier plugs. 'We're not into music, we're into chaos', ranted Johnny Rotten in *New Musical Express*, a point further demonstrated by a string of carefully engineered media events ('situations', McLaren called them, using best art college jargon) of which the Grundy interview was just one. And as the Pistols made their ramshackle progress through the colleges, pubs and clubs of the capital, so the punk cult gathered momentum and a string of bands sprang up in their shadow – some just established pub bands in a new uniform, some (like the Clash, the Damned and Siouxsie and the Banshees) managed by former McLaren aides and collaborators, and the rest mainly self-managed outfits formed from within the ranks of Pistols followers.

Specific events also had a formative effect on the growing scene, notably the 100 Club Festival of punk bands held over two nights in September 1976 and the opening during December of the Roxy Club in Neal Street, Covent Garden, which became the premier punk venue. The decision of the much larger Roundhouse in Camden Town to stage punk gigs on Sundays was equally crucial, as were the London appearances of Patti Smith, the Ramones and the Heartbreakers, the latter led by ex-New York Dolls pair Johnny Thunders and Jerry Nolan. In style and sound, these bands

Above: the New York Dolls on stage in Manhattan in 1973. Just like the Sex Pistols (led by Johnny Rotten, below) three years later, their scruffy sound and bizarre dress sense left no room for indifference

were models for countless emerging punk groups, and it was the imported notion of 'street credibility' – credited to Smith and her sidekick, rock critic-turned-musician Lenny Kaye – that became the key critical canon by which the groups liked to be judged. According to this thinking, musicianship mattered far less than a band's street-level awareness and the closeness of its members to their peer-group roots: the superstar trip was out, and to play the record industry game was to risk losing touch with those roots.

Despite all the anti-industry rhetoric however, the majority of punk bands found the lure of a record contract irresistible, though many followed the Pistols' example and made a point of being as obnoxious and unco-operative as possible with their respective companies. The companies themselves trod very gingerly at first, signing only those bands with an established live following,

but by the middle of 1977 the Jam (Polydor), the Stranglers (United Artists), the Clash (CBS) and pub combo-turned-punk band the Rods (Island) were all seeing chart action. The Pistols, meanwhile, went from EMI to A & M and along the way sacked Glen Matlock for becoming too proficient; a week later, the group were once again label-less after the behaviour of his replacement, the musically incompetent Sid Vicious, caused ructions at their first and only A & M press reception. Finally, Virgin Records – hitherto most associated with just one release, the triple-million selling *Tubular Bells* by multi-instrumentalist Mike Oldfield – took a calculated gamble and signed them just in time for 'God Save the Queen', the Pistols' gruesome tongue-lashing of Her Majesty's England, to hit the Silver Jubilee week chart. The record peaked at Number 2 despite a blanket radio ban, and Virgin maintained that it had been kept from the

FROM PUNK ROCK TO NEW WAVE

top only by chart compilers anxious to protect the Queen from embarrassment.

Punk variations

As the year went on, punk bands grew in number, popularity and – to the scorn of some of the original punks – musical ability. Many religiously followed the Pistols' blueprint – recorded for posterity on their late 1977 album *Never Mind the Bollocks, Here's the Sex Pistols* – of unmodulated guitar chords, venomous mock-cockney vocals and rabble-rousing, screw everything lyrics, but there were variations. The Clash led punk's

political school of bands with their own brand of riot charge rock, giving credence to the fashionable analysis of punk as a reaction against repression and the drudgery of the dole queue. Offering a battery of songs littered with social issues and a musical range that took in reggae and even a hint of Chuck Berry – echoing leader Joe Strummer's earlier spell with pub rockers the 101ers – they were punk's true heavyweights from the start and never lost their polemical edge. An equally committed but more individualistic note was struck by the Jam, a threesome from Woking who raised the ire of their first Roxy audience in late 1976 by taking the stage in Sixties mod gear. Unashamedly evocative of the best of the Who, the Kinks and other mod bands, their songs – mostly written by lead singer/guitarist Paul Weller – had not only punk anger and attack but wit and literacy, locating the enemy in the British class system and drawing acidic word pictures ('Eton Rifles', 'Down in the Tube Station at Midnight') of class war in microcosm.

Different again were the Buzzcocks, whose strength was fast, quirky, high-energy punk romance, their approach typified by the deliberate gaucheness of their 1978 hit 'Ever Fallen in Love (With Someone You Shouldn't've)'. A Manchester-based band and as such a reminder of punk-rock's impact way beyond London, they were also one of the first punk bands to produce and distribute their own record on their own label, thereby keeping their punk integrity intact. In content, style and demeanour they could not have been more different from a band like the Damned, who personified punk's more laughable extreme: Hammer horror caricatures with a Dracula-like lead singer and a heavy metal bent, their motives were at least candid – 'Anyone with any honesty will admit', mused drummer Rat Scabies,

'that all they want out of this business is a colour TV and £25,000 a year' – and they did manage to outlast nearly all their punk rivals by still figuring in the charts some eight years later.

Perhaps the real ground-breakers of punk, however, were its women – performers like Poly Styrene of X-Ray Spex and Arri Up of the Slits, who turned the traditional role of women in rock completely on its head by not only leading bands but using their position to scream out contempt for conventional standards of femininity. Traditionally, female singers peddled male fantasy, singing sweetly or sexily as the (usually male-written) song required; frilly frocks or low-cut dresses enhanced the effect. Poly Styrene, by contrast, shrieked messages like 'Oh Bondage, Up Yours' through a toothbrace, while Arri wore Jubilee knickers over wet-look trousers and sang of boredom, prowlers, life in the new towns and shoplifting for kicks. Siouxsie and the Banshees, the Raincoats and others followed up some of the same themes and dressed and sang with similar stridency, in a deliberately mannered and alienating vocal style that was soon adopted to great effect by Hazel O'Connor.

Punk was all about upsetting conventional values and stereotypes – and bands like the Slits (below) led an onslaught on rock's innate sexism. A harsh, shrill vocal style was a characteristic of female punk, and one imitated successfully by Hazel O'Connor (below right), star of the first of several pseudo-punk films, Breaking Glass

A NEW WAVE BREAKING

A longside its performers and McLaren-like hustlers, punk-rock had key propagators and pioneers behind the scenes, in the industry and in the media – men like BBC Radio One disc jockey John Peel and *New Musical Express* journalists Nick Kent, Charles Shaar Murray and Tony Parsons, whose coverage of un-signed bands was often instrumental in winning them contracts. Peel's surpris-ing conversion to punk after years of association with the progressive rock fringe was especially important: obliged by BBC-Musicians Union agreements to feature specially recorded sessions, he and producer John Walters went out to find bands rather than wait for the record companies to provide them. Sometimes they found them in the clubs, but just as often they discovered exceptional, un-tried talent among the huge pile of home-made demonstration tapes that began arriving daily at Radio One. Getting a Peel session became the recognised way of catching the ear of a record company, and Siouxsie and the Banshees, the Undertones, Joy Division and Altered Images were among scores of groups to benefit directly from his endorsement.

In the absence of such a benefactor – and there was a limit to the number of bands that Peel could promote so self-lessly – some bands found that a little self-help and a comparatively modest outlay could pay rich dividends. As the Buzzcocks showed by their example, any band could create and finance their own one-off label, limit their initial production run to anything between 1,000 and

25,000 copies, sell them all to fans via personal appearances and local record dealers, and still make a small profit out of an initial outlay of £500. The precedent was intensively followed, by managers and agents as well as bands: in London, for instance, UK-based American accountant Miles Copeland replaced the expense accounts of his faltering British Talent Management company with a shoestring operation under which his group of labels (Illegal, Step Forward, Deptford Fun City) released short runs of singles by unknown bands, his brother Stewart's new outfit the Police among them. The expanding independent scene also prompted a dealer in West London, Geoff Travis of Rough Trade, to start his own mail-order and shop service for the distribution of what was termed 'alternative' product. For the committed rock fan, such discs were the only credible source of punk and new wave music, while the bands themselves found that a place on Rough Trade's independent chart (initiated in late 1977) was an invaluable indication of their potential to any major label thinking of signing them.

All this amounted to a radically new approach to the economics of record-making in Britain, though small-scale, local independent labels had been a fixture of the US recording scene for years. It was partly in honour of the famous US indie labels of the past – Sun, Philles, Chess, Motown – that Britain's most successful punk-era independent, Stiff, was established in 1976, though the label's name (industry slang for an unsaleable record) was a sign of the initially tongue-in-cheek nature of the whole operation. Like Philles, Stiff released

Ian Dury was one of 1977's rising new wave stars, but prior to his success with the Blockheads he led one of the most acclaimed bands on the London pub rock circuit, Kilburn and the High Roads (above)

Dr Feelgood (above) and Graham Parker (above right) had two of the biggest followings on the London pub scene but – a handful of minor hit singles apart – failed to make the national impact they deserved. Parker was managed in his early pub-playing days by Dave Robinson, who formed Stiff Records in 1976, partly as an outlet for pub-rock talent. Stiff's first chart hit however, came from punk band the Damned (below right), whose line-up included future UK chart-topper Captain Sensible (pictured second from left)

records selectively, avoiding the scatter-shot release-ten-and-one's-bound-to-stick policy of the majors, and promoted each one individually: by using eye-catching picture bags and witty, skilfully-placed advertising, and marketing their releases through specialist shops, they managed to publicise their product without incurring vast expense. Like Motown, the label sent all its artists on a big cross-country tour, grandly hiring a special train and holding meet-the-people sessions on station platforms. Like Sun's Sam Phillips, Stiff bosses Jake Riviera and Dave Robinson based their A&R policy firmly on their own personal taste, to the extent of signing numerous ex-pub band buddies – Nick Lowe of Brinsley Schwarz, Jona Lewie of Brett Marvin and the Thunderbolts, Ian Dury of Kilburn and the High Roads – to the label in its early days. Legend even had it that Stiff was started on a £400 loan from yet another pub circuit regular, Lee Brilleaux of Dr Feelgood.

Pub connections

Stiff's first punk signing was The Damned in late 1976, but the label became most associated with a more general wackiness, favouring art school eccentrics and

uncategorisable acts that major labels would not touch. It had a punk *attitude*, born in the sweaty, boozy atmosphere of London's popular pub music scene in which both Robinson and Riviera had worked as managers of R&B specialists Graham Parker and Chilli Willi and the Red Hot Peppers respectively, and its sense of adventure and nose-thumbing at the rest of the industry were right in keeping with punk-style alternativism. That many of the Stiff acts were somewhat older and certainly more musically accomplished than their punk counterparts disgruntled those of a more purist

punk persuasion, but such people tended to forget the clear influence of pub rock stalwarts like Ian Dury on the punk-rockers themselves: Johnny Rotten, for instance, had been a frequent visitor to the shows of Kilburn and the High Roads and had obviously based his microphone mannerisms, hunched posturings and audience-baiting on the albeit less alienating Dury model.

Dury himself was Stiff's most surprising success of 1977-78, a disabled, overcoat-wearing, blunt-speaking singer-songwriter with a runt-of-the-litter image and a set of songs (written with keyboardist Chas Jankel) that spoke plainly and often hilariously of personal paranoia and sexual frustration. Although pictured in the press as a cheerful cockney-type with music-hall leanings, his *New Boots and Panties!!* album (1977) had a maniacal, on-the-edge quality reminiscent of the best of US singer-writer Randy Newman but without his sense of detachment. He was the first Stiff artist to reach Number 1, with 'Hit Me With Your Rhythm Stick' in 1978, and he also wrote the all-time perfect encapsulation of punk ennui in 'Sex and Drugs and Rock and Roll', released as a single in 1977.

Dury apart, Stiff's most significant long-term discovery – though he left the label with Jake Riviera in 1977, when the latter formed Radar Records – was another former pub rocker, Flip City's guitarist/singer Elvis Costello. Modelling his image on Buddy Holly and affecting a sneering, rapid-fire vocal delivery that was widely imitated, Costello had no cheery veneer to make his unsparingly condemnatory songs more palatable: he was an updated version of a Fifties angry young man, bristling with belligerence towards anybody or anything that smacked of phoniness, dishonesty or self-interested conservatism. His targets included the creeping threat of neo-

fascism ('Night Rally', 'Goon Squad'), the fripperies of fashion ('[I Don't Want to Go to] Chelsea'), the power and influence of the media ('Watching the Detectives', 'Radio Radio'), and the 'murder mile' of mercenary life ('Oliver's Army'), but he was not above turning his rage on himself, as the self-mocking title of *This Year's Model*, his second and biggest-selling album, showed. An outstanding song craftsman and a musician well prepared to look beyond the familiar rock mode for inspiration – witness his stabs at soul and country styling in *Get Happy!!* (1979) and *Almost Blue* (1981) –

Above: Elvis Costello started out in a pub band, Flip City, and made his mark with the Nick Lowe-produced My Aim is True *on Stiff in 1977. One of contemporary rock's most caustic and unpredictable figures, his career has encompassed excursions into soul and country music, production work for the Specials, Robert Wyatt and others, and an acting role in the film* No Surrender, *released during 1986*

195

FROM PUNK ROCK TO NEW WAVE

he was for many the most genuinely provocative voice of the time, occasionally over-prone to self-conscious cynicism but rarely less than challenging.

Punk fragments

Stiff, Costello and Dury between them helped broaden the punk perspective, maintaining the anarchic spirit and anti-authority pose of punk but re-introducing the traditional skills of musicianship and songwriting. Their impact could be clearly seen on first-generation punk bands like the Boomtown Rats and Squeeze, who rose majestically out of 1977's punk group glut by switching away from punk's familiar buzzsaw drone and featuring songs that explored something other than the stock themes of discontent and the lure of the barricades. The Rats, under Bob Geldof, progressed from neat but conventional teenage runaway tales like 'Rat Trap' to the melodramatic but affecting 'I Don't Like Mondays', which encouraged the listener to sympathise with or at least understand the motives of a teenage killer. Squeeze attempted to bolster their punk credentials by calling in ex-Velvet Underground bassist John Cale to produce their first album, but found their real niche under folk-rock producer John Wood, who gave their Ray Davies-like portraits of south London life ('Up the Junction', 'Cool for Cats') a

smoother, cleaner setting.

Newly-formed bands also took the hint. The Pretenders, put together by ex-Malcolm McLaren shopgirl and one-time *New Musical Express* journalist Chrissie Hynde, hired Nick Lowe to produce their first recordings in studio time donated by Elvis Costello. Their sound, built on Chrissie's Dusty Springfield/Dionne

Warwick-inspired vocals and the jingle-jangle Byrds-like guitar work of James Honeyman-Scott and Pete Farndon, had a mid-Sixties feeling also typical of the music of two other newcomers, Joe Jackson and Dire Straits. Neither act could claim any punk connections whatsoever, but both combined street-wise songwriting, soaked in urban images, with solid musical ability – in Jackson's case, a clever ear for re-working half-forgotten sounds and song-hooks (like the introductory riff of 'Is She Really Going Out With Him', lifted straight from Wayne Fontana's 'The Game of Love'), and Mark Knopfler's crystalline lead guitar playing in the case of Dire Straits.

The change in emphasis from punk-rock to what was increasingly called 'new wave' music suited the record industry: not only was the music more accessible and less controversial, it had the potential to cross national frontiers and reach the US market in particular. From 1977 onwards, the A&R departments of the major companies worked overtime, either signing new bands that vaguely fitted the new wave concept or making national distribution deals with independents for the release of material by already contracted bands. Within a year or so, new wave was a term applied to anything from the hard-edged R&B of Dr Feelgood and Graham Parker – belatedly making a chart impact – to heavily derivative groups like the Pleasers, the Yachts, the Smirks and the Rich Kids, who played a more frantic version of Sixties UK beat music and were briefly lauded as pioneers of 'power-pop'. All became victims of the period's volatile rock environment, though the Rich Kids featured the promising line-up of ex-Sex Pistol Glen Matlock and later Ultravox front-man Midge Ure, who before Johnny Rotten appeared had been pencilled in by Malcolm McLaren as the Pistols' vocalist. Such was the new wave preoccupation

FROM PUNK ROCK TO NEW WAVE

By 1979, Britain's punk-inspired music scene was fast fragmenting and even Kate Bush (above) was being touted by EMI as a 'new wave' talent. It was a time of political activism on a broad scale: the Tom Robinson Band played in support of many political causes, including Gay Pride Week (top)

during 1978 that even Kate Bush, brought to EMI fresh from school by Pink Floyd guitarist Dave Gilmour, was so bracketed: her wailing voice, other-worldly songs and idiosyncratic use of mime and choreography made her a new and very different talent, but she was as far removed from the original punk explosion as it was possible to get.

For the diehard punks, such developments signalled the beginning of the end, a final negation of everything that the first punk bands had set out to achieve. But it was myopic to blame the demise of punk on industry exploitation alone, or on the understandable desire of its early heroes to make musical and career progress: the facts were that the original punk scene in London had already changed beyond recognition and punk's initial sense of unity was fast dissipating into a dangerous factionalism. This was partly a

consequence of the political atmosphere of the time, which found extremist right-wing organisations like the National Front and the British Movement exploiting the aggression and fascistic iconography of punk for their own ends; in response to this, the Anti-Nazi League was formed with the backing of punk's most politically aware acts – the Tom Robinson Band, the Gang of Four, Crass and the Ruts among them. Fighting at gigs between punks, skinheads and fringe ANL supporters became commonplace, and the emergence of the so-called 'Oi!' movement, led by skinhead bands roaring football-terrace-like chants with explicit racist sentiments, heightened the tension. One such band, the Four Skins, sparked off a full-scale riot after appearing at a pub in the predominantly Asian district of Southall, West London: the punk era had reached its nadir.

AMERICAN ECHOES

The year 1979 also saw the death of Sid Vicious (below, pictured with his equally ill-starred girlfriend, Nancy Spungen) in New York, a matter of months after the departure of Johnny Rotten from the Sex Pistols

Reaction in the US to the British new wave was at first muted, the attitudes of record-buyers and radio programmers alike heavily coloured by the debacle of the Sex Pistols' American tour in 1978. Violence had been a feature of virtually every date on the tour, and it ended with Johnny Rotten leaving the group in disgust and making a prophetic comment. 'Steve can go off and be Peter Frampton', he snorted, finally tired of acting the slob, 'Sid can go off and kill himself and no-one will care. Paul can go back to being an electrician, and Malcolm will always be a wally'. A few months later Sid Vicious did indeed take his own life, with a heroin overdose, following his arrest in New York for the murder of his girlfriend Nancy Spungen. When, just a few weeks after that, Elvis Costello undertook his first US tour and provoked fierce demonstrations against his allegedly racist remarks about Ray Charles and James Brown, the mood of some industry people towards UK music turned to outright hostility. It would be 1982 before UK bands made any real breakthrough.

For America's own 'new wave' acts – and the term was an American one, first applied to the likes of Patti Smith and the Heartbreakers – mainstream acceptance was equally long in coming, thanks in part to the country's late Seventies obsession with all things disco. That particular boom, abetted by the enormous success in 1977 of the film *Saturday Night Fever* and its Bee Gees-originated soundtrack album, inspired even rock's leviathan performers – the Rolling

FROM PUNK ROCK TO NEW WAVE

Stones, Rod Stewart and the Beach Boys included – to flirt with dance floor rhythms, while also generating its own 'underground' culture of exclusive night clubs and gay bars. If new wave rock had its heart in the streets and took pride in its sense of realism, disco belonged to the plush, escapist fantasy world of leisure holes like the notorious Studio 54 in Manhattan, where Grace Jones – staring, impenetrable, androgynous – performed unsmilingly with an assortment of male dancers in various stages of semi-nudity. Against this kind of competition in their own New York backyard, punk acts such as Television, Wayne County and Mink de Ville found it hard to get taken seriously beyond the new wave ghetto.

US new wave also faced another problem: while UK punk-rock was a shared experience, a movement in which it was difficult to tell consumers from performers, its American equivalent lacked this participatory base. Clubs like CBGBs and Max's Kansas City catered for a largely passive clientele, as footage shot at the former venue and featured in

the 1977 film *Blank Generation* showed – here were long-haired college types sitting politely in rows and staring up bemusedly at the seedy posturings of Wayne County, the ripped T-shirt and spiked hair of Richard Hell and the ghostly pallor of Television lead singer Tom Verlaine. Neither did the New York new wave scene throw up its own network of successful independent labels, despite the pioneering efforts of Seymour Stein at Sire, who secured world-wide distribution for his artists' releases by signing a deal with Warner Brothers. Other indies like Ork, Shake and Goli never grew into more than one-shot operations, their inability to get past the format-minded, 'quality'-demanding FM

At the vanguard of the American new wave stood figures like Richard Hell (above left), who played alongside Tom Verlaine in Television and ex-New York Dolls Johnny Thunders and Jerry Nolan in the Heartbreakers before forming his own band, Richard Hell and the Voidoids. Devo (above) were five graduates from Kent State University who played jagged, angular, metallic music with a manically comic edge

Jonathan Richman (top right) and Television (centre right) were both bracketed as new wave acts, yet had vastly different approaches. Richman favoured an avowedly naive pop minimalism, which he developed on an increasingly eccentric series of albums; Television drew on the expansiveness of Sixties San Francisco rock and the avant-garde jazz of John Coltrane and Albert Ayler. The B-52s (bottom right) revelled in Fifties and Sixties kitsch and recorded tracks with titles like 'Rock Lobster', 'Quiche Lorraine' and 'Throw That Beat in the Garbage Can'

radio gatekeepers costing them the wider exposure they needed.

The transatlantic trek

To the New York bands who heard and read of the mysterious and exciting punk-rock on the other side of the Atlantic, London was really the only place to be in 1977. Demand for suitably 'street credible' New York acts had grown there since the 1976 appearances of Patti Smith and the Ramones, and there was also an increasing cult appreciation – fuelled by New Musical Express, Time Out and the trusty John Peel – of wayward, punk-type acts from other parts of the US like Jonathan Richman and the Modern Lovers, Devo and the B-52s. It was one of the lesser-known New York groups however, called Blondie, who took the bold decision to forsake their home ground for a while and concentrate solely on making a name in Britain. Their reward was major album and singles success, a surprisingly young, teenybopper following, extensive national press and television coverage, and eventual acceptance back in the US, where their sales far eclipsed those of any of their new wave contemporaries.

Blondie grew out of a minor CBGBs band called the Stilettoes, who performed mostly girl-group material of the early Sixties in a camp style. Singer Debbie Harry and guitarist-boyfriend Chris Stein renamed the group in 1974 and brought in a new rhythm section that included drummer Clem Burke, who was

Debbie Harry (below and opposite page, top) led Blondie out of America's new wave ghetto to huge success in Europe, their style a pot-pourri of swiftly-assimilated influences ranging from punk to disco, from reggae to rap

steeped in Sixties pop and British beat in particular. Together, Harry, Stein and Burke devised Blondie as a vehicle for a new kind of pop that would echo the past yet project a modern, urban veneer, and they used Britain as the testing ground. Signed by Chrysalis, an independent label established at the height of the progressive era in the late Sixties, they planned each step with precision, first building up a cult following via live appearances and then making a startling television debut on BBC's traditionally sedate *Old Grey Whistle Test* to promote their single 'Denis'. Dressed only (or so it seemed) in an oversize man's shirt and putting on an image of Sunday school innocence laced with Monroe-like sensuality, Debbie was revealed as a sex symbol for the new age. Following that

dance rhythms that would be a characteristic of early Eighties rock. Commercially, too, Blondie set a major precedent in their use of video as a promotional technique and were one of the first bands to release an album on record and video-cassette simultaneously – *Eat to the Beat* in 1979.

Manhattan transfers

Blondie's success was a classic marketing coup, but it left the genuine American new wavers unimpressed. Although it did encourage companies to sign new wave acts – or re-investigate their deals with New York independents – there was no chart takeover on the UK scale and those who benefited most were bogus imitation-punk bands from the west coast like the Knack, whose discs were also produced by Mike Chapman. Taking many of their ideas from bands like the Raspberries and the Flamin' Groovies, who had started in the late Sixties as straight pop-rock bands and never deviated from that course, the Knack were launched in 1979 as beat revivalists in the manner of Britain's power-pop bands. They were well-drilled and professional, but the smutty nature of their teenage-lust songs – typified by 'Good Girls Don't'

with appearances on every television music show going, including children's Saturday morning programmes, Blondie became almost instant stars.

Musically, Blondie remained true to their plan and they brought in producer Mike Chapman to help them achieve the next stage. He had been responsible for writing and producing dozens of UK pop hits in the early Seventies for artists like Sweet, Suzi Quatro and Mud, and his appreciation of the requirements of AM radio programmers was second to none. Their first album with Chapman, *Parallel Lines* (1978), contained four major hit singles, among them the most innovative record in marketing terms of the late Seventies – 'Heart of Glass', which daringly featured Harry's voice over a streamlined, synthesiser-based disco backing. The track gave them their long awaited US breakthrough and paved the way not only for Blondie's subsequent work with Eurodisco producer Giorgio Moroder, but for the widespread matching of new wave sensibility to disco

The eventual American success of Blondie aside, the new wave bands of the US east coast found it notoriously difficult to make commercial progress in their homeland. It was left to a California band, the Knack, (below), to take on some of the visual and musical attributes of the new wave bands and turn them to their advantage, though the group's single-minded pursuit of the teenybopper audience was unpalatable to many

FROM PUNK ROCK TO NEW WAVE

Patti Smith (below) was labelled 'the high priestess of punk' early in her career and built her reputation via her vastly influential Horses album in 1975. Her biggest commercial success came with a single, 'Because the Night' (1978), written in collaboration with Bruce Springsteen. Her contemporaries in the New York club scene included Talking Heads (bottom, pictured on a 1980 tour), whose own success and influence developed on an international scale during the Eighties

and 'Baby Talks Dirty', both big Top 40 hits – and the contempt for their audience implicit in album titles like *But the Little Girls Understand* . . . caused offence to many both inside and outside the rock business.

As the Seventies drew to a close, the Manhattan clubs played host to a number of new bands of whom the Fleshtones, the Raybeats, the Bongos and the Lenny Kaye Connection were the pick, but to some the old energy was missing. The original club bands had mostly moved on or broken up: Patti Smith signed off with *Wave* in 1979 before disbanding her Group and settling down to married life with former MC5 guitarist Fred 'Sonic' Smith, and the Ramones – undeviatingly and ecstatically moronic in their endless regurgitation of punk's basic three-chord trick – carried on playing songs like 'Teenage Lobotomy', 'I Wanna Sniff Some Glue' and 'Judy is a Punk' before audiences in large arenas and halls, later branching out into films and a short-lived association with Phil Spector. Of all the Manhattan originals, only Talking Heads made the transition into the big league of internationally respected, critically acclaimed, platinum album-selling bands, a status that had much to do with their move into the realm of electronic funk

around 1979. With ex-Roxy Music keyboard player and Bowie collaborator Brian Eno becoming almost a fifth member – he co-produced *More Songs About Buildings and Food* (1978) and *Fear of Music* (1979) – they rose to determinedly intellectual heights with *Remain in Light* in 1980, building up rhythm patterns from tape loops made from studio jam sessions and adding on layer after layer of intricate cross-rhythms. To these, Heads founder David Byrne added lyrics adapted from broadcasts by radio evangelists he had taped for an earlier solo album. One of the tracks, 'Once in a Lifetime', became a hit single in 1981, but all this was a far cry from their beginnings as CBGBs regulars, when their bare, angular sound and studiedly ordinary image revealed the particular influence of Jonathan Richman, with whom Heads guitarist Jerry Harrison had once played.

It was Richman who exemplified the minimalist tendencies of new wave, emerging in the mid-Seventies as a champion of the simple and commonplace in music. His songs were loopy love celebrations set to plain garage band rhythms and sung in a warbly, bleating voice, and he was infatuated with the idea of paring them down to their most basic elements. 'The whole reason we're doing what we're doing is to be contrary' was his explanation for his oddball approach, which in time extended to dropping all amplification from his stage performances and a policy of writing only children's songs. 'Roadrunner' brought him a Top 20 hit in Britain during 1977, but his ideas had a considerably wider impact. He stayed truer than any other artist to the do-it-yourself philosophy of punk, which he summed up in his own way: 'We have to learn to play with nothing, with our guitars broken, and it's raining'. Richman's 1977 album, *Rock 'n' Roll with the Modern Lovers* summed up his musical philosophy.

Easily the most laudable aspect of the punk and new wave boom was that rock underwent a much needed process of demystification, with young people realising that there was just as much fun and satisfaction to be gained from making music as from spending hard-earned money on some superstar band's latest platinum-album concoction. In terms of encouraging the formation of new bands, punk had an impact comparable with skiffle in the Fifties and the beat group explosion of the Sixties – the difference being that the late Seventies groups stood a much better chance of being heard, thanks to the mini-revolution in recording, pressing and distribution that was another legacy of the punk years.

Yet although undeniably radical in intent, punk-rock was in form a very traditional music, rooted in the Sixties beat ethic and as regressive in some ways as the professionally made rock it sought to expiate. As with skiffle and beat music, in the end it was what the new musicians made of the lessons learned that was so significant – how they, like their predecessors, could fashion a new music for their particular time, one that reflected the special tensions, problems and pleasures of the late Seventies and after. If punk-rock itself died because it stood still, its great contribution was to renew hope for the creative and commercial future of rock music at large.

Punk-rock was important in itself and also for what it made possible. Few bands kept the punk flag flying as single-mindedly as the Clash (above), who – despite occasional bouts of critical censure – survived into the Eighties with their original goals intact

CHAPTER 10

KARMA CHAMELEONS
Rock in the Eighties

How reggae, disco rhythms and the new technology pointed the way to a multi-faceted rock future

The Police (opposite) based their style on a synthesis of rock and reggae, while the Specials (below) revived Jamaican ska. Although very different in appeal and approach, the two bands shared roots in the punk era and were among the most influential new acts of 1979-81

In July 1981, the Specials entered the UK chart with 'Ghost Town', a bleak and unsettling lament for a once-booming city in the grip of economic recession. 'Bands don't play no more/too much fighting on the dance floor ... can't go on no more/people getting angry', ran the lyric, while the track ended with the sound of distant police sirens and wind whistling through a derelict factory. It was a record with despair and disquiet all but ingrained in its grooves, made by a group who had come together partly to escape the dole queue, and it was released on an independent, provincially-based label – 2-Tone, in industrial Coventry – that made no secret of its anti-government leanings. But 'Ghost Town' packed a particular punch because of its topicality:

it reached Number One at the very height of some of the worst rioting ever seen in mainland Britain, when youthful discontent erupted into violence and open confrontation with authority in the decaying inner city areas of London, Liverpool, Manchester, Birmingham and elsewhere. There were few other moments in rock history when a hit disc so chillingly reflected the climate of its time.

The Specials were typical of numerous bands in the early Eighties who believed, in the words of UB40 drummer Jim Brown, that 'a dance band is a package to sell your politics'. Cloaking their didactic songs about unemployment, racism and the threat of nuclear war in the light West Indian rhythms of ska, rocksteady and reggae, such groups attempted to radicalise teenage dance music and to reclaim rock – at a time when a few old

The Selecter (above) sang angrily of unemployment, racism and inner city boredom. They followed their 2-Tone stablemates the Specials into the UK chart during 1979 with 'On My Radio' but broke away from the label a year later, claiming that the 2-Tone sound had become stereotyped

warhorses like Rod Stewart and the Bee Gees were freely giving support to Margaret Thatcher – as left-of-centre territory. Their influence was perhaps overstated by a music press anxious to maintain its left-wing credentials, but on a general level they did highlight the social context in which all UK rock in the first half of the Eighties was created and sold – that of increasing youth unemployment and changing leisure patterns. In practical terms, lack of jobs meant more leisure time for those affected, and there were many instances of school leavers and the long-term jobless forming bands to fill that time constructively and, maybe, find a route out of what politicians were starting to call 'the urban wasteland'. Even the much derided 'new romantics' cult of 1980, started by young London élitists with a passion for over-dressing and self-aggrandisement, was in its own way a creative response to the prevailing no-hope atmosphere of the period – a naïve but attractive invitation to ignore day-to-day realities and commit oneself to self-achievement and the pursuit of pleasure for its own sake. As one leading 'romantic', Gary Kemp of

Spandau Ballet, put it, 'Our music is about enjoying yourself, looking good and having a laugh . . . we are trying to tell kids not to condemn themselves into thinking opportunities are slim. What kids do have is their individuality'.

Unemployment among the young was also blamed for the record industry's own mini-recession from 1979 onwards, although other factors like the increased home taping of records, the competition for leisure expenditure from video games and computer software, and the success of the new independent labels at the expense of the majors contributed equally to the slump in sales of nationally distributed albums and singles. The net effect was that major UK companies were forced to cut back on staff and output, to streamline their A & R policies and to intensify their promotional efforts around the most obvious sources of profit – the big selling bands. New marketing devices like expensively-produced video films (offered free to television programmes), picture discs, limited-edition releases of singles in 12in format and free gifts to retailers as a reward for large orders, were widely seen as examples of industry profligacy, but in fact they were signs of panic, indications of how far the labels were prepared to go in an effort to secure sales and a return on their investment. Pressure for results also meant that the time gap between an individual act's releases became ever shorter, with a follow-up often hitting the shops at the first hint of its predecessor slipping down the chart: bands therefore tended to burn themselves out very quickly and experience a much shorter chart career than their counterparts in previous pop eras. In general, the scope for risk-taking was narrower than ever – and this, ironically, at a time when the creative state of UK rock, as measured by the number and quality of new bands forming, had never been healthier.

REGGAE MEETS ROCK

Chris Blackwell (bottom right) used his label, Island Records, to pioneer Jamaican music in Britain. His release policy encompassed numerous reggae productions by leading Jamaican producer Coxsone Dodd (bottom), who worked with many of the music's best-known names. Among them were Toots and the Maytals (below) – Toots Hibbert (centre), flanked by Nathaniel 'Jerry' Mathias (left) and Henry 'Raleigh' Gordon

T he real risk-takers and innovators were, as usual, the independent companies, and it was they who spearheaded one of the key stylistic developments of the new decade – the incorporation of West Indian music and reggae in particular into mainstream rock. 2-Tone was at the forefront of this, but the essential groundwork had been laid some years before by a longer established independent with solid Caribbean connections – Chris Blackwell's Island label. A white Jamaican, Blackwell formed Island in 1962 as a UK outlet for Jamaican product and later expanded its base by signing progressive rock acts like Traffic, Free and Cat Stevens. In 1972, he sold his interest in the Trojan label – effectively an Island subsidiary – to the similarly reggae-based B & C Records but retained two acts who, in his judgement, had the potential to reach a worldwide rock audience. One, Toots and the Maytals, won a respected critical following but made only a limited commercial breakthrough; the other, Bob Marley and the Wailers, justified Blackwell's faith by becoming not only international ambassadors of reggae but semi-legendary figures, as important to the struggle for black identity in Jamaica and in Britain as soul stars like James Brown and Sam Cooke had been in the US.

The Wailers' career mirrored the various changes within Jamaican music since the early Sixties, particularly the evolution of ska – essentially a hybrid of traditional West Indian calypso-like 'mento' music with imported and hugely popular American R & B – into the more soul-inflected rocksteady and reggae itself. At the time of their formation in 1962, the Jamaican music scene was dominated by disc jockeys like Coxsone Dodd, Leslie Kong and Duke Reid, who ran customised mobile sound systems

Above: Bob Marley with a portrait of Haile Selassie. The Ethiopian emperor – whose original name was Ras Tafari Makonnen – was a figurehead for the Rastafarian faith, which finds much expression in reggae music. Marley set one of Haile Selassie's speeches to music to form the song 'War' on his 1976 album, Vibration

and produced records made by local talent for their own turntable use. It was Dodd who took the Wailers under his wing and championed their first local success in 1964 with 'Simmer Down' – a ska song directed, typically, at the 'rude boys' or tough shanty town youths of Kingston among whom the Wailers had a special following. They disbanded in 1966 but original members Marley, Peter Tosh and Bunny Livingston came together again two years later and, after flirting unsuccessfully with the newly popular rocksteady mode, found their real niche in the reggae style perfected and polished by producer Lee 'Scratch' Perry on discs by the Upsetters and others. Working with Perry from 1969

onwards, the Wailers developed into a tight rock-oriented unit, with Bob Marley's plaintive, reedy voice well to the fore and brothers Aston and Carlton Barrett joining from the Upsetters (on bass and drums respectively) to give an extra sense of power and density to the group's sound.

Their association with Island began with *Catch a Fire*, which was recorded in Kingston on an £8,000 loan from Blackwell and was considerably revised, rearranged and edited by him before release. Wayne Perkins, a Muscle Shoals session man, overdubbed lead guitar on the album's nine songs, while Texan keyboard-player John 'Rabbit' Bundrick made substantial additions to the sound,

Peter Tosh (above) had a dual career in Jamaica in the Sixties, recording solo under various aliases and with the Wailers. He left the group in 1973, claiming Bob Marley had become too much of a focal point within it, and built up a dedicated international reggae following. He had a spell with Rolling Stones Records in the late Seventies and early Eighties

the idea being to create a saleable rock-reggae synthesis. The ruse worked and the Wailers' reputation – and that of Marley in particular – grew as their music took on a new air of militancy, typified by 'Get Up, Stand Up', on their 1973 album *Burnin'* and fed by Marley's increasing commitment to Rastafarianism, a religious movement that drew inspiration from the Bible and the teachings of black Jamaican nationalist leader Marcus Garvey. Believing in Ethiopian emperor Haile Selassie (real name Ras Tafari) as 'the Living God' and looking to Africa as their spiritual homeland, Rastafarians were regarded as dissidents by both the Jamaican music establishment and the authorities at large, but lyrics quoting

Rasta scripture and promoting back-to-Africa sentiments became intrinsic features of Jamaican reggae throughout the Seventies. For Marley himself, more of a figurehead than ever following the departure of Tosh, Livingston and the Barrett brothers from the Wailers in 1974, the political goal of freedom from oppression and the Rasta's promise of spiritual salvation were inseparably linked.

The Marley legacy

Despite a difficult relationship with the Jamaican powers-that-be, the respect for Marley in his home country was such that he alone was able to call a truce, in 1978, between the politicians and gunmen who were threatening to plunge the island into civil war. Two years later, he consolidated his growing statesmanlike status in Africa itself with an appearance at Zimbabwe's official Independence Day celebrations in Harare, while his song 'Zimbabwe' (included on *Survival* [1979]) was adopted as the party song of the country's ruling Patriotic Front. By the time of his death from cancer in 1981, he had become a true third world superstar and was on the verge of breaking through into the one market that had so far remained resolutely cool towards him and to reggae in general – the US.

Marley's international success opened commercial doors for a wide range of Jamaican reggae acts – Toots and the Maytals, former Wailer Peter Tosh, Burning Spear and Big Youth among them – and was a vital inspiration to such up-and-coming UK reggae bands as Aswad, Black Slate, Steel Pulse and the uncompromisingly militant Misty in Roots. Island built on its own success with Marley by exploring other ethnic idioms like salsa and Nigerian juju, finding a particular market for the sweet melodicism and muscular rhythms of juju star Sunny Ade in the Eighties, while

Virgin set up its own reggae subsidiary called Front Line as a specific British outlet for the records of Big Youth, Burning Spear and other major Jamaican names. In the last years of his life and in the years following his death, Marley was a symbol of musical liberation and independence, even if the degree of his creative influence on reggae as a developing style was arguable: some cited Tosh and Burning Spear as of at least equal importance, while the emergence of 'rockers' reggae – a hard, skeletal sound pioneered by Jamaica's top studio rhythm men, Sly Dunbar and Robbie Shakespeare – and the softer, floating 'lovers rock' ballad style favoured by Sugar Minott, Dennis Brown and others denoted a local departure from Marley's internationalist approach.

Whatever the variations in style, however, reggae did become heavily indentified – in Britain as in Jamaica, and largely thanks to Marley – as a rebel music, and in this respect it had an affinity with punk-rock. The hippest punks declared

Dennis Brown (left) was a versatile reggae performer whose records included 'Promised Land', cut in a London studio during 1983 with the young lions of UK reggae, Aswad (bottom). Brown was one of many reggae stars to work with the music's most illustrious production team, Sly Dunbar (below) and Robbie Shakespeare (opposite below)

the Beat in Birmingham drew particular inspiration: with multi-racial line-ups and a distinctive instrumental sound that drew equally on punk and reggae sources, such bands personified the RAR ideal and became its most articulate and respected voices.

The 2-Tone beat

The Specials were formed in Coventry in mid-1977 by white art student Jerry Dammers and first became nationally known as the support band on the Clash's On Parole tour during the following year. Clash boss Bernie Rhodes offered them a management deal at the end of the tour but they chose not to take it, preferring to keep Coventry as their base and maintain control of their own affairs through a specially created label, 2-Tone, which Dammers insisted would be an operation 'run by musicians instead of businessmen'. Their first disc, 'Gangsters', was entirely self-financed and distributed through Rough Trade: a sharp attack on music business practices, it reached Number 6 in the UK and led to Dammers signing a no-interference distribution deal with Chrysalis for the release of all 2-Tone material, which by late 1979 included discs by the Selecter, the Beat and London-based Madness.

As a rebel music, punk rock had close affinities with reggae. DJ Don Letts (above, pictured with club owner Andy Czezowski) played reggae discs between acts at the premier punk venue, the Roxy in London's Covent Garden

that reggae was the only music to which they listened, and one of the Roxy club's key attractions was Rastafarian disc jockey Don Letts, who played imported reggae discs between sets. The punk-reggae connection was acknowledged by artists in both genres: Bob Marley recorded 'Punky Reggae Party' in 1977, the Clash covered Marley backing guitarist Junior Murvin's 'Police and Thieves' as a single, and Dennis Bovell of Matumbi produced records by the Slits and the Pop Group. A further link was established with the formation of the Rock Against Racism movement, whose numerous benefit concerts featured such acts as the Clash and the Ruts playing alongside lesser known black reggae bands in a gesture of racial harmony and solidarity. It was from these gigs that bands like the Specials in Coventry and

The starting point for all the 2-Tone groups was mid-Sixties ska rather than its later variant, reggae, and to this end they adopted not only the frantic performing style but the pork-pie hat and two-tone suit uniform of ska personalities like Prince Buster, whose Jamaican-produced records had been particularly popular among Midlands mods a decade or so earlier. But if the spirit of 2-Tone music was revivalistic, its message was determinedly contemporary, as the Specials sang stridently of life in the urban jungle in 'Stupid Marriage' and 'Rat Race' and the Selecter lambasted racism and joblessness in 'Black and

Blue' and 'Too Much Pressure'. Only Madness (named after a Prince Buster song) seemed less than interested in making political points, and they left the label for Stiff after just one release to become one of the most successful singles acts of the post-punk era. Retaining the Buster-inspired 'nutty boy' image that first brought them to 2-Tone's attention, they developed a winning, inoffensive line in chummy, music hall-type songs like 'Baggy Trousers', 'Embarrassment' and the macabre 'Cardiac Arrest' – most of them comic reflections on school or council estate life accompanied by marvellously inventive promotional videos.

For a label conceived not so much as a commercial enterprise but more as a musical manifesto, 2-Tone was spectacularly successful: its first eleven releases all charted – an unprecedented achievement for a new independent – and critical acclaim for its acts was unanimous, reaching a peak with the release of the Specials' self-named debut album, which Elvis Costello produced. Its very success caused problems – the Beat quit to form their own label, Go-Feet, in early 1980

and the Selecter, claiming the 2-Tone sound was becoming too stereotyped, followed a few months later – but the label continued to flourish until the original line-up of the Specials broke up late in 1981. Vocalists Terry Hall and Neville Staples and guitarist Lynval Golding formed the Fun Boy Three, leaving Jerry Dammers to reconstitute the group (under its original name, the Special AKA) with ex-Bodysnatcher Rhoda Dakar, ex-Selecter Stan Campbell and Egidio Newton from Animal Lightlife. Their music became yet more polemical, and of their next three releases, 'The Boiler' (a broadside against attitudes to rape), 'War Crimes' (an indictment of Israeli involvement in Lebanon)

Coventry's 2-Tone operation had parallels elsewhere in the UK. UB40 (singer Ali Campbell, below) ran their own label from their home base of Dudley in the West Midlands, while the Beat (below right) set up the Go-Feet label in their native Birmingham as an outlet for their own releases. Meanwhile, Madness (right) built on their initial success with 2-Tone by recording a long string of quirky hit singles for Stiff in London

and the anti-apartheid 'Free Nelson Mandela', only the latter gained enough airplay to secure a chart placing.

The 2-Tone sound had parallels elsewhere, most obviously in the contrasting 'white reggae' styles of UB40 and the Police, both of whom were of 1977 vintage and were inspired by the ideology if not the form of punk. UB40 were an eight-piece multi-racial band with a built-in three-man brass section, whose name – taken from the identity card issued to recipients of unemployment benefit – reflected their dole queue origins and political concerns. The band was run as a musical co-operative from Dudley in the West Midlands, and they recorded for an independent (Graduate Records) before starting their own label in DEP International, but there was a lack of humour and a holier-than-thou arrogance about their political stance that set them apart from the equally committed but less intense bands of the 2-Tone stable. The Police, formed by seasoned R & B professionals Stewart Copeland (ex-Curved Air) and Andy Summers (ex-Zoot Money) with Newcastle jazz-rock bassist Gordon 'Sting' Sumner, had no political position to speak of and were generally far less deferential towards their reggae sources: they simply applied the basic elements of the reggae sound – rimshot drumming, prominent bass, high-pitched Bob Marley-like vocal – to the dynamics of a well-oiled three-piece rock line-up and performed songs that ran the gamut of subject matter from adolescent neuroses ('Can't Stand Losing You', 'Does Everyone Stare') to Jungian philosophy ('Synchronicity'). Not surprisingly, they fitted most easily into the post-punk mainstream, trading on the charisma of lead singer Sting – whose film career began in 1979 with a cameo role in *Quadrophenia*, adapted from the Who's album – and leading the wave of UK-based acts who flooded the US charts in the Eighties.

The charismatic Sting (above, pictured during his Live Aid appearance in 1985) supplemented his Police career with roles in the films Quadrophenia, Radio On *(both 1979) and* Brimstone and Treacle *(1982). Fellow Policemen Stewart Copeland and Andy Summers (left) embarked on their own solo projects, the latter collaborating with King Crimson founder Robert Fripp on the 1982 album* I Advance Masked

ELECTRO-POP AND THE VIDEO VOGUE

Adam Ant (far right) and Bow Wow Wow (bottom right) looked the part of tribal leaders, while Brian Seltzer of the Stray Cats (below right) inspired scores of young rockabillies to copy his dazzling quiff

T o their credit, the 2-Tone bands confronted head on, in their music and in their public statements, the often violent factionalism that had hastened the demise of punk in the late Seventies. They attempted to forge a unity between black and white, punk and skinhead, and did not always succeed. Their gigs, frequently held in ballrooms and clubs rather than concert halls and theatres to give the audience the freedom to dance, were marred by outbreaks of fighting and, during one performance in Cambridge, Specials Jerry Dammers and Terry Hall were themselves arrested on a charge of threatening behaviour after trying to pull the warring factions apart. It was difficult to preach unity at a time of fragmentation within the teenage culture itself – and the early years of the Eighties saw any number of newly emerging yet oddly retrospective youth tribes take the streets, from shaggy-haired, heavy metal-loving 'headbangers' and scooter-driving mods to self-styled 'rockabilly rebels' (the Teds of old) and so-called 'new psychedelics' who wore granny glasses and paisley patterned shirts and spoke mistily of the spirit of 1967. Each had its own adopted rock style, but only rockabilly (as played by the Stray Cats, Matchbox and the Polecats) and heavy metal (as represented by Rainbow, Iron Maiden, Judas Priest and Status Quo, who had been charting since the late Sixties) made any sustained impact on either the singles or the album chart.

The existence of fringe cults, however, told only part of the story of UK rock in the early Eighties: in the face of all this tribal diversity, the chief feature of the charts themselves was the way they continued to reflect the punk legacy – or at least the continuing assimilation of new wave ideas and artists into the pop mainstream. The most successful new act of 1980-81 was Adam and the Ants, who started in 1976 as a particularly derivative and self-consciously decadent punk band and slowly evolved into a vehicle for the theatrical fantasies of leader Adam

The youth tribes of Eighties England were many and varied, but the heavy metal hordes were no new phenomenon. Mop-haired and denim-clad, they – or their older brothers – had been around since the late Sixties, when Status Quo (below) were just starting out. Playing a simple brand of infectious, remorseless 12-bar boogie, Quo had by 1986 scored more hit singles than any other band in UK pop history

Ant (art student Stuart Goddard). So intent was Adam on rock stardom that he paid Malcolm McLaren a £1,000 consultancy fee to re-shape the group's sound: McLaren introduced him to the drum beat of the African Burundi tribe – a sound that Goddard's mentor, Gary Glitter, had unconsciously brought to pop in the early Seventies – but persuaded the Ants to part company with their leader and join Bow Wow Wow. Unabashed, Adam formed a new Ants and re-launched the band in pirate togs and Red Indian warpaint – a swashbuckling image designed (he said) to bring colour, showmanship and romanticism back to pop. Re-styling his own image for each Ants single and acting the parts in a series of visually stunning videos – a highwayman in 'Stand and Deliver', a 19th century dandy in 'Prince Charming', a knight in shining armour in 'Ant Rap' – he turned himself into the first major teenybopper star of the decade and had his face splashed across a whole new batch of young teen and children's pop magazines. Others followed his blueprint – notably Bow Wow Wow, lead by the Mohican hairstyled Annabella Lwin – and his success revealed the wisdom of cultivating a very young audience to even the hippest and most musically ambitious bands.

Adam Ant was one type of post-punk star – a traditional, egotistical pop entertainer whose only interest in punk was to use it as a stepping stone. Another type was represented by Gary Numan, who climbed aboard the punk bandwagon in 1977 with a band called the Lasers (later renamed Tubeway Army): using record company support to further his acquaintance with synthesisers and develop his own in-studio skills, he turned the band into a one-man operation, writing all the material, playing all the synthesiser parts and handling all the production. If Adam Ant's hero was Gary Glitter, Gary Numan's model was David Bowie, and his image (dyed blonde hair, all-black stage gear, ghostly white make-up), vocal style and high-tech musical approach all drew clear inspiration from Bowie's mid-Seventies electronic experimentalism. He seemed at first like a throwback to an earlier era but it quickly became clear that he was a sign of things to come: with the synthesiser gaining in popularity and revealing all kinds of facets and qualities that conventional instrumentation lacked, Numan set the stage for a major shift in rock's technical and musical vocabulary. Numan was far from the first new-wave act to explore the possibilities of electronics – the Normal had a hit in the independent chart with 'TVOD' and the Human League with 'Being Boiled', both in 1978 – but his doom-laden songs presaged the gloomy, introspective synth-based sounds of such Eighties acts as Kissing the Pink, Howard Jones, Bronski Beat and New Order.

High-tech hymns

A series of technological innovations in the Seventies culminated in the launching of a synthesiser – the Wasp – that was comparable in price to a cheap electric guitar, and this fact alone was enough to ensure its widespread adoption by post-

Avatars of the electro-pop era included would-be aviator Gary Numan (opposite top), Depeche Mode (opposite bottom) and one-time multi-media experimentalists Human League (left). Striking a gloomier, more melancholic vein were New Order (above), whose 'Blue Monday' (1983) was the first single in a 12-inch format to reach the UK chart

punk groups. The advent of mass market computer technology and devices like the sequencer – which could store whole passages of music and play them back as required – gave added flexibility and made the whole process of music-making more accessible to non-musicians. This had a kind of 'democratising' effect on UK rock, very much in keeping with the punk principle, although the first wave of synthesiser bands tended to stick to a style of music that was strictly danceable – an inevitable consequence of the level of the musicians' skills and the availability of drum computers which could be most easily programmed to play steady dance tempos. This style was labelled 'electro-pop' and was well showcased on a compilation album called *Some Bizarre*, released on the label of the same name, which featured the first recorded efforts of Soft Cell, Blancmange and Depêche Mode and showed once again the pervasive influence of

Eurodisco pioneer Giorgio Moroder. Soft Cell, a vocal and synthesiser duo from Leeds, scored a Number 1 with a track taken from the album, 'Tainted Love'.

Other bands took a more studied approach to the use of synthesisers and drum machines. New Order, from Manchester, evolved out of Joy Division, a seminal local band with a cult status built on the grim, tortured singing of Ian Curtis, who committed suicide on the eve of their first US tour. The new band – with Gillian Gilbert joining on keyboards – carried on in much the same bleakly atmospheric vein, typified by their first two singles 'Ceremony' (written by Curtis) and 'Procession'. While maintaining their image as melancholic recluses, they developed a brighter rhythmic base with 'Temptation' and 'Blue Monday' – a massive hit despite its availability only in 12in format – and championed a new form of white electro-disco with 'Confusion' in 1983, which was recorded with

New York disco producer Arthur Baker. The Human League, from Sheffield, took a similar direction after establishing a small local following as an experimental, art school-oriented multi-media band: original members Martyn Ware and Craig Marsh left in 1980 to form their own British Electric Foundation (and subsequently Heaven 17 with vocalist Glenn Gregory), and Philip Oakey re-structured the group with two female backing singers, Joanne Catherall and Susanne Sulley, and new bassist Ian Burden. With their sound now an assured blend of mainstream vocal pop with Moroder-like electronic efficiency, they worked with producer Martin Rushent to create the quintessential electro-pop album of the Eighties, *Dare* (1981). Their use of insistent Linndrum electronic percussion, repetitive keyboard riffs and synthesised basslines was much copied, though the League themselves seemed unable to match these commercial and creative heights with later releases.

Elsewhere, there were further variants on the electro-pop blueprint. Some bands took their cue from Bowie's collaborations with Brian Eno on *Low* and *'Heroes'*, others from the German school of electronic avant gardists headed by Tangerine Dream and Kraftwerk. The latter were of special importance: a four-man electronics workshop, they saw

Foremost among Merseyside's contribution to UK rock in the aftermath of punk were Echo and the Bunnymen (opposite, bottom left) and Orchestral Manoeuvres in the Dark (opposite top). Like the Human League, whose Dare (opposite, bottom right) was one of the most technically imaginative albums of the early Eighties, OMD were synthesiser specialists who became chart regulars, though their real interest lay in emulating the electronic ingenuities of German band Kraftwerk (above)

Right: Spandau Ballet, one of the loosely linked gaggle of groups labelled 'new romantics', play to an attentive audience. Their television exposure in mid-1980 took the movement out of the London clubs and into the national spotlight

themselves more as studio technicians than as musicians and even utilised uncannily realistic dummies for photo sessions, to free them to get on with their work. Their attitude to music-making was clinical, scientific, unemotional, but in no sense were their records – as was frequently assumed – mindless hymns to high technology. As member Ralf Hutter put it, explaining the thinking behind their 1981 album *Computerworld*, 'Our idea is to take computers out of the context of control functions and use them creatively in an area where people do not expect to find them ... it's about time technology was used in resistance, it shouldn't be shunned, reviled or glorified'. Kraftwerk's techniques – though little of their wit and sense of irony – were mirrored particularly in the music of Orchestral Manoeuvres in the Dark, products of a thriving Merseyside postpunk scene that also threw up chart bands Wah!, Echo and the Bunnymen and the Teardrop Explodes. OMD came to exemplify the pretentious stream of electro-pop, *Dazzleships*, their 1983

album, a rather comical attempt to explore the aural possibilities of yet more new gadgetry, namely an Emulator synthesiser into which any sound – from a lawn mower to a banshee – could be programmed and then slowed down or speeded up.

Synthetic fantasies

A synthesiser-based sound was also the most obvious aural aspect of the new romantics fad, which won instant exposure when the newly formed and contract-less Spandau Ballet were the subject of TV's *20th Century Box* programme and were seen gigging in exclusive, unpublicised locations before an in-crowd of young professionals from the worlds of advertising, publishing, design and fashion. The five Spandaus, from Islington, wrapped themselves in billowing tartans and wove tinny, pseudofuturistic sound patterns out of their synths, while in their songs and in their statements they propounded their belief in the work ethic, in old-fashioned romanticism and dance-floor hedonism.

As the music scene expanded and the Spandaus reached the chart with the meaningless 'To Cut a Long Story Short', attention switched to laser-decorated venues like the Music Machine in Camden Town, now renamed the Palace under the new ownership of young entrepreneur Steve Strange. There, London's new dilettantes gathered nightly, dressed as anything suitably 'romantic' – cowboys, Robin Hoods, pirates, spacemen, safari hunters, dashing white sergeants – while Strange himself plotted his own, brief pop career with ex-Rich Kids Midge Ure and Rusty Egan and John McGeoch and Dave Formula of Buzzcocks spin-off band Magazine. Under the name of Visage, they created a string of languid tales of romantic despair, each set to a pounding Eurodisco beat overlaid with pseudo-classical synthesiser.

Midge Ure, meanwhile, joined much respected pre-punk synthesists Ultravox, who were in danger of disintegrating following the departure of their enigmatic leader John Foxx for a solo career. With founder members Billy Currie (another one-time Visager), Chris Cross and Warren Cann, he refined and streamlined the smooth electronic anthems on which they had built their cult reputation and fashioned them into grandiose, clinically clean new romantic pop songs. Their

image changed to suit the new style and they began, like the Spandaus and Visage, to take the filming of promotional videos into new, 'artistic' areas – their accompanying film to 'Vienna', directed by Ure, was for example packed with visual allusions to the 1948 film classic *The Third Man*. A video could play up an artist's larger-than-life appeal and tell its own story, making it an ideal vehicle for new romantic fantasies, and the lessons were quickly learned by two groups from the regions – Duran Duran from Birmingham, who found chart fame via a steamy, mildly pornographic promo for 'Girls on Film' (1981), and ABC from Sheffield, whose spectacularly seductive videos for 'Poison Arrow' and 'All of My Heart' (both 1982) rehashed the imagery of Hollywood romance and detective films without apparent irony or humour.

The success of both groups underlined the concern with glamour and image that was the new romantics' chief legacy, and Duran Duran were quickly accepted as the natural successors to Adam Ant's teenybopper mantle, boasting not only pretty boy looks and a whiff of decadence

The new romantics renewed pop music's love affair with visual extravagance and musical flamboyance, typical of which were the startling videos and elaborate productions of ABC (bottom left) and Ultravox (above). ABC's producer was Trevor Horn (opposite left, with Buggles partner Geoff Downes), who also lent his expertise to records by Dollar (inset), Frankie Goes to Hollywood and the Art of Noise. At the same time, the new pop vogue brought forth artists with old-fashioned teen appeal in Eighties dressings, including Eurovision Song Contest winners Bucks Fizz (opposite, top right) and Marty Wilde's daughter Kim (opposite, below right)

but the crucial big-money backing of EMI and the formidable packaging skills of ex-10cc members turned video-makers Kevin Godley and Lol Creme. The group's rise paralleled and helped consolidate that of new teen magazines like the phenomenally successful *Smash Hits*, which managed to outsell each of the established music papers by sticking to a simple formula of song lyrics, uncritical features, gossip and pin-up pictures. And following in Duran Duran's steps came others – Bucks Fizz, Kim Wilde, Haysi Fantayzee, Haircut 100, Altered Images, Shakin' Stevens, Dollar – all of whom could count on well-organised publicity machines and the excellence of in-demand producers like Trevor Horn, Andy Hill, Martin Rushent and Stuart Colman.

ATLANTIC CROSSCURRENTS

The fresh importance placed on record production was another sign of the times. Having been very much undervalued during the punk years, producers now found themselves called upon to add what one writer called a 'prefabricated sheen' of gloss, colour and opulence to the musically unfocused creations of new and inexperienced acts. Trevor Horn, who learned his trade as one half of the Buggles duo who reached Number 1 in 1979 with the timely 'Video Killed the Radio Star', set new standards with his work on ABC's debut album *The Lexicon of Love* in 1982, when he embellished their rather wooden brand of pop-funk with crashing drum treatments and epic flurries of synthesised strings. Two years later he launched white Liverpool soul boys Frankie Goes to Hollywood into the top bracket with his pounding, multi-layered disco productions of 'Relax' and 'Two Tribes' – this to the accompaniment of an unprecedented campaign of hype by Island Records and ex-*New Musical Express* journalist Paul Morley that involved the release of countless remixed 7in and 12in versions of 'Relax', two calculatedly controversial videos, the creation of a whole new line in street fashion in the form of 'Frankie Say' T-shirts, and much ridiculing of the BBC for its decision to ban 'Relax' over references in the song to gay sex.

Right: Holly Johnson of Frankie Goes to Hollywood, whose domination of the 1984 charts was due in no small measure to one of the craftiest publicity campaigns in the history of the music business. Their first three single releases all went to Number 1, a feat previously achieved by only one group, fellow Liverpudlians Gerry and the Pacemakers, back in 1963

The trend towards big production values and co-ordinated marketing campaigns indicated that the UK record industry was intent on winning back some degree of control over the market after the new wave onslaught, but the type of act signed and promoted by the major companies in the early Eighties was influenced by one particular factor – that act's potential appeal to the US rock market. After years of resistance to new wave sounds, America finally began to open its eyes and ears to British acts in 1982, with the setting up of 24-hour cable channel MTV: part-owned by Warner Communications, it featured live concert telecasts and bulletins of rock news, but most of its airtime was filled with the most readily available (and inexpensive) material – the unending stream of music videos produced on the other side of the Atlantic. British bands suddenly discovered that they could build up a sizeable American following without even setting foot in the country, while even US bands like the Stray Cats – unknown in their homeland but established in the UK as popular video stars – found themselves with totally unexpected US Top 40 hits as a result of MTV coverage. With its audience swelling to an estimated 16 million by the end of 1983, MTV assumed a promotional significance comparable to US radio, and the American record companies responded by creating their own video departments and giving a major push to those British artists already signed to their UK subsidiaries.

As welcome as these developments appeared to the UK record business, they in fact imposed a new kind of straitjacket upon those major British labels with American connections. In signing new artists, they were now obliged to concentrate their attention on acts with 'transnational' appeal – i.e. wholesome and anodyne enough for prime-time US viewing – rather than the quirky, offbeat talents that had characterised the late Seventies new wave. The result was that, despite the proclamation by American trade papers of a British pop 'invasion' of the Top 40 on the mid-Sixties scale, UK music actually became insidiously Americanised, dominated by acts whose chief skill was to cheerfully replicate the two most globally acceptable US styles – soul and disco. Wham!, a lithe-limbed, high-energy duo (comprised of George Michael and Andrew Ridgeley) from suburban Hertfordshire, fitted the bill perfectly with their mélange of Motown sound, New York street rap and Elton John-like balladry. Under the ever-sharp influence of Sixties hustler Simon Napier-Bell, they switched from minor independent Innervision to the major Epic and topped the US chart during 1984 with 'Wake Me Up Before You Go Go'. Alison Moyet left Yazoo and her synthesiser

Below: unemployed disco-goers Andrew Ridgeley and George Michael (below) emerged from Watford near London in 1982 with the strutting, self-celebrating 'Young Guns (Go for It)' and quickly became the UK's biggest home-made pin-up stars for years

Among the most distinctive voices in Eighties rock were Genesis singer Phil Collins (above), Alison Moyet (above right) and former Q-Tips lead singer Paul Young (right), all of whom peppered the international charts with polished retreads of old soul material

partner Vince Clarke for a lucrative contract with CBS, who gave her rich, soulful voice a series of bland AOR-like settings typified by 'All Cried Out' (1985). Her stablemate Paul Young, once lead singer with pub rock band the Q-Tips, carved his niche with likeable but undistinguished revivals of Marvin Gaye's 'Wherever I Lay My Hat' and Nicky Thomas' early reggae classic, 'Love of the Common People'. Virgin, meanwhile, enjoyed major success with Genesis drummer Phil Collins, who figured high in the international charts of 1984-85 with a revival of the Supremes' 'You Can't Hurry Love' and a duet with ex-Earth, Wind and Fire vocalist Philip Bailey, 'Easy Lover'.

The funk factor

Simple Minds, Joe Jackson, the Thompson Twins and Spandau Ballet were among the many other British acts to crack the US market in the wake of MTV's opening, but there was no such easy passage for those with more parochial appeal or those less willing to gear their music and image to American audiences. The UK's main rock talking point of 1983-84, Culture Club, created a minor stir in the US because of the notoriety of lead singer Boy George (christened George O'Dowd) who wore make-up, dressed in frocks and talked freely about his bisexuality. The central idea behind the group however – that they represented, in their music and in their membership, a coming together of black, white Anglo-Saxon and Jewish cultures – was missed completely by American commentators. Eurythmics, comprising Royal Academy of Music-trained singer Annie Lennox and keyboard player Dave Stewart (both ex-members of new wave band the Tourists), made a greater musical impact in the US, but bewildered American audiences with their eclectic, uncategorisable plundering of different idioms – a lilting calypso rhythm on 'Right By Your Side', a lurch into electro-disco for 'Sex Crimes' (from the film *1984*, for which they provided a score), a nod to Sixties era Motown on 'There Must Be An Angel', which even included a Stevie Wonder-type harmonica break. Their videos also caused problems: MTV refused to show the film made to accompany 'Who's That Girl' for fear that Lennox, pictured removing a long wig to expose her own close-cropped hair, might be promoting transvestism.

Although initially much misunderstood in the US, Eurythmics (left) and Culture Club (singer Boy George above) were soon in the forefront of the UK onslaught on the MTV-influenced American rock scene

White UK bands who embraced soul wholeheartedly but used it for unorthodox or conspicuously political ends (Dexy's Midnight Runners and Style Council respectively) found the US similarly unyielding. Dexy evolved from mod revivalists to purveyors of a Van Morrison-inspired brand of what was labelled 'Celtic soul' – R & B laced with Irish folk – but had only one US hit to show for it, 'Come On Eileen', also a chart-topper in Britain. Similarly, Paul Weller broke up the Jam in 1982 to form the Style Council with Mick Talbot of the Merton Parkas: taking a strident Curtis Mayfield-influenced early Seventies funk sound as its base, the Council attacked the inequalities of class and privilege in 'Money Go Round' and the occupants of 10 Downing Street in the 1985 UK hit, 'The Lodgers'. Weller's pointed anti-Americanism however and his insistence on using records as vehicles for personal manifestoes were not calculated to please either American radio programmers or the bosses of MTV. Black UK soul bands like Imagination, Linx and Central Line also had difficulty breaching MTV, but for different reasons: many observers claimed that MTV discriminated against black performers – the official explanation was that the channel played only 'rock'n'roll'.

In the US itself, black music was one of the biggest growth areas of the Eighties, and Michael Jackson, Lionel Richie and Shalamar all managed to cut through the restrictive programming policies of MTV and AOR radio to dominate both the rock and soul charts. Shalamar recorded for Solar Records in Los Angeles, a black label that unrepentantly followed the Motown principle of launching its product at the white dance market, while the success of Richie (ex-lead singer with the Commodores) and the evergreen Stevie Wonder kept Motown well to the

Led by Kevin Rowland, Dexy's Midnight Runners (right) first became known to British audiences as third on the bill to the Specials and the Selecter on the 2-Tone winter tour of 1979. After a series of changes in music, personnel and image, they re-emerged in 1982 dressed in Romany gear and playing self-styled 'Celtic soul'. Their 'Come On Eileen' was a Number 1 in the UK in 1982 and in the US a year later

forefront of mainstream rock and pop for a third decade. Most dazzling of all was the success story of ex-Motown, ex-Jackson Five member Michael, who followed up his disco-oriented *Off the Wall* album of 1979 with the blockbusting *Thriller* (1982), which sold over ten million copies worldwide and provided hit singles in 'Beat It', 'Billie Jean' and the title track. The album merged elements of Motown soul, disco and even heavy rock, with guitarist Eddie Van Halen's lead break in 'Beat It' singlehandedly starting a craze for a rock-soul synthesis. Jackson set a new precedent in video-making, too, by hiring Hollywood director John Landis – whose credits included spoof horror film *An American Werewolf*

in London – to produce a 20-minute long visual treatment of 'Thriller'. Besides bringing the disciplines as well as the techniques of cinema to video for perhaps the first time, the resulting mini-masterpiece made history by becoming the fastest and biggest selling video-cassette ever on its international retail release in 1983.

Street corner jive

Jackson's youth, his edgy and reclusive image, and his fabulous command of new, street-originated black dance forms like robotics and breakdancing, gave him a credibility among young black audiences that very few other soul or disco superstars could claim. While an artist

Above: Disbanding the Jam in 1982, Paul Weller (right) teamed up with Mick Talbot (ex-Merton Parkas and Dexy's Midnight Runners) to form the Style Council. They played soul with a political edge, taking their cue from the declamatory early Seventies funk of Curtis Mayfield and the Isley Brothers

Michael Jackson (right) revitalised American soul in 1982 with his Thriller *album, from which was drawn a clutch of transatlantic hit singles. Jackson challenged the trend towards faceless, mechanistic dance-floor funk by backing each release with an inventive promotional video; he even hired Hollywood director John Landis to supervise the video interpretation of the title track*

like Lionel Richie worked hard at smoothing down the edges of soul and blurring the distinction between it and other musical genres – his song 'Lady', for example, became a major hit for country singer Kenny Rogers in 1980 – Jackson demonstrated a much closer affinity to the dance-based urban R & B sounds still favoured by black radio. Foremost among those sounds in the early Eighties were two connected yet superficially contrasting subgenres, each of which had roots in New York's black disc jockey fraternity – rap and 'cybernetic soul'.

Rap's key element was the fast-talking rhyme spoken over a stripped-down rhythm track, and much of its appeal to black listeners lay in its street-corner subject matter and its apparent incomprehensibility to whites. Black radio in the US had long had a 'rapping' tradition, with disc jockeys introducing records in a high-speed rhyming patter, but the technique was transferred to record only after

taking a very circuitous route: ska producer Coxsone Dodd brought the tradition to Jamaica in the Sixties and encouraged DJs in his employ to adopt it, soon after which the first 'dub' tracks (recordings with the vocals mixed out, specifically for DJs to talk over) began appearing commercially. The dub principle was brought to the US in the Seventies and DJs like Kool Herc, a Jamaican emigré now resident in the Bronx, developed rapping into a fine art during their stints at New York clubs. Shortly after came the Grand Wizard Theodor's propagation of the 'scratching' technique – literally, moving the stylus back and forth in the record groove – and DJ Grandmaster Flash's use of a drum machine in combination with montaged fragments of records. By the end of the decade, the rapping and scratching scenes had coalesced under the collective term of 'hip-hop' and the first custom-made rap records were on sale – the Fatback

Left: Grandmaster Flash and the Furious Five brought rap to an international stage in 1982 with 'The Message'. Like fellow DJs Kool Herc and Grand Wizard Theodor, Flash was one of the early figureheads of New York's hip-hop culture, his major innovation being the use of a drum machine in combination with montaged fragments of records

Below: Lionel Richie was most interested in writing and performing old-fashioned, romantic soul ballads for the mainstream music audience

Band's 'King Tim III (Personality Jock)' and the Sugarhill Gang's 'Rapper's Delight'.

Rap became an identifiable part of black street culture in the US, as gangs gathered on corners to show off their verbal and improvisational prowess in much the same way as doo-wop vocal groups had done over two decades earlier. The doo-wop analogy is appropriate in that many of the managers and label-owners who capitalised on the rap craze were themselves former street-corner singers. Rap had its dark, almost paranoid moments – notably the Furious Five's 'The Message' (1982), with its arresting hook line, 'don't push me 'cos I'm close to the edge' – but mostly it was a boasting, comic declaration of ghetto bravado – an aural equivalent of spray-can graffiti and the head spins and acrobatics that constituted breakdancing.

Cybernetic soul, on the other hand, was a more exclusive affair, fashioned at

Afrika Bambaataa (below) embodied the new era of cybernetic soul. Once the leader of a street gang called the Black Spades, he first made his name as a rapping DJ at the turntables of New York's Roxy Club. In 1982, he pulled off one of the music's most daring coups by adding a rapping track to Kraftwerk's 'Trans Europe Express' and issuing the mix as 'Planet Rock'

the mixing desk of a recording studio and given life in the environment of a hip club like the Manhattan Funhouse or New York's Roxy. A harder, funkier brand of European electro-disco, its stars were disc jockeys turned producers (and in some cases performers) like John 'Jellybean' Benitez, Paul Rodriguez and Larry Levan. The new soul had the sound and look of a stark, metallic celebration of the new technology and all things space age, with leading bands like Afrika Bambaataa and the Soul Sonic Force, Arcade Funk, Orbit, Cybotron and Planet Patrol evoking the era of video games and inter-

planetary fantasies in their very names. It was an old hand, however, who produced the consummate statement of cybernetic soul in 1983: George Clinton – founder of premier funk bands Parliament and Funkadelic in the late Sixties – took the genre to new technical heights with *Computer Games*, a bizarre journey into the infotech world of computers, synth drums, tape loops, vocoders and Lyricon synthesisers.

A static scene

If the efforts of Clinton and company represented a break with the past – and

particularly with the notion of black music as a music of struggle – white US rock music in the Eighties seemed as static as ever. With certain welcome exceptions, the early decade was a period of consolidation rather than innovation, in which the US record industry's own experience of recession imbued a sense of caution bordering on paralysis. The twin pillars of AOR and heavy metal, upon which the industry placed its faith in the Seventies, stood unchallenged even by the British renaissance in chart fortunes – the most successful UK bands in the US in album sales were those established acts who conformed to either the AOR or hard-rock stereotypes, like Foreigner (formed by ex-King Crimson keyboardist Ian McDonald) and ex-patriate Sheffield boys Def Leppard. There was even a vogue in the US in the Eighties for bands who blended the riff-based attack of heavy metal with the pop hooks and vocal harmonies characteristic of AOR: Meat Loaf and REO Speedwagon proved especially adept at this, each producing a loud, gothic-like sound that appealed as much to rock fans in their twenties and older as to heavy metal's traditional teen audience.

The acts who meant most to American record-buyers in the Eighties were seasoned professionals rather than newcomers – bands with members

Hard rock meant huge business in the US in the early Eighties, with Meat Loaf (left), Foreigner (lead singer Lou Gramm, bottom left) and Def Leppard (below) leading a highly populated field. The latter hailed from Sheffield, England, and consistently enjoyed bigger success in the States than back in their native land

whose rock pedigree stretched back to the Sixties, like Journey (featuring ex-Santana regulars Neil Schon and Gregg Rolie) and Toto, an AOR 'supergroup' made up entirely of Los Angeles-based session musicians. Fleetwood Mac was another example: the leading band in Britain's brief blues revival of 1969-70, they came to the US in the early Seventies but reshaped themselves as a hip, rock-based middle-of-the-road outfit with the addition of Americans Lindsey Buckingham and Stevie Nicks in 1974. The complex personal relationships between the five members became a favourite talking point among the west coast rock fraternity, and their 1977 album *Rumours* –one of the biggest sellers of the whole decade – was widely interpreted as a frank documentation of the emotional and sexual conflicts within the group. The Eighties found the band on the apparent brink of breaking up, yet still attracting massive sales for both their collective efforts – *Fleetwood Mac Live* (1980) and *Mirage* (1982) – and their various solo outings. Fleetwood Mac had enough individual talent (especially instrumentally) to place them above most of their AOR rivals, but they shared the common AOR reluctance to deviate from a proven hit album formula.

Among those providing some relief from the AOR/heavy metal duopoly were white Philadelphians Daryl Hall and John Oates, who wrote and produced a series of immaculate albums and singles in the very best tradition of east coast 'blue-eyed soul'. Their partnership dated officially from 1972, when they were signed as an acoustic singer-songwriter duo by Atlantic, but they reached their commercial peak in 1982 with 'I Can't Go For That', 'Maneater' and the *Private Eyes* album. And while Hall and Oates made their mark working within a black idiom, black singer-writer Prince (real name Prince Rogers Nelson) made his by echoing caucasian psychedelia with punk and heavy metal overtones. Specialising in acid-laced, heavily erotic material like the singles 'When Doves Cry' and '1999', he prompted a campaign by the Parents Music Resource Center pressure group to purge the airwaves of records with such explicitly sexual content – a campaign that appeared to have some effect.

Hall and Oates and Prince apart, protagonists of US rock could point approvingly to the growing strength of the country's independent sector, in which small labels were mushrooming on the UK scale and providing a home for some of the more esoteric, determinedly alternative new US bands. Of these acts, R.E.M. from Georgia were the best received in critical quarters, with the Dream Syndicate, the Violent Femmes, Jason and the Scorchers and Rain Parade close behind: all drew on mid- to late Sixties west coast influences – the Byrds,

Buffalo Springfield, the Doors and Love in particular – but the problem for each remained the intransigence of radio stations and the lack of a co-ordinated distribution system for independently-released records. By the middle of the decade this new American 'underground' remained commercially insignificant, but bands in the R.E.M. mould were beginning to make some national impact through exposure on the vast network of voluntarily run campus stations – the true upholders of the play-anything late Sixties FM tradition.

Not all the major US acts of the early and mid-Eighties travelled well. Fleetwood Mac (opposite top left and right; Christine McVie, inset) were perennial sellers overseas, but both Hall and Oates (opposite, bottom) and Prince (below) had been US chart fixtures for some years before European success beckoned

Right: Madonna Louise Ciccone – the face of the 80s? In her appearance, her dancing, and her singing, she mined a vein of street-wise sexuality virtually untouched by female singers of earlier eras. She was one of several US acts whose international sales rocketed as a direct result of an eye-opening Live Aid performance

Opposite: the first half of 1985 belonged to Bruce Springsteen, who embarked on an extraordinarily long and physically punishing world tour that left a powerful impression on all who patronised it. For many, he was the past, present and future of rock all rolled into one

Rocking with the Boss

Overall, US rock in the Eighties lacked real creative clout – and only one of its artists could properly claim international superstar status. He was Bruce Springsteen, a singer-songwriter whose tough, working man's music was labelled 'blue-collar rock', and who had the dubious distinction of being quoted by *both* Ronald Reagan *and* Walter Mondale in their attempt to woo the youth vote during the 1984 Presidential campaign. Politically, Springsteen was ambivalent – a born patriot with a streak of gut liberalism, whose songs verged between celebrating the America of highways, small towns and big city excitement and mourning the loss of old values and the influence of the state and big business on individual lives. Musically, he recalled Fifties' rock'n'roll and mid-Sixties garage band beat in equal measure and developed a stage act as electrifying as that of any performer in rock's thirty year history – and his *dedication* to rock was such that he kept touring tirelessly while lesser artists took sabbaticals, he played two-hour sets in intimate concert halls rather than perfunctory 45-minuters in soulless

sports arenas, and he steadfastly refused to make promotional videos until his record company (Columbia) forced him to relent in 1984 with 'Dancing in the Dark'; the result showed his influence though in its resemblance to a live performance.

Springsteen was admired for his integrity as much as his music: to many he seemed the personification of the Anglo-American rock tradition, a rock'n'roller at heart and probably the music's greatest-ever romantic – a man in love with not just the pleasure of performing or the power of the music, but with the *idea* of rock as a uniting force and as a carrier of hope for the generation weaned upon it. As he himself once explained, 'What I heard in the Drifters, in all that great radio music, was the promise of something else. Not the politicians' promise, y'know, that everything is gonna be alright . . . that would be a false promise anyway. I mean the promise of *possibilities*, the promise that the search and the struggle matter, that they affirm your life. That was the original spirit of rock'n'roll, and that's what I hope we carry on, a message that no-one has the right to tell you you gotta forfeit'.

The thirtieth anniversary of the hit record that heralded the birth of rock – Bill Haley's 'Rock Around the Clock' – went almost unnoticed during 1985, but it was a fitting occasion on which to look back at the many changes in rock and assess just how far the music had come. The success of Bruce Springsteen, star of a back-breaking world tour that grossed £37 million by mid-1985, suggested that rock still possessed the same traditional qualities and the same basic appeal, but he was fundamentally a symbol of rock's past rather than its future. Elsewhere, the new interest in African music, the flirtation with jazz that brought such artists as Pat Metheny, Working Week and Sade to the fore, and the fact that it was now perfectly possible for producers to make decent, danceable records without employing a single musician, all indicated how rock was continuing to take on board new influences and plunder many different ethnic and technological sources in its restless search for inspiration.

Another major change after thirty years of rock was the sheer scale of its appeal across age groups, classes and cultures. Rock was truly a world-popular music by the midway stage of the Eighties, its status ensured by the expansion of the US-dominated record business into a multi-million dollar, multi-national industry. Although the remorseless encroachment of the US companies into the record markets of overseas countries provoked allegations of cultural imperialism, one of the most encouraging features of the decade was the emergence of lively, productive rock scenes in countries traditionally seen as rock outposts – Australia, Japan, India, Poland and South Africa among them. In the latter two cases, rock took the form of a heavily politicised music, instrumental in articulating and spreading dissent against political oppression.

One event in 1985 celebrated rock's new-found global importance in grand and glorious fashion – the staging of Live Aid concerts at Wembley Stadium, London, and John F. Kennedy Stadium, Philadelphia on July 13th, and their relay to a record television audience of over 1.5 billion people. On a day of high emotion, over eighty top rock acts gave their services free to raise money for the relief of famine in Africa – a cause already highlighted by the worldwide success of the Band Aid single, 'Do They Know It's Christmas', on which dozens of leading UK rock names had pooled their talents. A total of £54 million was

raised and the man who was behind the venture, Bob Geldof, was nominated for the Nobel Prize, and created a Knight of the British Empire (KBE) in June 1986.

Apart from reflecting the global appeal of rock, Live Aid precipitated a fundamental change in people's perception of the music. The image of rock was transformed dramatically: here was the rock community – the musicians and the audience together – leading the world, kicking against the political hypocrisies and bureaucratic inaction that prolonged the horrors of famine, and forcing the music's detractors to reassess their dismissal of the rock world

as egotistical, selfish and money-grabbing. Perhaps Live Aid would prove to be, as some cynics suggested, just a one-off occasion, incapable of repetition: for one great moment, however, it reflected rock's traditional rebel image in its most positive light, by cutting through governmental inertia to ensure the survival of countless human lives.

Writers of 'Do They Know It's Christmas' and founders of Band Aid, Bob Geldof (left) and Midge Ure (below)

Below left: the Live Aid finale. 'Remember on the day you die', said Geldof, 'there is someone alive in Africa 'cos one day you watched a pop concert'

PLAYLIST 1: SINGLES

The following is a highly selective list of 75 of the most significant singles in over thirty years of rock music. The criterion for inclusion here is not the rather nebulous one of 'artistic merit' alone but also the record's influence on, and/or its encapsulation of, a particular era in rock. Not all the singles listed were major hits, although all but the first Elvis Presley track achieved chart placings in either the US or Britain or both. In each case, the artist(s) and title are followed by the US and/or UK record companies responsible for the track's release, and the year of issue.

'That's All Right, Mama'   **Elvis Presley** (Sun, US only, 1954)
A country boy sings the blues and a vital precedent is set. Early rock'n'roll at its best – relaxed, spontaneous, not yet encumbered by commercial restraints.

'Earth Angel (Will You Be Mine)'   **The Penguins** (DooTone, US only, 1954)
The first million-selling expression of pedestal-putting adolescent love, from an archetypal black harmony group discovered by Platters manager Buck Ram.

'Rock Around the Clock'   **Bill Haley and the Comets** (Decca/Brunswick, 1954)
Rock'n'roll's first great teenage anthem, a dance-hall stormer originally written as a 'novelty fox-trot' in 1948. It became a Top 20 UK hit on two further occasions, in 1968 and 1974.

'Ain't That a Shame'   **Fats Domino** (Imperial/London, 1955)
Pat Boone's cover version topped the US chart, but Domino's original (written with arranger Dave Bartholomew) had all the lazy, doleful charm of classic New Orleans R & B.

'Maybelline'   **Chuck Berry** (Chess, US only, 1955)
Pounding, rockabilly-flavoured R & B music and characteristically automobile-obsessed lyrics from rock'n'roll's poet laureate. A song much covered too, by British beat groups in the Sixties.

'Heartbreak Hotel'   **Elvis Presley** (RCA/HMV, 1956)
The track that launched Elvis as an international phenomenon, this was a contrived attempt to emulate the sound of his earlier Sun recordings, but for many a slice of Presley at his most smouldering and sexually-charged.

'Rock Island Line'   **Lonnie Donegan** (London/Decca, 1956)
The song that inspired a thousand skiffle groups, yet one for which Donegan was reportedly paid only a session fee. A surprise Top Ten hit in the US, it presaged a revival of interest in traditional American folk songs and idioms.

'Please Please Please'   **James Brown** (Federal, US only, 1956)
A minor R & B hit at the time but a million-seller over a period of years, this extravagantly emotional heart-wrencher remains the melodramatic high point of Brown's stage performances to this day.

'Blue Suede Shoes'   **Carl Perkins** (Sun/London, 1956)
Mockingly self-regarding lyrics and rip-snorting rockabilly licks from the man groomed by Sam Phillips as Presley's natural successor. Presley's own version was his follow-up to 'Heartbreak Hotel'.

'Bye Bye Love'   **The Everly Brothers** (Cadence/London, 1957)
Polished country harmonies from two of the Grand Ole Opry's most precocious young professionals, on a track that signalled a softer, more reflective era in teenage pop.

'That'll Be The Day'   **The Crickets** (Brunswick/Coral, 1957)
One of the most assured and confident performances of the rock'n'roll years and a track that set the standard and tone for head Cricket Buddy Holly's all-too-brief recording career.

'Yakety Yak'   **The Coasters** (Atlantic/London, 1958)
Written and produced by Jerry Leiber and Mike Stoller, this brilliantly comic cameo defined teenage tribulations and the drudgery of parental expectations better than any other record of the period.

'Move It'   **Cliff Richard** (Columbia, UK only, 1958)
Inarguably the finest British rock'n'roll disc of the Fifties, cut before Cliff made his transition from guitar-toting rock'n'roller to all-round family entertainer.

'To Know Him is To Love Him'   **The Teddy Bears** (Dore/London, 1958)
Quintessential home-made high-school pop of the *American Bandstand* era, from a threesome featuring a pre-'wall of sound' Phil Spector. The song was Spector's, inspired by the inscription on his father's gravestone.

'Summertime Blues'   **Eddie Cochran** (Liberty/London, 1958)
A much bigger star in the UK than in his native US, Cochran was killed in a car crash in England early in 1961. He earned rock immortality largely because of this track, a witty chronicle of the frustrations of working all summer.

'There Goes My Baby'   **The Drifters** (Atlantic/London, 1959)
Leiber and Stoller's no-holds-barred production almost relegated veteran black vocal group the Drifters to the role of backing singers, but in its unprecedented mixing of styles, sounds and technical effects it was a true pop milestone.

'What'd I Say'   **Ray Charles** (Atlantic, US only, 1959)
This consummate example of Charles' profane but revolutionary blond of gospel and blues began life as a twelve-minute on-stage improvisation. One of black music's great mavericks, he confounded many with his switch to country music two years later.

THE SIXTIES

'Shakin' All Over'   **Johnny Kidd and the Pirates** (HMV, UK only, 1960)
Kidd was a maverick UK rock'n'roller whose one great legacy was this nervous, mesmeric (and much covered) national chart-topper. Like that other classic UK rock track, Cliff Richard's 'Move It', this was initially intended as a flipside.

'Apache'   **The Shadows** (ABC-Paramount/UK Columbia, 1960)
The backing steps forward: Cliff Richard's sidemen, originally called the Drifters but renamed to avoid confusion with the US group, began a massively successful independent recording career with this crisp, clean and totally typical UK Number 1.

'Running Scared'   **Roy Orbison** (Monument/London, 1961)
A characteristic Orbison *tour de force* – a country-styled ballad racked with guilt and torment. He repeated the formula of foreboding lyrics over a gathering crescendo many times, but this 1961 track was impossible to equal for sheer emotional punch.

'Bring It On Home to Me'   **Sam Cooke** (RCA/RCA, 1962)
The premier black superstar of the early Sixties and a track that marked his transition from straightforward, gospel-influenced pop balladry to the beginnings of an identifiable 'soul' style.

'Blowin' in the Wind'   **Peter, Paul and Mary** (Warner Bros/Warner Bros, 1963)
Despite the ambivalence and imprecision of the lyrics, this Bob Dylan song became the anthem of the American Civil Rights movement, thanks largely to this sincere if somewhat prettified hit version by the nation's favourite folk trio.

'You've Really Got a Hold on Me' — **The Miracles** (Tamla/London, 1963)
Not a UK hit, but a Smokey Robinson song popular with innumerable British beat groups – including the Beatles, who recorded their own version on their second album. Faultless early Motown, with Smokey at his most vocally abandoned.

'Can I Get a Witness' — **Marvin Gaye** (Tamla/London, 1963)
Another much-recorded early Motown song – the Rolling Stones covered it on their debut album – and a track shot through with exuberant, delirious gospel passion.

'She Loves You' — **The Beatles** (Swan/Parlophone, 1964/1963)
Four lads from Liverpool on the verge of world acclaim – and sounding as if they know it. Three minutes of irresistible charm and cockiness that will forever evoke the madness of Beatlemania.

'House of the Rising Sun' — **The Animals** (MGM/Columbia, 1964)
Brilliant Alan Price R & B arrangement of a folk song that had been featured on an early Dylan album, and one of the most surprising transatlantic chart-toppers ever, in the light of its unusually long duration and distinctly un-poplike subject matter.

'Baby Love' — **The Supremes** (Motown/Stateside, 1964)
The newly sophisticated, lighter sound and face of Motown circa 1964, with the airy, well-tutored tones of Diana Ross well to the fore. The far greater vocal talents of fellow Supreme Florence Ballard were, however, shamefully neglected by Berry Gordy in his promotion of the group as a Ross vehicle.

'Remember (Walkin' in the Sand)' — **The Shangri-Las** (Red Bird/Red Bird, 1964)
Comic book romance ingeniously translated into girl group pop, with just a hint of tragedy in the song's dénouement. Produced by George 'Shadow' Morton for a specialised girl group label set up in New York by Leiber and Stoller.

'You've Lost That Lovin' Feeling' — **The Righteous Brothers** (Philles/London, 1965)
A magnificent exposition of love grown cold from America's greatest (and most underrated) blue-eyed soul duo. A doomy, atmospheric production by Phil Spector that marked the end of his preoccupation with the girl group idiom.

'We Can Work it Out' — **The Beatles** (Capitol/Parlophone, 1965)
A major step in the group's musical maturation that found Lennon and McCartney experimenting with different time signatures and exploring the politics of personal relationships. A double 'A'-sider with 'Day Tripper', John Lennon's slyly worded tale of an encounter with a sexual tease.

'(I Can't Get No) Satisfaction' — **The Rolling Stones** (London/Decca, 1965)
Jagger at his strutting, snarling, sneering best on arguably the most vehement and aggressive protest song of the Sixties – if not of the whole rock era.

'Mr Tambourine Man' — **The Byrds** (US Columbia/CBS, 1965)
Roger McGuinn's revised version of an apparently drug-influenced Dylan song defined folk-rock as a sound and style, with his own majestic twelve-string guitar work carrying strong echoes of Merseybeat band the Searchers.

'Concrete and Clay' — **Unit Four Plus Two** (London/Decca, 1965)
One of the most inventive discs of Britain's provincial beat era, with a lovely Drifters-inspired baion rhythm and a melody and lyric worthy of Goffin and King at their finest. The song was written by group members Tommy Parker and Bobby Moeller.

'Sunshine Superman'   **Donovan** (Epic/Pye, 1966)
Glasgow-born Donovan Leitch emerged with peaked cap and guitar in 1965, as the UK's answer to Dylan. Later, with Mickie Most producing, he struck a rich vein of psychedelic poeticism typified by this anticipatory flower-power anthem.

'Good Vibrations'   **The Beach Boys** (Capitol/Capitol, 1966)
Brian Wilson's *pièce de résistance*, originally intended for inclusion on what was to be the Beach Boys' definitive art-rock album, *Smile*. Brian's creeping paranoia and Leonard Bernstein's description of him as a 'genius' led him to abort the project in a fit of panic, though some of the tracks were rescued and issued later on *Surf's Up* (1972).

'River Deep, Mountain High'   **Ike and Tina Turner** (Philles/London, 1966)
Phil Spector's climactic production, the commercial failure of which in the US forced his temporary retirement. In 1970 he was back, doing a repair job on the Beatles' final *Let it Be* album and producing George Harrison's *All Things Must Pass*.

'Light My Fire'   **The Doors** (Elektra/Elektra, 1967)
Named after Aldous Huxley's novel *The Doors of Perception*, Jim Morrison's band played acid-laced garage band rock and were one of the few flower-power era outfits to make a consistent impact on the singles charts. This track was one of their less controversial, despite its sexual imagery and the insolence with which Morrison performed it on TV.

'Paper Sun'   **Traffic** (United Artists/Island, 1967)
After leaving the Spencer Davis Group in 1966, Stevie Winwood formed Traffic with Dave Mason, Jim Capaldi and Chris Wood. Fusing R & B, folk and fashionable psychedelia, they were one of 1967's most notable debutants: like *Sgt Pepper*, this single captured the incense-and-kaftans atmosphere of that summer quite perfectly.

'Pictures of Lily'   **The Who** (Decca/Track, 1967)
The quirky, obsessive side of mod spokesman-turned-pop artist Pete Townshend: a comic yet oddly affecting tale of a teenager's masturbatory fantasies. One of the best-ever rock songs on a sexual theme, infinitely more subtle than the same year's 'Let's Spend the Night Together' by the Stones.

'Strawberry Fields Forever'   **The Beatles** (Capitol/Parlophone, 1967?)
First intended for *Sgt Pepper*, the ultimate acid-rock record – eerie, unfocused, forbidding, but with moments of cackling humour. Listen, for instance, for John Lennon muttering 'cranberry sauce' over and over as the track fades out.

'Mrs Robinson'   **Simon and Garfunkel** (US Columbia/CBS, 1968)
Paul and Artie grew in maturity as the decade went on, creating a minor masterpiece in the *Bookends* album and recording this acerbic put-down of late Sixties American values for the soundtrack of *The Graduate*.

'Need Your Love So Bad'   **Fleetwood Mac** (US Columbia/Blue Horizon, 1968)
A beautiful reading of a Little Willie John blues composition from 1955, by a band who kept the flag of traditional, unadulterated UK R & B flying in the late Sixties under the leadership of guitarist/vocalist Peter Green. Much greater success followed Green's departure and the band's emigration to the US, but at great cost to their original blues leanings.

'Suite: Judy Blue Eyes'   **Crosby, Stills and Nash** (Atlantic/Atlantic, 1969)
Exquisite harmonies from a much-hyped supergroup whose early promise dissolved into squabbling and dissension. A Steve Stills song dedicated to leading Greenwich Village-era folkie Judy Collins, herself a blossoming west coast star in the early Seventies.

'Space Oddity'   **David Bowie** (RCA/Philips, 1973/1969)
Bowie in his first chart incarnation, as the alter-ego of doomed space scientist Major Tom. A timely release in the year of the first Moon landing, but also an important pointer to the later Bowie themes of space-age adventurism and the suicidal course of public superstardom.

'Honky Tonk Women'   **The Rolling Stones** (London/Decca, 1969)
As Lennon and band turned back to rock basics with *The Beatles* album and 'Get Back' (also 1969), so Jagger and friends returned to straight, no-nonsense sass and raunch with this sleazy, southern-styled macho rocker.

THE SEVENTIES:

'I Want You Back'   **The Jackson Five** (Motown/Tamla Motown, 1970)
The bubbling chart debut of America's first family of soul, who according to myth were discovered and brought to Motown by Diana Ross. 12-year-old Michael sings lead with precocious verve and confidence.

'Me and Bobby McGee'   **Janis Joplin** (US Columbia/CBS, 1971)
Written by rising country star Kris Kristofferson, a downbeat hippie hymn exactly suited to Joplin's wayward and vulnerable personality. Curiously for such an influential singer, her only US Top 40 hit.

'Maggie May'   **Rod Stewart** (Mercury/Mercury, 1971)
Long before he grew fat and complacent on conveyor-belt disco offerings, Stewart could reasonably claim to be the UK's finest white soul singer. This was the track that launched him: the decline began around five years later, with his split from the Faces and his move to California.

'All the Young Dudes'   **Mott the Hoople** (US Columbia/CBS, 1972)
Brilliant pre-punk summation of adolescent ennui, written and produced by David Bowie. Mott's lead singer, Ian Hunter, even sounded like Bowie on this, the first of five hits for his Herefordshire-based band.

'Virginia Plain'   **Roxy Music** (Atco/Island, 1972)
Mind-bendingly florid lyrics, electronic pyrotechnics and a joke ending combined to make this one of the most self-consciously avant-garde singles ever.

'American Pie'   **Don McLean** (United Artists/United Artists, 1972)
The story of rock from the death of Buddy Holly ('the day the music died') to the debacle that was Altamont, told entirely in metaphor. Cloaked references abound to Presley ('the king'), Dylan ('the jester'), the Beatles ('a quartet in the park') and Jagger ('Jack Flash').

'Layla'   **Derek and the Dominoes** (Atco/Polydor, 1972)
The band name was indicative of Eric Clapton's desire for a degree of anonymity and a return to old-fashioned rock simplicity. His most outstanding post-Cream recording, with Duane Allman of the Allman Brothers guesting on lead guitar.

'Walk on the Wild Side'   **Lou Reed** (RCA/RCA, 1973)
The freaks and poseurs of low-life early Seventies Manhattan, immortalised in song by the Velvet Underground's former leader. From the *Transformer* album, and given a deceptively sweet, orchestrated production by David Bowie.

'Rock Your Baby'   **George McCrae** (TK/Jayboy, 1974)
A key track in the expansion of the disco craze in the US, written and produced by H. W. Casey and Rick Finch of white soulsters K. C. and the Sunshine Band. McCrae proved a one-hit wonder, but the record's slinky rhythm track and subtle shifts in tempo were much copied.

'No Woman No Cry'   **Bob Marley and the Wailers** (Island/Island, 1975)
Eric Clapton's espousal of reggae and his cover version of Marley's 'I Shot the Sheriff' brought the Wailers much prestige in progressive circles in the mid-Seventies. Recorded live at London's Lyceum, this track was first heard on the album, *Bob Marley and the Wailers Live* (1975).

'Imagine'   **John Lennon** (Apple/Apple, 1975)
Recorded four years earlier for the album of the same name and a still bigger UK hit when re-issued following Lennon's murder in December 1980. A song that manages to be both dream-like and cutting, and the perfect distillation of the ex-Beatle's abrasive brand of peace-and-harmony politics.

'Bohemian Rhapsody'   **Queen** (Elektra/EMI, 1975)
Pompous and contrived, yet a suitable illustration of how the progressive rock legacy lasted well into the Seventies. Pretentiously described as a mini-opera, the track had a certain kitsch grandeur that the accompanying video (the first of its kind) played up to the full.

'Dancing Queen'   **Abba** (Atlantic/Epic, 1976)
Superior Eurodisco fare from a group who neatly straddled the camps of teeny-bopper glitter pop and adult-oriented rock. Scandinavia's only major contribution to the history of rock, they became the world's biggest selling group ever in 1980, when their sales passed the 150 million mark.

'Anarchy in the UK'   **The Sex Pistols** (EMI, UK only, 1976)
The definitive punk statement – noise, nihilism and nausea from the precursors of the late Seventies new wave.

'Sheena is a Punk Rocker'   **The Ramones** (Sire/Sire, 1977)
Named after a Paul McCartney pseudonym – he nicknamed himself Phil Ramone for a brief period during the Beatles' pre-fame days – the Ramones established the three-chord, high-energy, rapid-fire sound of punk-rock with seminal tracks like this. From the album *Rocket to Russia*.

'Roadrunner'   **Jonathan Richman and the Modern Lovers** (Beserkley/Beserkley, 1977)
Elementary and elemental minimalist pop from the court jester of the US new wave – a highway song stripped down to the bare essentials of rhythm and vocal.

'Because the Night'   **The Patti Smith Group** (Arista/Arista, 1978)
The high priestess of punk's only US or UK hit was, ironically, not her own composition but a somewhat romanticised sketch of love-on-the-run written by Bruce Springsteen. The record nevertheless had the crude passion and grace of her best album work.

'Sing If You're Glad to Be Gay'   **The Tom Robinson Band** (EMI, UK only, 1978)
Punk as a political platform: gay rights spokesman and socialist activist Robinson included this savagely sarcastic indictment of police and public attitudes to homosexuality on his EP, *Rising Free*. Predictably, however, it was another, less contentious track from the EP – 'Don't Take No For an Answer' – that EMI promoted and the radio stations played.

'The Eton Rifles'   **The Jam** (Polydor/Polydor, 1979)
Paul Weller at his most acidic, using a rugby match between a comprehensive school and elitist Eton as a metaphor for Britain's class war.

'Heart of Glass'   **Blondie** (Chrysalis/Chrysalis, 1979)
New wave meets disco. The band produced better, more original singles – 'Hanging on the Telephone', 'The Tide is High' – but none had greater impact or influence than this skilful mélange of two apparently disparate genres.

THE EIGHTIES:

'Love Will Tear Us Apart' — **Joy Division** (Factory/Factory, 1980)
Possibly the most angst-ridden record in rock history, this release ushered in a new and oddly English style of introspective, anguished pop at the start of the Eighties.

'Don't You Want Me' — **The Human League** (A & M/Virgin, 1981)
Multi-layered, clinically executed, seminal synthesiser pop from a band whose stated ambition was to become 'an electronic Abba'. They succeeded.

'The Message' — **Grandmaster Flash, Melle Mel and the Furious Five** (Sugarhill/Sugarhill, 1982)
Acid-tongued, no-compromise rap that even some black stations refused to play due to lines like 'They pushed that girl in front of the train/Took her to the doctor, sewed her arm on again/Stabbed that man right in his heart/Gave him a transplant for a brand new start'.

'Billie Jean' — **Michael Jackson** (Epic/Epic, 1983)
The best track from the 40 million selling *Thriller* album and a breathtaking amalgam of rock, soul and disco elements. Produced by Quincy Jones, with Michael himself performing the basic rhythm line on a drum machine, and jazzmen Tom Scott and Louis Johnson of soul duo the Brothers Johnson on bass. The song was Jackson's own.

'Karma Chameleon' — **Culture Club** (Virgin-Epic/Virgin, 1983)
Boy George and friends broke with their lightweight brand of white reggae for this, their biggest-selling international hit, and instead toyed with a jaunty, almost country-style harmonica-based accompaniment. Engaging and optimistic early Eighties pop, tailored for global sales.

'Blue Monday' — **New Order** (Factory/Factory, 1983)
Nervy, traumatised bed-sit pop set to a stolid disco rhythm, and a track that appealed to both Joy Division cultists and the dancers in the clubs. A UK hit twice during 1983, on the second occasion because of its success in Europe and its popularity with returning holidaymakers.

'Two Tribes' — **Frankie Goes to Hollywood** (Island/ZTT, 1984)
An over-sold group but a great contemporary production (by Trevor Horn) of a chilling anti-nuclear song, complete with four-minute warning sirens and the voice of actor Patrick Allen giving take-cover instructions.

'Nelson Mandela' — **The Special AKA** (Chrysalis/2-Tone, 1984)
The reconstituted Specials with a simple, danceable political chant calling for the release of jailed African National Congress leader Mandela. A rare UK chart triumph (it reached Number 9) for such specifically issue-related politicising – other 'issue' records like Elvis Costello's anti-Thatcher broadside 'Pills and Soap' (1983) and Robert Wyatt's Costello-composed anti-Falklands War song, 'Shipbuilding', were cold-shouldered by daytime radio and sales suffered accordingly.

'We Don't Need Another Hero' — **Tina Turner** (Capitol/Capitol, 1985)
Tina's was the comeback of the decade, culminating in her starring role in *Thunderdome* and her show-stealing appearance with Mick Jagger in Live Aid. Her new sound was straight mid-Sixties R & B with booming, semi-gothic accompaniments, the elements cleverly shaped and refined by a succession of UK-based producers.

'Sisters Are Doin' It for Themselves' — **Eurythmics and Aretha Franklin** (RCA/RCA, 1985)
Inspired matching of two immaculate soul voices, Annie Lennox and Aretha, on a feminist anthem for the Eighties. Produced by Eurythmic Dave Stewart.

PLAYLIST 2: ALBUMS

Listed here are representative album releases by the main artists and groups described in the text. The majority of the listed selections are either compilation albums highlighting a particular act's finest or best-known material, or key 'career' albums – those representing an important stage in a singer's or band's creative development. The US and UK record labels responsible for releasing the albums are listed in parentheses. Do bear in mind, however, that a 'US only' or 'UK only' listing does not necessarily mean that the album in question was or remains unavailable in the other country – most import shops will stock or offer to order the required item.

CHAPTER 1: ROCK'N'ROLL IS HERE TO STAY

Fats Domino
The Fats Domino Story Vols 1 to 6
(United Artists/United Artists)

Little Richard
The Fabulous Little Richard
(Sonet/Specialty)

The Platters
20 Classic Hits
(Mercury/Mercury)

Bill Haley and the Comets
Golden Hits
(MCA, US only)
Rock the Joint
(London, UK only)

Elvis Presley
The Sun Sessions
(RCA/RCA)
Elvis
(RCA, US only)
Elvis' Golden Records Vols 1 to 4
(RCA/RCA)

Carl Perkins
Blue Suede Shoes
(Sun, US only)

Jerry Lee Lewis
Jerry Lee's Greatest
(Sun, US only)

Charlie Rich
The Early Years
(Sun, US only)

Gene Vincent
The Best of Gene Vincent Vols 1 and 2
(Capitol, UK only)

RECOMMENDED MULTI-ARTIST COLLECTIONS:
Echoes of a Rock Era: The Early Years
(Roulette, US only)
Artists featured include Bo Diddley, Chuck Berry, Penguins, Moonglows and Frankie Lymon and the Teenagers.

Echoes of a Rock Era:
The Groups Vols 1 and 2
(Roulette, US only)
Classic doo-wop from the Crows, the Harptones, the Heartbeats, and the latter's offshoot, Shep and the Limelites.
The Sun Collection
(RCA/RCA)
Includes the major Sun singles and a number of unreleased takes.
Elvis, Scotty and Bill: The First Year
(Virgin Golden Editions, UK only)
Elvis plus Scotty Moore and Bill Black, captured live in concert during March 1955. Includes an early Elvis interview.
CBS Rockabilly Classics Vols 1 to 3
(CBS, UK only)
Commercial rockabilly from the US Columbia label, including tracks by Marty Robbins, Johnny Horton, Rose Maddox and Chuck Murphy.

CHAPTER 2: HIGH SCHOOL USA

Chuck Berry
Chuck Berry's Golden Decade
(Chess/Chess)

The Crickets
The Chirping Crickets
(Brunswick/Brunswick)

Buddy Holly
The Complete Buddy Holly
(Coral, UK only – 6 LP boxed set)

The Everly Brothers
Songs Our Daddy Taught Us
(Cadence/London)
Walk Right Back
(Warner Bros/Warner Bros)

Paul Anka
21 Golden Hits
(RCA, UK only)

The Coasters
The Coasters' Greatest Hits
(Atco, US only)

The Drifters
24 Original Hits
(Atlantic/Atlantic)

The Shirelles
Sing Their Very Best
(Springboard, US only)

RECOMMENDED MULTI-ARTIST COLLECTIONS:
American Graffiti Vols 1 and 2
(MCA/MCA)
Excellent compilations of late Fifties US hits, released to tie in with 1974 film of the same name. Artists featured include the Platters, Johnny Burnette, The Big Bopper, Buddy Holly, Mark Dinning, the Flamingos, Jerry Butler, Johnny Tillotson, Little Anthony and the Imperials.

Only in America
(Atlantic/Atlantic)
Compilation of hits and lesser known tracks written by Jerry Leiber and Mike Stoller. Includes tracks by the Coasters, the Drifters, Ben E. King and many more. Double album.
The Dimension Dolls
(London, UK only)
The pick of early Sixties releases on Don Kirshner's Dimension label, including tracks by Carole King, Little Eva and the Cookies.
Echoes of the Sixties
(Phil Spector International/Phil Spector International)
Phil Spector's greatest productions. Track listing includes biggest hits of the Crystals, the Ronettes, the Righteous Brothers and Ike and Tina Turner.

CHAPTER 3: ENGLAND SWINGS

Lonnie Donegan
Lonnie Donegan Showcase
(Pye-Nixa, UK only)

Tommy Steele
The Tommy Steele Story
(Decca, UK only)

Cliff Richard
40 Golden Greats
(EMI, UK only)

The Shadows
The Shadows
(UK Columbia, UK only)
Billy Fury
The Sound of Fury
(Decca, UK only)
The Beatles
Live at the Star Club in Hamburg, Germany 1962
(Atlantic/Atlantic)
Please Please Me
(Parlophone, UK only)
With the Beatles
(Parlophone, UK only)

Meet the Beatles
(Capitol, US only)
The Searchers
Golden Hour of the Searchers
(Pye, UK only)

RECOMMENDED MULTI-ARTIST COLLECTIONS:
They Called it Rock'n'Roll
(Decca, UK only)
Compilation featuring highlights (and lowlights) of UK rock in the Fifties. Artists include Tommy Steele, Wee Willie Harris, Terry Dene, Joe Brown, Lord Rockingham's XI.

The Fantastic Skiffle Festival
(Decca, UK only)
Recordings by the more professional skiffle outfits of 1955-57, including the groups of Alexis Korner, Bob Cort, Ken Colyer and Ray Bush.
Hits of the Mersey Era
(Capitol/EMI)
British beat group pop, 1963-65. Includes hit tracks by the Swinging Blue Jeans, the Hollies, Gerry and the Pacemakers, Billy J. Kramer and the Fourmost.

CHAPTER 4: TALKING 'BOUT MY GENERATION

The Rolling Stones
Out of Our Heads
(London/Decca)
Aftermath
(London/Decca)
High Tide and Green Grass
(London/Decca)
Between the Buttons
(London/Decca)
Georgie Fame
Rhythm and Blues at the Flamingo
(UK Columbia, UK only)
The Pretty Things
The Pretty Things
(Fontana, UK only)
The Kinks
Face to Face
(Reprise/Pye)
The Kink Kronikles
(Reprise, US only)
Manfred Mann
Semi-Detached Suburban
(EMI, UK only)
The Animals
Animal Tracks
(MGM/UK Columbia)
Most of the Animals
(UK Columbia, UK only)
Them
Them featuring Van Morrison
(Parrot, US only)

The Spencer Davis Group
Their First LP
(Fontana, UK only)
Sandie Shaw
Golden Hits
(Pye, UK only)
Dusty Springfield
Golden Hits
(Philips/Philips)
The Who
A Quick One
(Reaction, UK only)
The Who Sell Out
(MCA/Track)
The Story of the Who
(Polydor, UK only)
The Small Faces
From the Beginning
(Decca, UK only)
The Move
Move
(Regal Zonophone, UK only)
The Yardbirds
Five Live Yardbirds
(UK Columbia, UK only)
The Yardbirds Great Hits
(Epic, US only)
The Beatles
A Hard Days' Night
(United Artists/Parlophone)

Help!
(Capitol/Parlophone)
Rubber Soul
(Capitol/Parlophone)
Revolver
(Capitol/Parlophone)

RECOMMENDED MULTI-ARTIST COMPILATIONS:
History of British Blues
(Sire, US only)
Artists include Cyril Davies, Blues Incorporated, John Mayall's Bluesbreakers, Fleetwood Mac, Yardbirds, Graham Bond Organisation.
History of British Rock Vols 1 to 3
(Sire, US only)
A mixture of UK R & B, beat and straight pop performers appear, among them the Kinks, Dave Clark Five, Donovan, Sandie Shaw, the Hollies, the Small Faces and Chris Farlowe.
Hard-Up Heroes
(Decca, UK only)
Thoughtfully compiled album of mid-Sixties R & B/beat tracks from the Decca archives. Includes tracks by the Small Faces, the Yardbirds, the Who and a young David Bowie.

CHAPTER 5: THE TIMES THEY ARE A-CHANGIN'

The Beau Brummels
The Best of the Beau Brummels
(Warner Bros, US only)
Sir Douglas Quintet
Mendocino
(Smash/Oval)
Bob Dylan
The Freewheelin' Bob Dylan
(US Columbia/CBS)
The Times They Are A-Changin'
(US Columbia/CBS)
Bob Dylan
(US Columbia/CBS)

Another Side of Bob Dylan
(US Columbia/CBS)
Bringing It All Back Home
(US Columbia/CBS)
Highway 61 Revisited
(US Columbia/CBS)
Blonde on Blonde
(US Columbia/CBS)
Phil Ochs
I Ain't A-Marchin' Anymore
(Elektra, US only)

The Byrds
Mr Tambourine Man
(US Columbia/CBS)
Turn! Turn! Turn!
(US Columbia/CBS)
Fifth Dimension
(US Columbia/CBS)
Tim Hardin
Tim Hardin Vols 1 and 2
(Verve/Verve)
Simon and Garfunkel
Sounds of Silence
(US Columbia/CBS)

The Lovin' Spoonful
Hums
(Kama Sutra/Kama Sutra)
The Mamas and Papas
Deliver
(Dunhill/RCA)
The Beach Boys
Pet Sounds
(Capitol/Capitol)
Best of the Beach Boys Vols 1 and 2
(Capitol/Capitol)
Buffalo Springfield
Buffalo Springfield
(Atco/Atlantic)
The Monkees
The Monkees
(Colgems/RCA)

The Young Rascals
Greatest Hits
(Atlantic/Atlantic)
The Fugs
The Fugs
(ESP, US only)
The Velvet Underground
The Velvet Underground and Nico
(Cotillion/Verve)
Loaded
(Cotillion/Atlantic)

RECOMMENDED MULTI-ARTIST COLLECTIONS:
Nuggets
(Sire, US only)

Excellent compilation (by Patti Smith's guitarist, Lenny Kaye) of US garage band tracks from the mid-Sixties. Bands featured include the Standells, the Electric Prunes, the Shadows of Knight, Nazz, the Amboy Dukes and the Chocolate Watch Band.
Anthology of Folk Music Vols 1 and 2
(Sire, US only)
Some obvious omissions (Dylan, Joan Baez), but a selection indicative of the various faces and styles in late Fifties/early Sixties US folk music. Artists include Pete Seeger, Woody Guthrie, Judy Collins, Odetta and the Dillards.

CHAPTER 6: LOVE IS ALL YOU NEED

Jefferson Airplane
Surrealistic Pillow
(RCA/RCA)
Moby Grape
Moby Grape
(US Columbia/CBS)
Big Brother and the Holding Company
Cheap Thrills
(US Columbia/CBS)
Janis Joplin
Pearl
(US Columbia/CBS)
Electric Flag
A Long Time Comin'
(US Columbia/CBS)
Quicksilver Messenger Service
Happy Trails
(Capitol/Capitol)
The Steve Miller Band
Living in the USA
(Capitol/Capitol)
Grateful Dead
Live Dead
(Warner Bros/Warner Bros)
Van Dyke Parks
Song Cycle
(Warner Bros/Warner Bros)

The Beatles
Sgt Pepper's Lonely Hearts Club Band
(Capitol/Parlophone)
The Beatles
(Capitol/Apple)
The Moody Blues
Days of Future Passed
(Deram/Deram)
King Crimson
In the Court of the Crimson King
(Atlantic/Island)
Procol Harum
Procol Harum
(Deram/Deram)
Pink Floyd
Relics
(Harvest/Starline)
Piper at the Gates of Dawn
(Tower/UK Columbia)
Atom Heart Mother
(Harvest/Harvest)
Cream
Fresh Cream
(RSO/Reaction)
Disraeli Gears
(RSO/Reaction)
Jimi Hendrix
Are You Experienced?
(Reprise/Track)

Axis: Bold as Love
(Reprise/Track)
Electric Ladyland
(Reprise/Track)
Led Zeppelin
Led Zeppelin
(Atlantic/Atlantic)
The Doors
Strange Days
(Elektra/Elektra)
The Rolling Stones
Beggar's Banquet
(London/Decca)
Bob Dylan
John Wesley Harding
(US Columbia/CBS)
RECOMMENDED MULTI-ARTIST COLLECTION:
Woodstock
(Atlantic/Atlantic)
The soundtrack of the film of the festival, featuring many of the major names in late Sixties US and UK rock. Artists include the Who, Jimi Hendrix, Ten Years After, Sly and the Family Stone, John Sebastian, Crosby, Stills and Nash, Joe Cocker, the Band, Country Joe and the Fish, Melanie, the Grateful Dead, Janis Joplin and Jefferson Airplane.

CHAPTER 7: DANCING IN THE STREET

Ray Charles
The Ray Charles Story
(Atlantic/Atlantic)
Ray Charles Live
(Atlantic/Atlantic)
Clyde McPhatter
The Best of Clyde McPhatter
(Atlantic/Atlantic)
Jackie Wilson
My Golden Favourites
(Brunswick/Coral)

James Brown
Live at the Apollo Vols 1 and 2
(King/Polydor)
Sex Machine
(King/Polydor)
Sam Cooke
Two Sides of Sam Cooke
(Specialty/Specialty)
The Best of Sam Cooke
(RCA/RCA)
The Miracles
Greatest Hits
(Tamla/Tamla Motown)

Marvin Gaye
Anthology
(Motown/Tamla Motown)
What's Going On
(Tamla/Tamla Motown)
Let's Get it On
(Tamla/Tamla Motown)
The Four Tops
The Best of the Four Tops
(K-Tel, UK only)
Booker T. and the MGs
The Best of Booker T. and the MGs
(Atlantic/Stax)

Solomon Burke
The Best of Solomon Burke
(Atlantic/Atlantic)
Wilson Pickett
Greatest Hits
(Atlantic/Atlantic)
Otis Redding
History of Otis Redding
(Atco/Volt)
Otis Blue
(Atco/Atlantic)
Aretha Franklin
Aretha's Gold
(Atlantic/Atlantic)
I Never Loved a Man
(Atlantic/Atlantic)
The Temptations
Greatest Hits
(Gordy/Tamla Motown)
Curtis Mayfield
Superfly
(Curtom/Buddah)
Stevie Wonder
Talking Book
(Tamla/Tamla Motown)
Music of My Mind
(Tamla/Tamla Motown)
Innervisions
(Tamla/Tamla Motown)

The Supremes
Anthology
(Motown/Tamla Motown)
Diana Ross
Diana Ross
(Motown/Tamla Motown)
Lady Sings the Blues
(Motown/Tamla Motown)
Barry White
Greatest Hits
(20th Century/20th Century)
Donna Summer
Love to Love You Baby
(Casablanca/GTO)
Sly and the Family Stone
Dance to the Music
(Epic/Direction)
Al Green
Let's Stay Together
(Hi/London)
RECOMMENDED MULTI-ARTIST COMPILATIONS:
Ain't That Good News
(Specialty/Specialty)
Near-perfect selection of top gospel performances from the Fifties, including Sam Cooke and the Soul Stirrers' legendary 'Touch the Hem of His Garment'.

Soul Years
(Atlantic/Atlantic)
Two-LP set highlighting the contribution of the Atlantic and Stax labels to the story of soul music, with well-chosen selections by Otis Redding, Aretha Franklin, Solomon Burke, Percy Sledge, Ray Charles and others.
The Motown Story
(Motown/Tamla Motown)
Five-LP boxed-set offering a chronological history of the Motown corporation, from early hits by Barrett Strong and the Marvelettes to early Seventies best-sellers by the Jackson Five and the Supremes.
The Sound of Philadelphia
(CBS, UK only)
Sampler album of early Seventies 'Philly Sound' creations featuring hits by Harold Melvin and the Blue Notes, the Intruders, the O'Jays and MFSB.
Saturday Night Fever
(RSO/RSO)
Included here by virtue of its popularity and impact rather than any particular excellence. Clinically-clean blue-eyed disco from the Bee Gees, Yvonne Elliman, K.C. and the Sunshine Band.

CHAPTER 8: AFTER THE GOLDRUSH

The Beatles
Abbey Road
(Capitol/Apple)
Let it Be
(Apple/Apple)
Paul McCartney
McCartney
(Capitol/Apple)
John Lennon
John Lennon/Plastic Ono Band
(Apple/Apple)
Imagine
(Apple/Apple)
George Harrison
All Things Must Pass
(Apple/Apple)
James Taylor
Sweet Baby James
(Warner Bros/Warner Bros)
Crosby, Stills, Nash and Young
Déja Vu
(Atlantic/Atlantic)
Van Morrison
Astral Weeks
(Warner Bros/Warner Bros)
Carole King
Tapestry
(Ode/A & M)
Joni Mitchell
For the Roses
(Reprise/Reprise)
Court and Spark
(Reprise/Asylum)

Bob Dylan
Self-Portrait
(US Columbia/CBS)
The Byrds
Sweetheart of the Rodeo
(US Columbia/CBS)
The Band
Music from Big Pink
(Capitol/Capitol)
The Band
(Capitol/Capitol)
Creedence Clearwater Revival
Greatest Hits
(Fantasy/Fantasy)
Leon Russell
Leon Russell and the Shelter People
(Shelter/A & M)
The Allman Brothers
Brothers and Sisters
(Capricorn/Capricorn)
The Eagles
On the Border
(Asylum)
Steely Dan
Can't Buy a Thrill
(ABC/ABC)
Alice Cooper
Killer
(Warner Bros/Warner Bros)
Mothers of Invention
We're Only in It for the Money
(Verve/Verve)

T. Rex
Electric Warrior
(Reprise/Fly)
Elton John
Goodbye Yellow Brick Road
(MCA/DJM)
Rod Stewart
Every Picture Tells a Story
(Mercury/Mercury)
Slade
Sladest
(Reprise/Polydor)
David Bowie
Hunky Dory
(RCA/RCA)
The Rise and Fall of Ziggy Stardust and the Spiders from Mars
(RCA/RCA)
Aladdin Sane
(RCA/RCA)
Diamond Dogs
(RCA/RCA)
Young Americans
(RCA/RCA)
Station to Station
(RCA/RCA)
Low
(RCA/RCA)
'Heroes'
(RCA/RCA)
Lou Reed
Transformer
(RCA/RCA)

Roxy Music
Roxy Music
(Atco/Island)
For Your Pleasure
(Atco/Island)
Stranded
(Atco/Island)

RECOMMENDED MULTI-ARTIST COLLECTIONS:
The Last Waltz
(Warner Bros/Warner Bros)
Soundtrack of Martin Scorsese's film of the Band's last concert. Included are appearances by Bob Dylan, Joni Mitchell, Ronnie Hawkins, Dr John, Neil Young, Eric Clapton and Van Morrison.
The South's Greatest Hits Vols 1 and 2
(Capricorn/Capricorn)
A showcase for the best southern rockers of the Seventies, among them the Allman Brothers, Wet Willie, Dr John and the Charlie Daniels Band.

CHAPTER 9: THIS IS THE MODERN WORLD

The Sex Pistols
Never Mind the Bollocks, Here's the Sex Pistols
(Warner Bros/Virgin)
The New York Dolls
Too Much Too Soon
(Mercury/Mercury)
The Clash
The Clash
(US Columbia/CBS)
The Jam
This is the Modern World
(Polydor/Polydor)
The Buzzcocks
Love Bites
(United Artists/United Artists)
The Damned
Damned Damned Damned
(Stiff/Stiff)
X-Ray Spex
Germ Free Adolescents
(EMI, UK only)
Siouxsie and the Banshees
The Scream
(Polydor/Polydor)
The Slits
Cut
(Polydor, UK only)
Ian Dury and the Blockheads
New Boots and Panties!!
(Stiff/Stiff)
Elvis Costello
My Aim is True
(Columbia/Stiff)
This Year's Model
(Columbia/Radar)

The Boomtown Rats
A Tonic for the Troops
(Columbia/Ensign)
Squeeze
Argy Bargy
(A & M/A & M)
The Pretenders
The Pretenders
(Sire/Real)
Joe Jackson
Look Sharp
(A & M/A & M)
Dire Straits
Dire Straits
(Warner Bros/Vertigo)
Dr Feelgood
Stupidity
(United Artists/United Artists)
Graham Parker
Stick to Me
(Mercury/Vertigo)
Kate Bush
The Kick Inside
(Capitol/EMI)
Television
Adventure
(Elektra/Elektra)
Blondie
Parallel Lines
(Chrysalis/Chrysalis)
Patti Smith
Horses
(Arista/Arista)
The Ramones
Rock'n'Roll High School
(Sire/Sire)

Talking Heads
More Songs About Buildings and Food
(Sire/Sire)
Fear of Music
(Sire/Sire)
Jonathan Richman and the Modern Lovers
Rock'n'Roll with the Modern Lovers
(Beserkley/Beserkley)

RECOMMENDED MULTI-ARTIST COLLECTIONS:
The Roxy, London WC2 (January-April 1977)
(EMI/EMI)
Live tracks from the heyday of punk-rock, including contributions from X-Ray Spex, Buzzcocks, Slaughter and the Dogs, Wire, the Adverts and Johnny Moped.
20 of Another Kind
(Polydor, UK only)
First-rate compilation of classic punk singles from the Jam, Plastic Bertrand, the Stranglers, the Heartbreakers, Sham 69, Generation X, the Skids, the Cure and others.
That Summer
(Arista/Arista)
An inspired selection of early new wave tracks, all of 1977 vintage and all featured in the film of the same name. Ian Dury, Elvis Costello, Nick Lowe, Eddie and the Hot Rods, Patti Smith, Mink de Ville and the Boomtown Rats are among those artists included.

CHAPTER 10: KARMA CHAMELEONS

The Specials
The Specials
(Chrysalis/2-Tone)
More Specials
(Chrysalis/2-Tone)
Bob Marley and the Wailers
Catch a Fire
(Island/Island)
Exodus
(Island/Island)
Uprising
(Island/Island)
The Selecter
Too Much Pressure
(Chrysalis/2-Tone)

The Beat
Wh'appen
(Go-Feet, UK only)
Madness
Complete Madness
(Stiff, UK only)
UB40
Signing Off
(Graduate, UK only)
The Police
Regatta de Blanc
(A & M/A & M)
Adam and the Ants
Kings of the Wild Frontier
(US Columbia/CBS)

Gary Numan
The Pleasure Principle
(Atco/Beggars Banquet)
Joy Division
Unknown Pleasures
(Factory, UK only)
New Order
Power, Corruption and Lies
(Factory/Factory)
Human League
Dare
(A & M/Virgin)
ABC
The Lexicon of Love
(Mercury/Neutron)

Duran Duran
Rio
(Capitol/EMI)
Frankie Goes to Hollywood
Welcome to the Pleasuredome
(Island/ZTT)
Wham!
Fantastic
(US Columbia/Innervision)
Alison Moyet
Alf
(US Columbia/CBS)
Paul Young
No Parlez
(US Columbia/CBS)
Phil Collins
Face Value
(Atlantic/Virgin)
Culture Club
Kissing to Be Clever
(Epic/Virgin)

Eurythmics
Touch
(RCA/RCA)
Dexy's Midnight Runners
Too-Rye-Ay
(Mercury/Mercury)
The Style Council
Introducing the Style Council
(Polydor/Polydor)
Michael Jackson
Thriller
(Epic/Epic)
Lionel Richie
Lionel Richie
(Motown/Tamla Motown)
Shalamar
Greatest Hits
(Solar/Solar)
George Clinton
Computer Games
(Capitol/Capitol)

Fleetwood Mac
Mirage
(Warner Bros/Warner Bros)
Daryl Hall and John Oates
Private Eyes
(RCA/RCA)
Prince
Purple Rain
(Warner Bros/Warner Bros)
Bruce Springsteen
The River
(US Columbia/CBS)
Nebraska
(US Columbia/CBS)
Born in the USA
(US Columbia/CBS)

GLOSSARY

A & R Abbreviation for 'Artists and Repertoire', the division of a record company responsible for discovering, signing and grooming new talent.

a cappella Singing without instrumental accompaniment, commonly found in gospel music ('*a capella*' means 'as in chapel' in Italian). Many doo-wop and R & B vocal groups began in this way, but hit records featuring vocals alone have been very few.

acid-rock Music that simulates the effects of the hallucinogenic drug LSD ('acid'). Particularly associated with San Francisco rock c. 1966-69.

advance Payment given by a record company to a new signing as an advance against future earnings, usually to finance the rehearsing and recording of a debut album.

arrangement The setting out, customarily in manuscript form, of the individual instrumental parts required on a particular recording session. The 'arranger' may also supervise the hiring of session musicians.

baion A Latin rhythm in which the offbeat is accentuated to create a jaunty effect. It was brought to rock music by Leiber and Stoller in their late Fifties productions for the Drifters. Later examples of records using the baion rhythm include Peter and Gordon's 'World Without Love' and Dionne Warwick's 'Do You Know the Way to San José'.

bluebeat Alternative name for 'ska' music, the precursor of rocksteady and reggae. The name derived from the Jamaican record label, Blue Beat, which was a subsidiary company of the larger, calypso-based label, Melodisc, and released early records by Prince Buster, Laurel Aitken and Derrick Morgan.

blue-eyed soul Music in a black soul style played by white musicians. Examples: the Young Rascals, Daryl Hall and John Oates, the Style Council, Go West.

bluegrass A sub-genre of country music and an instrumental, banjo- and fiddle-based style associated particularly with the Appalachian mountain areas of Kentucky. The terms derives from the blue grass common to Kentucky and neighbouring southern states.

bootleg A recording made or procured by clandestine means (eg via concealed taping equipment at a concert) and issued without the consent of the artist involved.

bubblegum General term applied to any pop music aimed at a pre-teenage (supposedly bubblegum-chewing) audience, but usually characterised by nursery rhyme lyrics and simple pipe-organ accompaniments. Buddah in New York was the leading bubblegum label in the late Sixties and the home of such hits as the 1910 Fruitgum Company's 'Simon Says' and the Ohio Express' 'Yummy Yummy Yummy (I Got Love in My Tummy)' (*sic*).

cajun The popular music of French-speaking natives of Louisiana. Cajun rock is a gliding mix of rock'n'roll with country dance music, with the accordion its most prominent instrument. Musicians bearing the cajun imprint include J. J. Cale, Clifton Chenier, Doug Kershaw and Dr John. The word 'cajun' is a corruption of 'Acadian', a reference to 'Acadia', the old name for French Canada, from where many of the original Louisiana settlers migrated.

calypso (1) A traditional folk style based on a lightly syncopated rhythm, that is indigenous to Trinidad in the West Indies.

(2) A song performed calypso-style, as a vehicle for topical comment.

charts The listing of currently popular records according to volume of sales. In the US, the main source of chart information is *Billboard* magazine, though for many years rival trade publication *Cashbox* produced its own, marginally less reliable chart. In the UK, there are two rival charts – the BBC's Top 40, compiled by the Gallup organisation, and Independent Radio's Network chart, which apportions chart positions according to both sales and a rather dubious airplay factor.

concept album An album of songs or extended musical pieces exploring a particular philosophical, political or personal theme. Prime examples include the Beatles' *Sgt Pepper's Lonely Hearts Club Band*, the Who's *Tommy*, and Pink Floyd's *Dark Side of the Moon*.

cover The *original* version of a song is generally defined as its first recorded treatment. A cover version is any subsequent recording of the song by a different artist or group.

crossover A crossover hit is any record which, although aimed at a specific musical market like country or soul, achieves sufficient sales to earn a national chart placing.

disco (1) An abbreviation of 'discotheque', a venue in which recorded dance music is played and sometimes augmented with live performances.

(2) A generic term applied to rock- or soul-based dance music played and danced to in discotheques.

dub (1) A term with reggae associations, applied to the instrumental tracks over which 'toasters' (usually disc jockeys) improvise rhyming patter.

(2) As a verb, to 'dub' means to add instrumental and/or vocal accompaniments on to an original recording.

easy-listening A marketing term given to any undemanding, lightweight musical fare bought by adult (ie non-adolescent) consumers. First coined by the Polydor record label in Germany in the late Sixties to describe the big-band music of James Last and Bert Kaempfert, the term now takes in everything from the slick vocal styling of Frank Sinatra to the laid-back contemporary AOR of Toto and Air Supply.

echo A reverberative effect beloved of record producers in the late Fifties, but used regularly since. Echo can be produced naturally, by recording in an 'echo chamber' (usually a specially modified room with walls made of materials that reflect rather than absorb sound), or by electronic means.

fill Short instrumental links between the verses of a song.

fuzztone The effect achieved by deliberate electronic distortion of the guitar's usual amplified sound.

Grand Ole Opry Originally a radio show broadcast from Nashville's Ryman Auditorium and syndicated throughout the American south, the Opry was for years country music's most famous institution and premier talent showcase. The show transferred to television in the Fifties, and changed venues to 'Opryland' – a Disneyland-type fantasy theme park – in the mid-Seventies.

groupies Female rock fans whose lifestyle revolves around providing touring rock bands with sexual favours.

heavy metal Loud, guitar-based rock music associated with UK progressive bands like Led Zeppelin and Deep Purple. The chief elements in heavy metal are 12-bar blues riffs, ear-shattering vocals and macho posturing. The term is generally credited to the rock writer Lester Bangs, though the phrase has its origins in William Burroughs' novel, *The Naked Lunch*.

hook The most memorable musical phrase in a song or record.

hype Short for 'hyperbole'. A hype campaign involves the making of exaggerated artistic claims by a record company in furtherance of a particular rock act's sales, but the word can also be applied to any kind of promotional overkill.

improvisation Spontaneous musical creation by instrumentalists, usually within the context of a live performance. In rock as in jazz, the term improvisation encompasses any unrehearsed elaboration of or departure from a melody line or pre-set arrangement.

jug band Jug bands were aggregations of folk musicians who played traditional repertoire on everyday utensils like washboards, tissue-paper combs and tea chests. Empty earthenware jugs were particularly favoured – hence the name – because of the tuba-like sound produced by blowing down them. Jug band music was raucous and basic, and it shared many characteristics with the British skiffle music of the Fifties.

juju A Nigerian musical style of increasing popularity in the UK and US during the Eighties, thanks mainly to its championing by guitarist King Sunny Ade. Juju is derived from the talking-drum music of the Yoruba tribe, but it also shows clear Spanish and Caribbean influences, the result of sustained importation of records from these countries from the Forties onwards.

lick A distinctive instrumental phrase highlighting the dexterity of the individual musician. Used in reference to a whole range of jazz instruments, the term is mainly applied to guitar playing in rock jargon.

melisma A vocal effect much favoured by soul, gospel and blues singers, involving the stretching of a word or syllable over several notes.

Mellotron An electronic sound synthesiser used extensively by progressive rock musicians in the late Sixties. It could simulate the sound of massed banks of strings and for this reason was favoured by rock bands seeking to give their efforts a pseudo-classical veneer.

mix The balancing of vocal and instrumental tracks, overdubs and production effects by a producer or engineer once all the required elements are recorded. Recordings can be mixed endlessly to play up different features, eg to emphasise the rhythm in a 'dance mix'. In the Eighties, the releasing of numerous 're-mixes' of a popular record became common-place, the idea being to generate extra sales at minimal cost.

MOR Abbreviation of 'middle of the road', a once perjorative term for anything safe and unspectacular. Now synonymous with 'easy-listening'.

monaural A monaural or monophonic record is that made for dissemination through one sound source.

multi-media The use of more than one medium – music, dance, light shows, film – in live performance.

multi-tracking Multiple recording of the same vocal or instrumental track to create a sense of aural density. Brian Wilson of the Beach Boys and Phil Spector were two of the technique's first exponents.

novelty A one-off hit record with a strong comic element, usually incorporating a particularly 'novel' vocal or production gimmick. Examples include the Chipmunks' 'The Chipmunk Song', the Toy Dolls' 'Nellie the Elephant', and Bobby 'Boris' Pickett's horror-movie lampoon, 'Monster Mash'.

psychedelia Literally, 'mind-expanding'. Psychedelic rock is a term synonymous with acid-rock.

quadrophonic In contrast to monaural sound, quadrophonic sound is that disseminated through four separate sources. The early Seventies saw the launch of quadrophonic records by the US and UK record industry, but the public of both countries proved reluctant to invest in four-speaker quad equipment and such releases were quickly abandoned.

race music An early trade term for rhythm and blues music.

raga rock Raga is the Indian word for a musical scale, 'raga rock' a neat if strictly inaccurate term for the incorporation of Indian influences into western rock music.

R & B Abbreviation for rhythm and blues, which in strict musical terms was the old acoustic blues newly amplified for playing in city bars and clubs. However, R & B was soon adopted as a catch-all term for any music made by blacks *for* blacks. In the Sixties, when white rock bands began playing in an R & B style, the term came to mean any rock music with obvious black origins.

riff A repeated musical phrase.

rimshot The clattering percussion sound made by striking the metallic rim of a drum rather than its skin.

salsa A Cuban dance music first brought to mainstream rock by Stevie Wonder in the mid-Seventies and popular with UK dance-oriented bands in the early Eighties. 'Salsa' is the Spanish word for sauce.

sequencer An electronic device that stores sounds electronically and repeats them sequentially, as required.

soft-rock Descriptive term applied to harmony- or acoustic-based rock music, eg that of vocal groups like the Beach Boys, Association and Harpers Bizarre, or of singer-songwriters of the James Taylor/Joni Mitchell ilk.

stereophonic The channelling of sound through two sources (speakers), each transmitting different features of a record's production, e.g. voice, rhythm track, orchestration. The stereophonic effect is best appreciated when the listener is positioned halfway between the two speakers.

stiff A single that achieves no chart placing.

Tin Pan Alley Not a genuine street name but, in its original meaning, a cluster of office blocks on and around Broadway in Manhattan that housed America's music publishing companies. Denmark Street in London, home of the UK's principal music publishers, is known by the same description.

toasting A reggae technique that gave birth, in the late Seventies, to New York rap. 'Toasters' – usually disc jockeys – introduce particular records on their sound-systems with a distinctive, showy and often self-celebrating rhythmic patter.

trade papers Publications offering news, gossip, information and statistics to the record industry. In the US, *Billboard* is the main 'trade'; in the UK, *Music and Video Week* has been the most widely read trade newspaper for many years, its prominence challenged only briefly by *Record Business* in the Seventies.

wah-wah Onomatopoeic term for the manipulation of the electric guitar sound to create a wailing effect. Since the late Sixties, this effect has been achieved electronically by the operation of a foot pedal. Jimi Hendrix was the wah-wah specialist *par excellence*.

FURTHER READING

A short list of recommended books on rock music and the record industry

Reference:

Billboard Book of US Top 40 Hits, The
  Ed. Joel Whitburn (Guinness Books)
Guinness Book of British Hit Albums, The
  Ed. Rice, Rice, Gambaccini and Read (Guinness Books)
Guinness Book of British Hit Singles, The
  Ed. Rice, Rice, Gambaccini and Read (Guinness Books)
New Rock'n'Roll, The: The A-Z of Rock in the 80s
  Stuart Coupe and Glenn A. Baker (Omnibus)
New Rock Record: A Collected Directory of Rock Albums and Musicians
  Ed. Terry Hounsome and Tim Chambre (Blandford Press)
Record Producers File, The
  Ed. Bert Muirhead (Blandford Press)
Rock Files Vols 1 to 4
  Ed. Charlie Gillett and Simon Frith (Panther)
Rolling Stone Encyclopedia of Rock'n'Roll, The
  Ed. Jon Pareles and Patricia Romanowski (Rolling Stone)
Rolling Stone Record Guide, The
  Ed. Dave Marsh with John Swenson (Virgin)

Histories and artist profiles:

After the Ball
  Ian Whitcomb (Allen Lane)
Awopbopaloobop Alopbamboom
  Nik Cohn (Paladin)
Beatles, The: An Illustrated Record
  Roy Carr and Tony Tyler (New English Library)
Black Gospel: An Illustrated History of the Gospel Sound
  Viv Broughton (Blandford Press)
Bob Dylan
  Anthony Scaduto (Abacus)
Born to Run: The Bruce Springsteen Story
  Dave Marsh (Doubleday)
Boy Looked at Johnny, The: The obituary of rock'n'roll
  Tony Parsons and Julie Burchill (Pluto Press)
Brother Ray: Ray Charles' Own Story
  Ray Charles with David Ritz (Macdonald and James)
Buddy Holly: His Life and Music
  John J. Goldrosen (Granada)
Clive: Inside the Record Business
  Clive Davis (Morrow)

Country Music USA
  Bill C. Malone (University of Texas)
Electric Muse, The: The Story of Folk into Rock
  Dave Laing and others (Methuen)
Elvis
  Jerry Hopkins (Abacus)
Eric Clapton
  John Pidgeon (Panther)
Girl Groups: The Story of a Sound
  Alan Betrock (Omnibus)
Lennon Remembers: The Rolling Stone Interviews
  Ed. Jann Wenner (Penguin)
Mystery Train
  Greil Marcus (Omnibus)
Nowhere to Run: The Story of Soul Music
  Gerri Hershey (Pan)
Out of His Head: The Sound of Phil Spector
  Richard Williams (Abacus)
Punk
  Ed. Julie Davis (Davison)
Record Producers, The
  John Tobler and Stuart Grundy (BBC)
Revolt into Style
  George Melly (Penguin)
Rolling Stones, The: An Illustrated Record
  Roy Carr (New English Library)
Shout!: The True Story of The Beatles
  Philip Norman (Elm Tree Books)
Signed, Sealed, Delivered: True Life Stories of Women in Pop
  Sue Steward and Sheryl Garratt (Pluto Press)
Solid Gold: The Popular Record Industry
  Serge R. Denisoff (Transaction)
Sound Effects
  Simon Frith (Constable)
Sound of the City, The: The Rise of Rock and Roll
  Charlie Gillett (Sphere)
Stones, The
  Philip Norman (Corgi)
Walking to New Orleans: The Story of New Orleans R & B
  John Broven (Flyright)
When the Music Mattered: Rock in the Sixties
  Bruce Pollock (Holt, Rinehart and Winston)

INDEX

Picture references are set in *italic*.